A Concise Encyclopedia
of the Civil War

A Concise Encyclopedia
of the Civil War

Compiled by
Henry E. Simmons

THE FAIRFAX PRESS
New York

Copyright © MCMLXV by A.S. Barnes and Company, Inc.

This 1986 edition is published by the Fairfax Press, distributed by Crown
Publishers, Inc., by arrangement with A.S. Barnes and Company, Inc.

Printed and Bound in the United States of America

Library of Congress Cataloging-in-Publication Data

Main entry under title:

A concise encyclopedia of the Civil War.

   (Random House pictureback)
   Originally published: New York: A.S. Barnes, 1965.
   Includes index.
   1. United States—History—Civil War, 1861–1865—
Dictionaries. I. Simmons, Henry E. II. Series.
E468.C745 1986   973.7′03′21   86–1996
ISBN 0-517-61061-2

h g f e d c b a

To Dad
Whose faith in me never wavered

Contents

Introduction

PERHAPS THE DARKEST PERIOD IN our history was that of the mid-nineteenth century when the United States ceased to be truly united and the Union almost dissolved in the turmoil and hatred of tragic civil war.

Yet, out of these four years of fratricide came a stronger nation, with less accent on the rights of the individual state and more emphasis upon a united nation with a singleness of purpose in the eyes of the world. This nation became truly united, despite the deep and intense emotions of the period between 1861 and 1865.

Sadly, out of this period also came romantic tales of war adventure conjured up by pseudo-historians to cover the gore and disgusting slaughter which was the war. From this era came the realization that this young nation was not a territory of New Yorks, Bostons, Philadelphias, Richmonds, or Atlantas, but rather a unity built around previously un-heard-of places such as Cold Harbor, Wet Glaze, Big Shanty, Gum Swamp, Glorietta, Droop Mountain, and Bear Wallow. These, not the major cities, were the scenes of the glory that was to make this nation one of the world's foremost.

The young America of the 1860's was an adolescent, not too far past a war of independence, and not yet fully recognized by other nations as anything but a "group of crackpots" experimenting in the ridiculous democratic form of government.

To try to get into the essentials of the vital issues of the great conflict called the Civil War would necessitate many more pages than this work contains. Most historians differ on *some* aspect of the war, and Americans have not yet even agreed upon a name for this great conflict or many of its major contests. It is alternately called (depending upon your location and your point of view) "the Civil War," "the War Between the States," "the War of Northern Aggression," "the War of the Rebellion," "the Brothers' War," "the Confederate War," "the War for Southern Independence," "the Great Rebellion," and a host of other equally deserving titles. Still, all agree that this was the most important war in the young history of a new nation, and that it established that nation as a member of the world family.

INTRODUCTION

No single journal can list all of the people or places or events of this conflict which covered an entire nation and reached into the politics of major nations around the world. However, there is a need for some type of encyclopedic beginning. This is that beginning.

Xenia, Ohio.

Henry E. Simmons

A Concise Encyclopedia
of the Civil War

A

ABOLITIONISTS—Antislavery extremists who favored national legislation to sweep away slavery in the United States, regardless of vested interest, economic repercussion, or constitutional guarantee were called abolitionists. The movement began to gain momentum in the mid 1830's and mushroomed, with the first major organization being the National Anti-Slavery Society, formed in 1833 in Philadelphia, Pa.

Although most of the leaders in both the North and the South favored some form of gradual emancipation, extremists like Wendell Phillips, Charles Sumner, Gerrit Smith, Lucretia Mott, and William Lloyd Garrison kept the public inflamed with fierce and bitter denunciations of the system of slavery. It was largely due to these abolitionists that the Civil War evolved into an antislavery struggle. The movement included among its followers, orators, philanthropists, Northern politicians, and many ministers.

The abolitionists assisted in the escapes of runaway slaves, denying and defying (with public approval in the North) the constitutional clause warranting the Fugitive Slave Law. Its underground railroad (a system of escape stations) was designed to help the runaways from the South reach Canada.

In 1840, the abolitionist movement took two directions when the group differed over the best means of obtaining their goal. One segment favored the formation of a political antislavery party. The result was the existence of two lines of attack until the end of slavery. The pressure exerted by this political group did much to influence the war and the period of reconstruction which followed it. Among the members of Lincoln's cabinet, Salmon P. Chase was perhaps the most rabid abolitionist.

The political segment of the abolitionist movement became known as the "radical Republicans" and gained a reputation for extreme legislative measures and denunciations where slavery was concerned. It was this group which split with the Old Whig regime and formed the Republican party in 1858.

ADAIRSVILLE, Georgia, the trap at—Two wagon roads reach from Adairsville to Cassville, being about five miles apart at the widest point. Johnston set a trap on these roads hoping that the pursuing Federal force under Sherman would be divided to make travel easier along these roads, and the Confederate force could pounce upon one of the columns and destroy it.

The trap would have worked except for the fact that Lieutenant General John B. Hood faced his corps in the wrong direction as the result of an unconfirmed report that the Federals were coming in from the east. The trap was never sprung, and the Southerners continued their retreat towards Atlanta. Only the disobedience of orders by Hood saved the Federal force from suffering severe punishment.

ADAMS, CHARLES FRANCIS (1807–1886)—Born in Boston, Mass. Son of President John Quincy Adams. Most of his education was received in Europe, but he graduated from Harvard in 1825. In 1858, he was elected to Congress, and was later appointed ambassador to Britain by President Lincoln, arriving there in 1861.

It was largely through his efforts that England failed officially to recognize the Confederacy. It was also through his efforts that the United States was finally able to receive $15,500,000 in payment for damage done to U.S. shipping by British-built ships.

Adams served in Britain for seven years.

AFRICAN SQUADRON—A Union naval unit, recalled in 1861 to participate in the blockade of Southern coastal cities.

"AGATE" (See REID, WHITLAW)

AIR FORCE (See LOWE, T. C. S.)

"ALABAMA" CLAIMS — The name applied to the indemnity claims made by the United States upon Great Britain because of damage done to U.S. shipping by thirteen British-built ships which sailed for or in the interest of the Confederate states. One of these ships, the "Alabama," did extensive damage, and the claims took their name from this ship. The United States based its claim upon the alleged failure of Britain to observe the restrictions put upon neutral countries by international law in time of war. Britain contended that since the United States did not recognize the Confederacy as a separate nation, there actually was not an international war, and therefore, international law did not apply.

Among the ships involved were the "Alabama," which captured and sank between sixty-five and seventy United States vessels before being sunk outside of Cherbourg Harbor, June 19, 1864; the "Florida," like the "Alabama," built at Birkenhead, England, which cruised for twenty months before being disposed of by the U.S.S. "Wachusett" off Baia, Brazil; the "Georgia," which was active for a year before being sold by Confederate agents; the "Shenandoah," originally the "British Sea King," which specialized in ranging the Artic waters destroying United States whaling ships, before surrendering to the British at Liverpool, November 6, 1865 (this ship extended her operations long after the end of the war and was consequently turned over to the United States); and nine other ships.

Through U.S. minister to Britain, Charles Francis Adams, the United States continuously repeated its protests against the British government for failing to halt the building of ships to be used in the Civil War. His efforts resulted in the Treaty of Washington (1871), which set up a commission for arbitration to consider the claims. The commissioners, one appointed by the United States, one by Italy, one by Great Britain, one by Switzerland, and one by Brazil, met at Geneva, Switzerland, on December 15, 1871. On September 14, 1872, the commission awarded the United States $15,500,000 in gold. The captain and namer of the infamous "Alabama" was noted seaman Raphael Semmes.

"ALABAMA" — Confederate raider built at Laird's Shipyards in Birkenhead, England. Originally named the "290." The ship departed from Liverpool on July 29, 1862, with a small group of passengers aboard for a supposed "maiden run." Captain Raphael Semmes had the guests taken off by tug as soon as the ship left the harbor, and set out to sea, as a raider for the Confederacy.

The "Alabama" cost $250,000, and weighed over 1,000 tons. She was 32 feet wide and 230 feet long, with a depth of 20 feet. The raider was armed with eight assorted guns, and was designed to outrun and overtake unarmed merchant vessels.

It was this raider which caused so much damage to Northern shipping that the United States claims against England in 1877 were named after

her. The "Alabama" was finally sunk by the U.S.S. "Kearsarge," an armored man-of-war, outside of Cherbourg Harbor (France), on Sunday, June 19, 1864.

Her captain, Semmes, was ordered to trial by the United States after the war, but was set free by Presidential order. In twenty-two months, the "Alabama" had taken 2,000 prisoners, boarded 386 ships, and destroyed more than five million dollars in United States property— all according to international law. The "Alabama" sank U.S. ships as far away as the China Sea and the Indian Ocean.

"ALBEMARLE" — An ironclad ram which figured prominently in the capture of Plymouth, N.C. The "Albemarle" was sunk by a torpedo mounted on the tip of a 14-foot boom fastened to the bow of a small steam launch. The 150-pound torpedo hit the "Albemarle" and carried both the ironclad and the launch to the bottom.

The idea of mounting a torpedo on a launch was conceived by Lieutenant William B. Cushing, who led the assault upon the ironclad on the night of October 27, 1864. He and fourteen other volunteers slipped past a guard post and got within yards of the "Albemarle" before being fired upon by a 100-pound gun and a host of small arms from the shore.

Cushing drove the launch over a waterline barracade of logs surrounding the ironclad, and rammed her. Of the fifteen men aboard, only

15

Cushing and one other man escaped. Cushing was promoted for his deed and became lieutenant commander at the early age of twenty-one.

ALDEN, JAMES (1810–1877)—Union. United States naval officer born in Portland, Me. He served as a lieutenant in the Wilkes expedition around the world, 1838–1842, and during the Mexican War was attached to the Home Squadron.

During the Civil War, Alden commanded successively the "South Carolina," the "Richmond," and the "Brooklyn." In the latter, he took part in the Battle of Mobile Bay, where he was severly criticized by Admiral Farragut for retreating because of the threat of torpedoes ahead. Farragut later ascribed Alden's move as an error in judgement rather than an act of cowardice. Alden's subsequent career did not suffer because of the incident.

Following the war, Alden rose to the rank of rear admiral (1872).

ALEXANDER COLLIE & COMPANY—A British company engaged in blockade-running during the war. This company became one of the biggest and most successful firms engaged in shipping merchandise to the South. It served as agent for many Confederate states in Europe. In particular, the company handled the financial affairs of the blockade-runners of the state of North Carolina, receiving and paying for all purchases made by the state, and eventually becoming part-owner of blockade-running steamers.

Among the ships either owned fully or partially by the company were the blockade runners "Don Hansa," "Annie," "Constance," "Edith," and "Pet."

ALEXANDER, EDWARD PORTER (1835–1910)—Confederate. Born in Washington, Ga., and a graduate of West Point in the class of 1857. Alexander served in the Mormon troubles in 1858, and later taught at West Point.

At the outbreak of the war, he resigned his U.S. commission and became a captain of engineers in the Confederate army. Prior to this, he had been responsible for the development of the semaphore system of "wig-wagging." In the Confederate army, Alexander rose to the rank of brigadier general, serving in ordinance, artillery, and being commander of units in both branches. He served under Lee at Appomattox, with Longstreet in the Virginia campaign against Grant, at Fredericksburg, Chancellorsville, and Gettysburg.

Following the war, Alexander published his *Military Memoirs of a Confederate* (1907). He was considered one of the most capable generals in the Confederate army.

ALEXANDRIA, LOUISIANA—Rail center, located on the west bank of the Red River opposite Pinesville, La. A thriving town until the war, when many of its buildings were torn down by Union forces in an effort to dam the river and so float their gunboats over the rapids.

ALEXANDRIA, VIRGINIA—Rail center

16

on the Potomac river, seven miles south of Washington, D.C. This town was vital because of its transportation facilities and its proximity to the Capitol.

AMELIA COURT HOUSE—A station on the Danville railroad line which was to be used as a supply drop for Lee's army in the last days of the Virginia campaign, but which became, instead, a point of disappointment when Lee found that the supplies had erroneously been sent to Richmond instead, and were captured by Federal troops late in the war.

AMES, ADELBERT (1835 – 1933)— Union. Born in Rockland, Me., Ames graduated from West Point in 1861. He was not particularly outstanding during the war, but his post-war career was sensational. Following the war, he was appointed Reconstruction governor of Mississippi (1868). He resigned in 1870 to take a Senate seat which he held until 1873 when he resigned to become the elected governor of Mississippi.

Ames' behavior was such that the Mississippi legislature impeached him. He resigned in 1876 on the condition that the impeachment be withdrawn. It was, and he faded into political obscurity.

ANDERSON, RICHARD HERON (1821– 1879)—Confederate. Born at Statesburg, S.C., Anderson graduated from West Point in 1842. He served with the Dragoons in the Mexican War, and became a colonel of a South Carolina regiment at Fort Sumter.

In July, 1861, he was made a brigadier general and served as a brigade commander during the Peninsular campaign. July, 1862, found him being promoted to major general. His famous stand at Crampton's Gap during the second Manassas was the high-mark of his military career. His other campaigns included Antietam's "Bloody Lane" (where he was wounded), Fredericksburg, Chancellorsville, Gettysburg, and the Wilderness.

When Longstreet was wounded at the Wilderness, Anderson assumed command of Longstreet's corps and commanded ably at Spotsylvania. He was promoted to lieutenant general in May, 1864, and commanded a division for the remainder of the war. Although not exactly a dashing officer, Anderson was very efficient. As a subordinate leader, he ranked with the best on either side.

ANDERSON, ROBERT (1805–1871)— Union. Born in Louisville, Ky., Anderson graduated from West Point in 1825. He served in the Black Hawk wars, Florida, and the Mexican War before the outbreak of the Civil War. In Charleston Harbor, when his position was threatened, he moved his forces from Fort Moultrie to Fort Sumter. He was in command during the firing upon Fort Sumter, April 12–13, 1861.

After refusing several demands to surrender his forces, Anderson was forced to give in. Although he surrendered the first piece of United States property to fall into armed Confederate hands, there was never any concerted censure of this officer. He is generally recognized as having been a competent officer who found himself in an unenviable position. During the war, he was promoted to brigadier general, and commanded in Kentucky for the greater part of its duration. After his health failed in 1861, he saw very little action.

Prior to Fort Sumter, Anderson had commanded in Charleston Harbor as a major.

ANDERSONVILLE PRISON—A Confederate stockade for Union prisoners, particularly enlisted men, located at Andersonville, Ala. Established in November, 1863, it was usually overcrowded. The prison began operation in February, 1864, and processed a total of 49, 485 Union prisoners from that time until April, 1865, when it was closed. Andersonville, built to accommodate 10,000 prisoners, often had as many as 33,000 at one time. Equipped with a hospital, but no barracks, the stockade was an open enclosure of twenty-seven acres surrounded by twenty-foot walls of pine logs. The impure water and unsanitary conditions which prevailed made the name of the prison a hated byword in Northern circles.

During the thirteen months of the prison's existence, 13,700 men died as a result of the living conditions and poor treatment at Andersonville. Following an investigation of the prison by the Confederate War Department's Medical Commission, all but 4,000 of the prisoners were removed to Florence, S.C., and Millen, Ga., in 1864. There, better conditions were in evidence.

Following the war, Captain Henry Wirz, a Swiss mercenary who was superintendent of the prison, was tried by a military court and hanged for cruelty and mismanagement.

The Andersonville cemetery, now comprising twenty-seven acres and containing 13,700 graves, is a national cemetery. The prison grounds, now expanded to eighty-four acres, is a national park.

ANDREWS, JAMES A. (1826–1862)—The Union spy who led the daring steal of the Confederate train, the "General," which resulted in the "Great Locomotive Chase." He was hanged for his part in the episode in Atlanta, Ga., June 7, 1862. (see also, ANDREWS RAID.)

ANDREWS, JOHN A. (1818–1867)—Union, Abolitionist governor of Massachusetts who gave the Union vigorous support in his state. Andrews is responsible for raising one of the first Negro regiments of the war and offering it for service to the Union.

ANDREWS' RAID—April 12, 1862. Twenty-two volunteers from three Ohio volunteer regiments under the command of Brigadier General Ormsby Mitchell were assigned to Union spy James A. Andrews to participate in a raid deep in Confederate territory. The original plan was to steal a train and to rip up the tracks, tear down telegraph wires and burn bridges between Atlanta and Chattanooga, thus severing a vital Confederate communications line. Andrews had requested thirty men, and it is not certain as to whether only twenty-two volunteered, or whether he decided to cut the number of men to be used for the job.

After purchasing civilian clothes, the soldiers (and one civilian, an Englishman named Mark Wood) infiltrated as far south as Marietta, Ga., where they met with Andrews. On Saturday, April 12, 1862, they boarded the Confederate train the "General" and proceeded to a point above Marietta, Ga., called Big Shanty. Here, the raiders uncoupled all but three boxcars, a tender and the engine, and pulled out of the station while a group of Confederate soldiers across the track at Camp McDonald looked on in puzzled ignorance of what was taking place. All but four of the raiders were secreted in the boxcars.

Andrews calmly stopped about one mile up the track, ripped out telegraph wires, tore up some track, and refueled before moving on. Unknown to the raiders, however, conductor William Fuller, station superintendent Anthony Murphy, and the engineer of the "General" were pursuing on foot. This trio was under the impression that the train had been stolen by deserting conscripts from Camp McDonald, and they expected to find the train abandoned somewhere up the track. Their pursuit continued via rail after they came across a railroad handcar, but this mode of transportation was lost when the car hit a stretch of track ripped up by the raiders.

Andrews and the raiders proceeded to Cartersville, Ga., where they had to wait for almost an hour to allow a southbound train to pass. This gave Fuller and his trio (who had commandeered a small engine called the "Yonah" and were in hot pursuit until they ran across another stretch of ripped up track) a chance to gain ground. Continuing on foot, Fuller and the others stopped a train in Cartersville, Ga., "The William R. Smith," and continued after the stolen train. Meeting the "Texas" further up the track, they boarded this engine and proceeded after the "General" running backwards. The "Texas" ended the chase in this manner.

Not far up the track, the leisurely raiders became aware that they were being chased when they heard the sound of the "Texas" whistle. From this point on, the chase grew so hot that the raiders were unable to rip up track to stop the pursuing engine. They were unable to burn vital bridges as they had planned, and all attempts to pile ties across the track failed.

About ninety miles up the track from Big Shanty, the raiders found that they were running out of fuel, with the pursuing "Texas" in sight behind them. They attempted to set one of the boxcars afire with shavings, but it had begun to rain, and the car would not ignite. The raiders then attempted to drop off boxcars, hoping to smash the oncoming engine. The grade was slight, however, and the engineer of the "Texas,' Peter Bracken, simply reversed his engine, coupled on the boxcars, and continued the chase.

Finding they could not shake the pursuers, the raiders abandoned the "General," having done little damage to the line. Attempting to escape on foot, they were captured with the help of dogs in a week-long manhunt. Andrews and seven others were hanged on June 2, 1862. Later, all but six succeeded in escaping. The six who failed were paroled on March 17, 1863, placed aboard the "State of Maine," and returned to the North. Those six, the escapees who survived, and the relatives of those who did not, were awarded the first Congressional Medals of Honor ever issued by the United States. They were also promised promotions to the rank of first lieutenant.

Ironically, at all times during the chase, the raiders outnumbered the pursuers, and could have possibly overpowered them and continued their work of ripping up the track had they been aware of this fact.

ANTIETAM, the Battle of—Known also as the Battle of Sharpsburg. September 17, 1862. One of the most decisive battles of the war; also the bloodiest single battle of the war.

Immediately following the Battle of Second Manassas (Bull Run), General Lee decided to continue his march into Maryland after taking Harper's Ferry. His plan called for the Confederate force to be divided into four parts (see ORDER NO. 191), to march to South Mountain with

one, and to encircle Harper's Ferry with the other three. Despite misgivings by Longstreet, Lee proceeded with the execution of his plan. It was done mainly because of the overcautious manner in which McClellan was moving forward.

A copy of the order was sent to all of the commanders involved, but that copy intended for Confederate general D. H. Hill never reached him. A Union soldier found Hill's copy, wrapped around three cigars, at an abandoned camp site near Frederick, Md., and McClellan was handed a blueprint of Lee's plan of attack. For some unknown reason, McClellan delayed until the next morning to advance to the attack, and Lee, by that time, had been made aware that a copy of his order had been intercepted. Lee was then faced with the task of holding McClellan's 90,000 men off with 19,000 men until the remainder of his army could rejoin him at South Mountain. Stonewall Jackson, having captured Harper's Ferry and its 11,000 man garrison, hurried to Lee's assistance. Jackson aimed for Sharpsburg. Upon hearing that aid was near, Lee wheeled his small army to do battle with McClellan. Jackson was still, at this point, seventeen miles from Sharpsburg. For some reason, McClellan again procrastinated, giving Lee a full day to dig in before attacking on September 16. Hooker did push forward to engage in a light skirmish with the left flank of Lee's force, but refrained from becoming involved in a major battle. By the morning of the 16th, when

20

McClellan had finally decided to attack, Lee had been strengthened by three additional divisions and three more were en route.

Although not in a strong position (one of the rare instances when Lee had not chosen his own battlefield), the Confederate force dug in. On the left was a wooded area to the rear the Potomac River and to the right the winding Antietam Creek. All that kept the Confederate force from being smashed was the fact that McClellan seemed to have no set plan of attack for the situation. However, early on the morning of the 17th, the full-scale fight began, with five separate assaults taking place from left to right. None were seemingly coordinated.

First, Hooker hit the left flank under Jackson and was repulsed after four or five hours of hard fighting; next, Mansfield's Twelfth Corps (two divisions) hit Hood and Early again (they had been engaged in Hooker's thrust). Mansfield was killed, but his attack resulted in the capture of Dunkard Church across Hagerstown Turnpike. It was now past 9 A.M. and neither side had gained a decided advantage after hours of fighting.

The third thrust came from Edwin Sumner's Second Corps, newly arrived on the battlefield (two divisions short). Meanwhile, the "marching foot cavalry," of which the Confederates had plenty, had made a forced march from Harper's Ferry and were in the position to hit the unsuspecting Sumner on the left flank when he made his move. Under Lafayette McLaws, the Confederates

trapped Sumner, and slaughtered over 2,000 of his troops in less than one half hour. In the center of the Confederate line, the other two divisions of Sumner were assaulting a position held by D. H. Hill's division under Longstreet near a point later named "Bloody Lane." The fighting at this point was termed the bloodiest and most desperate of the entire war. First the Confederates had the advantage, commanding the approach to the fortification along a relatively narrow lane. Next, the Union forces gained access to a rise, which enabled them to pour rifle fire into the fortification at the lane.

The fifth and final Union thrust was made by Burnside's Ninth Corps (four divisions). Burnside, like McClellan, was slow to do battle. He had received his order to prepare to attack about 7 A.M.; later, at 10 A.M., he was ordered forward. This move would have coincided with Hill's move and would have exerted much pressure on the right and center of the Confederate line. Burnside did not move. At about 1 P.M., he finally overcame his fear of fording Antietam Creek, and carried his troops across the bridge below Sharpsburg. The tired Confederates had exhausted all of their ready reserves and were easily being pushed back by the rallying Union forces when the last Confederate reserve, a division under A. P. Hill arrived on the scene to turn the tide of battle. Hill's force had marched seventeen miles from Harper's Ferry to Antietam during the day; they hit the Union flank (Burnside) and drove it back to Antietam Creek. The Union drive was stopped, but so was the Confederate invasion of Maryland. On this day, more men were killed or wounded than on any other day of the war. Lee's first invasion of the North was ended, possibly because of the loss of a copy of Order No. 191.

The difference may be seen in the fact that all of Lee's 40,000 men were employed at one time or another during the heated fighting; while, on the other hand, 46,000 of the 70,000 Union troops saw battle. Neither the Fifth Corps nor the Sixth Corps saw battle that day. Had Lee foolishly remained at the scene of battle after the 17th, these two units of fresh troops would undoubtedly have been able to crush him. However, wisely, he slipped away on the 18th, late at night after McClellan failed again to follow up his advantage throughout the complete day of the 18th and even after receiving an additional 10,000 troops.

Losses were about one fourth of the total force used by both sides. The South lost 10,000 men killed, wounded, or captured; the North lost 12,000 of their 46,000 who saw battle. The national cemetery at Antietam contains the graves of 4,833 soldiers who fought in the battle. It is divided into cemeteries for each state, and was established in 1862.

APPOMATTOX COURTHOUSE—A small Virginia village situated between Lynchburg and Deatonville on an arm of the Appomattox river. The village is nine miles west of Rich-mond and 180 miles south of Washington, D.C., and became famous when Robert E. Lee and U. S. Grant met there to end the fighting in Virginia.

On Sunday, April 9, 1865, U. S. Grant accepted the surrender of the Confederate Army of Northern Virginia from Robert E. Lee in this village. Lee's army, though not the last of the Confederate forces in the field, was the last remaining army of any offensive or defensive potential at this time. For all practical purposes, the surrender ended the war. Strangely enough, the supposedly relentless "Unconditional Surrender" Grant showed great compassion and leniency in dealing with Lee.

The treaty site, resting on the Appomattox river, was actually the home of Wilmer McLean, a man in whose cornfields the first great battle of Manassas had been fought. McLean had moved south following this battle to escape the war in Prince William county, and was, ironically, the man whose home was used to serve as the meeting place of the two men destined to go down in history as the ones who signed the treaty which ended the major part of the fighting.

McLean, when asked about the site for the historic meeting, first suggested that another house be used. However, Lee's military secretary, Colonel Charles Marshall, was not satisfied with the house, and McLean then offered his own home. The meeting took place in his parlor.

The surrender details were arranged by three commissioners

from each side. Lee's committee consisted of Longstreet, Gordon and Pendleton; Grant's commissioners were Gibbon, Griffin and Merritt. They first met at the Clover Hill Tavern on April 10, 1865, and later adjourned to the McLean House and completed their discussions in the parlor. The final surrender papers were signed at that site at 8:30 A.M. April 10, 1865, by six officers.

Lee and Grant met only one time after parting at Appomattox, when Lee visited Grant at the White House in 1869.

The small cemetery at Appomattox Courthouse contains the bodies of eighteen Confederate soldiers and one unknown Union soldier. The park is administered by the National Park Service which has restored the Clover Hill Tavern. The park was authorized by an Act of Congress, August 13, 1935, and established April 10, 1940.

ARIZONA, the Confederate Territory of—This state came into the fold of both the Union and the Confederacy during a disputed interval from July, 1861, to March, 1863. During the period from 1857 to 1860, citizens of the section of the New Mexico Territory below 33° 40′ had made numerous unsuccessful attempts to get the United States to declare this area the territory of Arizona. Finally, the New Mexico assembly passed its own resolution in February, 1858, favoring a division of territory with

a north-south boundary line to run along the 109th meridian.

A pro-Confederacy convention at Mesilla, on March 16, 1861, declared Arizona to be a territory of the Confederate States. The Confederate government did nothing to recognize this declaration until January, 1862, when the Confederate Congress passed an act officially creating the Territory of Arizona. Prior to this, however, a lieutenant colonel, John R. Baylor, proclaimed the provisional Territory of Arizona in the name of the Confederacy. He set himself up as governor over a strip of land which covered the territory between the thirty-fourth parallel and Mexico, and from Texas to California. Mesilla was designated as the capital. Officers of the territory were: James A. Lucas, Secretary of the Territory; M. H. McWittier, Attorney-General; George M. Frazier, Marshall; E. Augorsteen, Treasurer; and Frank Higgins, Probate Judge.

Prior to this, in 1861 Lucas (as president of a secessionist convention at Mesilla) had submitted a resolution which read: "We will not recognize the present Black Republican Administration, and . . . we will resist any officers appointed to the Territory by said administration with whatever means in our power."

The territory which Baylor had designated covered an area 670 miles long, and was extended over an area which formed the bottom half of the territory designated by the Federal government as Arizona Territory. He reported his move to General Earl Van Dorn on August 8,

23

1861, and proceeded to request military support for the move from Van Dorn and General Henry H. Sibley. His call to Sibley came as the result of a move by Union Colonel E. R. S. Canby, who was bringing 2,500 troops down the Rio Grande to compel the Texans to abandon the territory.

On December 14, 1861, General Sibley, from Fort Bliss, Tex., assumed command of the Confederate forces in both New Mexico and the territory. Sibley issued a proclamation six days later which reaffirmed Baylor as military governor, and promised to liberate the New Mexicans from "the military despotism erected upon the ruins of the former free institutions of the United States."

When Jefferson Davis approved the Arizona Territory Organic Act, on January 18, 1862, he designated the northern boundary to be the thirty-fourth parallel; the eastern line at Texas; the western boundary at California; and Mexico and Texas in the South. Provisions of the act called for the following :

1. The Governor and other territorial officials were to be appointed by the President of the Confederacy.
2. The Legislature, elected by the white male residents over 21 years of age, was to consist of thirteen council members and a House of Representatives of thirteen, with a limited increase to thirty-nine allowable.
3. Military personnel who were not citizens of the Territory could not vote or hold office.

4. All legislative and judicial proceedings were to be conducted in English.
5. Legislation passed was subject to correction and modification by the Confederate Congress.
6. Slavery was legalized and was to be protected.
7. Mesilla was to be the capital.
8. The Territory was permitted to have one delegate in the House of Representatives in Richmond, Virginia.

On February 14, 1862, President Davis issued a proclamation declaring this act to be in full force and effect. He submitted the following names to the Confederate senate for confirmation :

Governor	John R. Baylor
Secretary	Robert Josselyn
Chief Justice	Russell Howard
Marshall	Samuel Jones
First delegate to the Confederate Congress	Granville Oury.

ARIZONA, the Union Territory of— The Union Territory of Arizona bill did not pass the Congress until February 20, 1863, although it had been introduced in December, 1861. It became a law on February 24, 1863. Charles D. Poston, later to serve as Indian agent for the territory, pushed the bill vigorously. He is known as "the Father of the Arizona Territory."

In March, 1863, Lincoln appointed John A. Gurley governor of the new territory, but Gurley died before he had a chance to take office, and was replaced by John N. Goodwin. The Union officials were :

Governor	John N. Goodwin
Secretary	Richard S. McCormich
Chief Justice	William F. Turner
Surveyor General	Levi Bashford
Indian Agent	Charles D. Poston
Marshall	Milton B. Duffield

Fort Whipple was established as the temporary seat of the government. When the war ended, Arizona had been in existence either two years or four years, depending upon your sentiments.

ASBOTH, ALEXANDER (1811–1868)— Union. Brevet Major General. Born in Keszthely, Zala, Hungary, on December 18, 1811, and died, January 21, 1868, Buenos Aires, Argentina. An Hungarian-American soldier who came to America in 1851 and became an American citizen. During the war, he served under Fremont and Samuel R. Curtis.

He was seriously wounded twice, once at Pea Ridge, and again at Mariana. He resigned his commission, and became United States minister to Uruguay and Argentina in 1866.

ASHBY, TURNER (1828–1862)—Confederate. Born in Fauquier County, Va., Ashby organized a company of horsemen and joined the Confederate army as a free agent at the outbreak of the war. He assumed command of a cavalry regiment late in 1861 as a captain. By March, 1862, he had been promoted to colonel and was assigned to Thomas Jackson's forces.

Among Ashby's campaigns and skirmishes are Winchester, Kernstown, Shenandoah Valley and Harrisonburg. He was killed while with the rear guard near Harrisonburg, on June 6, 1862, defending Jackson's retreat.

Although greatly respected by both sides, and although his actions usually brought about the desired results, Ashby was described by many as a "novice" or an amateur. His actions seldom followed a set military pattern, and were more on the guerilla style of warfare which later became a recognized part of Southern strategy.

When informed of Ashby's death, "Stonewall" Jackson wrote, "Poor Ashby is dead. He fell gloriously."

ATLANTA, Georgia, the Battle of— May 3—September 2, 1864. Perhaps one of the hardest battles of the war to define. It should be entitled "the Battle for Atlanta," because skirmishes leading up to this siege began when Sherman left Chattanooga. Kennesaw Mountain, New Hope, Adairsville, Resaca, and a host of other large and small engagements made up the Atlanta campaign, with Hood's 48,000 strategically retreating, fighting, and retreating, before the relentless oncoming might of 100,000 Federals under a Grant-like Sherman. Sherman, who had become an advocate of total war, pressed on to Atlanta in a systematic drive that followed a format laid down by Grant—divide the weakening enemy, defeat each segment individually, and push on regardless of the cost of lives and equipment as long as it shortened the war.

The Twelfth and the Eleventh Corps were consolidated to make one large Twentieth Corps under Hooker, allowing former Eleventh Corps commander O. Howard to relieve Gordon Granger at Laudon, Tenn., as commander of the Fourth Corps. By the 4th of May, Howard had brought his corps down to Ringold, Ga., to assemble with those of Schofield, McPherson, and Hooker. The Confederates were drawn up at Dalton, Ga., under the command of General Joseph E. Johnston.

Johnston took the initiative and moved north to occupy Taylor's Ridge, a gap through which any Federal troops coming into Georgia from Tennessee would have to pass. The Union forces numbered 99,000 men, outnumbering the Confederate army by 28,000 at this point. Thomas and Schofield were ordered to breast the enemy and occupy him while McPherson was to strike at the Atlanta railroad below Resaca. This part of the plan was dropped however, since McPherson was unable to bring his unit up to full strength.

The Fourth Corps under Howard cleared Tunnel Hill, a part of Taylor's Ridge, opening the route into the heart of the Confederacy. Under cover of Schofield's frontal action against Johnston, McPherson was able to skirt the enemy's line of defense and emerge at the eastern exit of the mountains without a major skirmish. His cavalry forced a detachment of Southern cavalry back to the breastworks at Resaca, but

failed to follow up their advantage and crush this force. Johnston, hearing about the Resaca situation, drew his forces back to Taylor's Ridge and formed a line of battle at Resaca, holding this point until Sherman began an encircling movement. On the 15th he withdrew under the cover of darkness to Adairsville, where he made a brief stand on the 17th.

Sherman moved portions of his army toward Rome, Cassville, and McGuire's Crossroads. However, until Sherman succeeded in cornering a portion of Johnston's army at Culp's Farm, the contacts were merely skirmishes and minor battles. At this point, Johnston's force repulsed all efforts of the Union force to dislodge them. Kennesaw Mountain was the same story. As a result, Sherman decided to bypass these pockets of resistance and forge on to Atlanta. Thomas pursued the Southerners through Marietta, but Johnston entrenched at Smyrna and on the bank of the Chattahoochee River.

However, when on the 9th of July, Schofield crossed the river and captured some of the Confederate artillery, Johnston withdrew again towards Atlanta. Thomas headed directly for Atlanta in pursuit; McPherson swung around through Roswell to Decatur; Schofield's force covered the ground between the two Union armies.

At this point, Johnston was removed from command for "failing to stand and fight Sherman," and Hood was placed in command. At this time, the Union army was drawn up in front of Atlanta, and the actual "Battle of Atlanta" began.

The move removing Johnston surprised even the Federal troops, for they had gained a great deal of respect for their shrewd opponent. His retreat had been masterly and costly to the Union.

Immediately after taking command, Hood attempted to smash the divided Union forces at Peachtree Creek. With Hardee and Stuart in command of cavalry units, he attacked Sherman's flanks. Another cavalry unit under Wheeler ran into a strong detachment under Gresham, and was pushed back to Bald Hill overlooking Atlanta. On the 21st, Blair dislodged the Confederates from this point with heavy losses, and the city of Atlanta was placed under Union artillery fire from this vantage point.

Hardee, coming out of Atlanta, circled southeast and came up near Decatur, which is north of Atlanta and to the rear of the attacking Union soldiers, in one of the quick night marches made famous by "Stonewall" Jackson. Here he encountered troops under Dodge, and a major skirmish took place during which McPherson was killed. McPherson had been consulting with Sherman at the Howard House, not far from the scene of battle, and ran into Confederate troops returning.

When Hood saw the smoke of battle, he sallied forth from the Atlanta breastworks and attacked Logan's line, breaking through and capturing a number of cannons. Sherman rushed re-enforcements, and the battle continued until nightfall when Hood withdrew to his position within the city.

At this point, Lincoln ordered Howard to be placed in command of the Army of the Tennessee to replace the fallen McPherson. Howard promptly began an encircling move which carried him around to the southwest of the city in an effort to sever the rail communications below the city.

At Ezra Church, Hood launched a counter attack, breaking through at a few points. Confederate cavalry kept re-enforcements from reaching Howard, but the Union line held, and again Hood was forced to withdraw into the city.

Sherman settled down to a siege operation which lasted over a month. The siege ended when Sherman, beginning another encircling move toward Jonesboro, was met by Hardee, S. D. Lee, and Cheatham. When this trio failed to dislodge the Federal force below the city, Hood abandoned the city and united with Hardee at Lovejoy Station near Jonesboro. On the 2nd of September, Sherman wired Lincoln: "Atlanta is ours, and fairly won."

Most of the battle scenes after the 20th July are now located inside the city limits of Atlanta. Yet, the battle for Atlanta actually began above Dalton, Ga., when the relentless Sherman began his march on the city.

ATLANTIC BLOCKADING SQUADRON—Union. The naval force assigned the task of blockading the Confederate ports along the Atlantic coast. Commodore Silas Stringham was assigned the post of flag officer of this squadron by Secretary of the Navy, Gideon Welles. At the beginning of the war, the squadron consisted mainly of converted merchant ships, armed with a wide assortment of artillery. However, before the war had lasted six months, the size of the fleet had grown to such an extent that the squadron was divided into two sections—one to blockade the ports north of the North Carolina–South Carolina state line, and the other to operate north of Florida's tip.

Eventually, the blockade was credited with working great hardships on the Southerners and contributing heavily to the ultimate defeat of the Confederacy.

AVERASBORO, NORTH CAROLINA — March 16, 1865. Johnston tried to stem the tide of Sherman's invasion of the Carolinas at this point, late in the war. The defensive maneuver was unsuccessful, and three days later (Bentonville), the last major battle of the East was fought.

AVERELL, WILLIAM W. (1832–1900)— Union. Brevet Major General. Born in Cameron, N.Y., on November 5, 1832. Graduated from West Point in 1855, and served on the frontier and in several Indian campaigns before the war. Appointed colonel of the Third Pennsylvania Cavalry and assigned to the defense of Washington when war broke out. Averell was noted as a delaying action raider, particularly in 1863–64. He re-

signed in 1865 to serve as U.S. consul general at Montreal, Canada. He became famous for his invention of a system of asphalt paving and the Averell insulating conduits for electric wires. He died at Bath, N.Y., February 3, 1900.

AYRES, ROMELYN B. (1825–1888)— Union. Brevet Brigadier General (later Major General). Born in Montgomery County, N.Y., December 20, 1825. Ayres remained in the service after the war as a colonel. He was a graduate of West Point in the class of 1847, and served in the Mexican War. He served at the first Bull Run (Manassas) as a captain, and later became chief of artillery under W. F. Smith. He commanded a division in the battle at Gettysburg, serving also at Chancellorsville, Antietam, and Fredericksburg. He died at Fort Hamilton, N.Y., December 4, 1888.

B

BABCOCK, ORVILLE (1835–1884)— Union. Brevet Brigadier General. According to the writings of Horace Porter, Babcock was a colonel at the time of the surrender of Lee. Babcock was born at Franklin, Vt., December 25, 1835, and served with distinction as a member of Grant's staff and as a brigadier general of the regular army. This last rank came at the end of the war for "meritorious and gallant service."

After the war, Babcock served as Grant's personal secretary from 1869 to 1877. He was indicted in 1876 for

28

taking part in the Whiskey Ring frauds, but was acquitted as the result of testimony given by Grant in regards to his excellent character. He died at Mosquito Inlet, Fla., June 2, 1884.

BADEAU, ADAM (1831–1895)—Union. Brigadier General. Born in New York City on December 29, 1831. He served on the staff of Thomas W. Sherman during the early part of the war. He was also on the staff of Quincy A. Gillmore. Badeau served as military secretary to Grant from April, 1864, until the close of the war. He served on Grant's staff until 1869.

Badeau became secretary of the London legation when Grant was elected President, and later became consul-general, in London. From 1870 to 1881, he held this post, and in 1882 became consul-general to Havana, Cuba. Resigning this post after a disagreement with the State Department over administrative policy, he settled down to write.

In 1868, Badeau had written a *Military History of Ulysses S. Grant* (3 vols.), and in 1887, he wrote *Grant in Peace*. Badeau died at Ridgewood, N.J., on March 19, 1895.

BAILEY, THEODORUS (1805–1877)— Union. Rear Admiral, born in Chateaugay, N.Y., April 12, 1805.

He entered the navy at the age of thirteen and served during the Mexican War on the western coast of Mexico. He was in command of the frigate "Colorado" when the Civil War broke out. The ship was a steam frigate. At New Orleans, he served under Farragut as second in command.

Bailey commanded the East Gulf blockading squadron from 1862 to 1864, was commissioned a rear admiral, and retired from active duty in 1866. He died at Washington, D.C., February 10, 1877

BAIRD, ABSALOM (1824 – 1905)— Union. Brevet Major General. Born in Washington, Pa., August 20, 1824. Graduated from West Point in 1849, served through the Seminole Wars as an artillery officer, and became an assistant professor of mathematics at West Point until the outbreak of the Civil War.

Baird fought in defense of Washington, and at the first Bull Run (Manassas). In April, 1862, he became commander of the Army of Ohio. Later, in 1862, he commanded the Third division of the Army of Kentucky. He served under Rosecrans in Tennessee, under Sherman in the Atlanta campaign and on the "March to the Sea."

Baird was present at the surrender of Confederate General Joseph Eggleston Johnston's army at Durham, N.C., in 1865. He retired from the army in 1888. He died at Relay, Md., June 14, 1905.

BAKER, LAFAYETTE C. (1826–1868)— Union. Chief of the Secret Police after 1862. Baker, who served as chief of the spy system of the Union after Allan Pinkerton was dismissed for supplying inaccurate information, acted as President Lincoln's personal bodyguard during Lincoln's stay in the White House. He was constantly at odds with Secretary of War Stanton, and, in 1961, one of the magazines owned by Baker was discovered with coded doodlings which implied that Stanton had engineered the assassination of Lincoln. This was not proven however, and most historians discount the find as vindictiveness on the part of Baker.

Baker was wounded twice by unknown assailants, and is credited with stopping any number of plots to assassinate Lincoln prior to the Ford Theatre murder. His official title was "Head of the Detective Bureau of the War Department."

Mystery surrounds Baker's death. He had a sum of money too great to have come from his salary as a detective and this sum disappeared from the house when Baker died. Doctors disagree with the presiding physician who claims that Baker died of natural causes. Most of the symptoms ascribed to his illness lean towards poisoning. He was believed insane at the time of his death. Subsequent trials and litigation involving his will caused quite a controversy in Washington circles.

BANKS, NATHANIEL PRENTISS (1816–1894)—Union. Born in Waltham, Mass. Banks could claim no formal education but was considered a well-educated man through his own self-teaching efforts. During his early prewar career, he was a lawyer, editor, politician and actor. Among his political prewar accomplishments were a term as congressman for 1853–1858, and a two-year term as governor of Massachusetts (1858–1860).

In 1861, he was commissioned a major general of volunteers. Not military in his thinking, Banks is known as one of the "political generals." He was badly defeated by Jackson's forces in the Shenandoah in 1862, fought passively at Cedar Mountain, but succeeded Butler in command of New Orleans in late 1862. Banks commanded Port Hudson in mid-1863, failed in the Red River Expedition in mid-1864 and, following the war, rushed back into familiar politics as a Congressman.

Throughout his military career, Banks attempted to use his position as a political stepping stone. He is generally considered one of the least capable generals on either side.

"BANSHEE"—The name was later changed to "Banshee No. 1." A Confederate blockade-runner. The ship made eight successful round trips before being taken. She was captained by J. W. Steele, but directed by "Supercargo" Tom Taylor in many instances.

The "Banshee" was built in Liverpool especially for the job of blockade-running. Often referred to as "the first steel ship ever laid down," the ship had a two-funneled paddle, a steamer with a 214-foot length, 217-ton weight, 20-foot beam, while drawing only 8 feet of water. This made the ship ideally fitted for the task of blockade-running and maneuvering within the shallow waters and shoals near Charleston and the Cape Fear River. Her speed was close to eleven knots, and her coal consumption was nearly thirty tons per day. She carried a thirty-six man crew.

The "Banshee" was carried on her maiden voyage early in 1863. However, faulty construction of plates, boiler room, etc., forced her back to port for repairs. It was not until mid-winter that she again took to the seas.

Her captain, Steele, and pilot, Tom Burroughs, were considered two of the best blockade-runners in the business.

BARLOW, FRANCIS CHANNING (1834–1896)—Born in Brooklyn, N.Y., October 19, 1834, Barlow received a good education, graduated from Harvard and became a lawyer. He enlisted as a private when war broke out, and became a major general of volunteers in less than three years. There is a monument dedicated to him at Gettysburg, Pa., testifying to his prowess in that battle. Barlow served in many of the major campaigns, most notable of which were Gettysburg and Spotsylvania.

He resumed his law practice after the war, becoming secretary of state for New York (1865–66 and 1869–70). He was made attorney general of that state (1871–1873). During his term as attorney general, Barlow initiated the prosecution of the famous "Tweed Ring." He died in New York City, January 11, 1896.

BARTLETT, JOSEPH J.—Brevet Major General. He commanded the First Division of the Fifth Corps at Appommattox. It was Bartlett to whom Colonel John Haskell of Lee's surrendering army turned over the artillery of the Army of Northern Virginia at McLean's House in Appomattox.

Bartlett was not a professional soldier, but volunteered for service when the war broke out. He was not officially a member of the party to whom Lee's lieutenants presented the request for terms.

BARTON, CLARA (1821–1912)—Union. Nurse. Born in Oxford, Mass., December 25, 1821. Clara Barton, a civilian worker during the war, was working as a patent office copyist in Washington, D.C., when war broke out. She began her career by giving aid to forty Massachusetts volunters who were attacked by a secessionist mob in Washington. After this, she obtained permission to travel to all areas of the Union front carrying supplies and medicines to the wounded. She traveled with a wagon train, and was called "the Angel of the Battlefield" by front line troops.

Not primarily a nurse, and never belonging to any organized aid group during the war, she dispensed aid to the wounded soldiers for four years. Through her work, 20,000 missing soldiers were identified. In 1881, Clara Barton founded the American Red Cross, and served as its president for nearly twenty-five years.

BARTOW, FRANCIS S.—Former mayor of Savannah. Later a member of the Confederate Provisional Congress and a brigade commander in the Confederate army. He was killed at the first Bull Run, and became a hero to the Confederacy. A monument is erected at the spot where he was killed.

BATE, WILLIAM B. (1826–1905)—Confederate. Major general. Born in Castalian Springs, Tenn., October 7, 1826. He served as a volunteer through the Mexican War, and graduated from the Lebanon Law School in 1852 following that conflict. He was elected attorney general of the Nashville district in 1854, and became a presidential elector in 1860. Bate enlisted in the Confederate army when war broke out, and rose from the rank of private to major general. He was wounded seriously three times.

He served as Governor of Tennessee in 1882 and 1884. He was also a U.S. senator in 1887, 1893 and 1899. Bate died at Washington, D.C., March 9, 1905.

BATON ROUGE, Louisiana—The seat of East Baton Rouge Parish, capital of the state and port of entry. Vital as a communications center during the war. The city was the location from which the state of Louisiana announced its secession from the Union.

The city was captured by a Union army on May 7, 1862, was under fire when Confederate Major General John C. Breckinridge and his forces attempted to retake the city on August 5, 1862. Their efforts failed, and the Federal forces occupied the city for most of the duration of the war. At the time of the Federal capture, Baton Rouge had a population of slightly over 5,000. It became the capital of Louisiana again in 1882, on March 1st, by an act of legislature.

BATTLE, CULLEN A. (1829–1905)—Confederate. Brigadier General. Born in Powelton, Ga., June 1, 1829. Battle studied at the University of Alabama, and was admitted to the bar in 1852. He was vehemently anti-Union and pro-slavery.

Battle served as a colonel and brigadier general of the Third Alabama Regiment of the Confederate army, and was in action at Gettysburg and Spotsylvania. He was severely wounded while with Early's forces in the Shenandoah Valley campaign (Cedar Creek) and retired from active service. Delegate to the Alabama Constitutional convention in 1874. He died at Greensboro, N.C., April 8, 1905.

BEAUREGARD, PIERRE GUSTAVE TOUTANT (1818–1893)—This 1838 West Point graduate was born outside of New Orleans, La. He served in the Mexican War prior to being appointed brigadier general at the outbreak of the war by the Confederate government.

Beauregard took command at the first Manassas, and was made a full general. During this engagement, he was working under Johnston. Prior to Manassas, Beauregard had been in command during the firing upon Fort Sumter, and was being hailed as the South's greatest hero.

Beauregard followed A. S. Johnston as commander at Shiloh, but was relieved from his post because of ill health and political disfavor. He was then put in charge of the defense of the south Atlantic coast region, an area which offered little chance for recognition. He took over the defense of Petersburg in 1864 when the situation was critical, and fought off Butler's attacks, bottled Butler up at the famous Bermuda Hundred, and held Petersburg until Lee arrived with relief. He, like most of the Confederate generals, was in constant conflict with Jefferson Davis, and this accounts for his military problems.

Generally aggressive, and inclined to discount the odds, Beauregard was a very able military man. Despite his argumentative nature, he was known as "The Great Creole" and as "The Napoleon in Gray."

BEAVER DAM CREEK (see MECHANICS-VILLE).

BEE, BARNARD E. (1824–1861)—Confederate General. A native South Carolinian who is credited with giving rise to Thomas Jackson's nickname, "Stonewall." His father was secretary of state of the Republic of Texas at the time that Bee received an appointment to West Point as a "cadet at large," in 1841. He graduated in 1845, but resigned from the army in 1861 to join South Carolina's troops. He was killed in the first Battle of Bull Run. Bee was described by his fellow officers as a man with tremendous potential. Most considered his death at such an early stage in the fighting a severe blow to the Southern cause.

BELKNAP, WILLIAM W. (1829–1890)—Union. Major General. Born in Newburgh, N.Y., September 22, 1829. Attended Princeton University, studied law at Georgetown, D.C., and was admitted to the bar in 1851.

Belknap joined the Union army in 1861, served in engagements such as Shiloh, Corinth, Atlanta, and Vicksburg. He became secretary of war in 1869. He was accused of malfeasance in office and resigned in 1876. He was later acquitted of the charges. Belknap died in Washington, D.C., October 13, 1890.

BELL, HENRY H. (1808 – 1868)—Union. Rear Admiral. Chief-of-staff to Farragut. Born in North Carolina, April 13, 1808. Became a midshipman in the U.S. Navy in 1823, and served in the Carribean campaign against pirates off the coast of Cuba (1828–1829). He served extended duty with the East India squadron, and was in command of one of the vessels of that squadron in November, 1856, when four forts near Canton, China, were destroyed.

Bell became fleet captain of the West Gulf squadron when war broke out and commander of one of the three divisions of Farragut's fleet during the capture of New Orleans. He became a commodore in 1865, taking command of the East India squadron in 1866.

Bell was drowned off the coast of Japan near the mouth of the Osaka River when his large barge capsized. He had resigned his commission at the time of the tragedy. The accident occurred on New Year's Day, 1868.

BENJAMIN, JUDAH PHILIP (1811–1884)—Confederate. Cabinet member.

Born on St. Thomas Island in the British West Indies. Benjamin was educated in Charleston and at Harvard. He was a New Orleans lawyer and businessman prior to the war. He also served as a senator for the state of Louisiana as a Whig, and as such advocated secession following the election of Lincoln.

Benjamin bolted the Whig party following the election and became a Democrat. In September of 1861, Jefferson Davis appointed him attorney general of the Confederacy. He was later transferred to the Confederate War Department, and was unjustly blamed for most of the Confederate failures. In March of 1862, he became the secretary of state, thus becoming the only one of the Confederate cabinet members to hold two different posts in addition to an influential outside post in the government. He fled to England following the war, and became one of that country's most successful lawyers.

Benjamin rates as one of the few genuinely outstanding men in the Confederate cabinet.

BERMUDA HUNDRED—A peninsula in Chesterfield County, Va., formed by the junction of the Appomattox and James Rivers. Bitter fighting took place over this strategic spot throughout the war.

In 1864, General Butler occupied this point with about 25,000 Federal troops in order to entrench and await the arrival of General Grant's forces. His forces were constantly skirmishing with those of Confederate P. G. T. Beauregard who commanded 20,000 Confederates in the vicinity. The location of the point was near both Richmond and Petersburg, and therefore hotly contested.

Except for the arrival of forces under Gillmore and Ames, Beauregard's forces would have captured the position on May 16 after destroying Heckman's Brigade. On the 19th, the Confederates again assaulted the strong positions of Ames and Alfred Terry, but without success. The battle lasted from May 16 through May 30. Because of the entrenching movement, Butler was charged with military incompetence for bottling himself up at the point.

The land received its name from a transaction that took place in 1622 (Order No. 212 of the Bermuda Company) which provided that a tract of land be made over to the Bermuda Company by the Virginia Company. This land, Chesterfield County, Va., is still known as the Bermuda Hundred.

BETHESDA CHURCH—In Montgomery County, Md., just inside the District of Columbia line, and only seven miles from downtown Washington, D.C. The town is known simply as Bethesda, but during the war, it was known as Bethesda Church or Darcy's Store, after William Darcy, who ran the post office and general store on the toll pike. It was a focal point of the fighting around Washington.

The town developed around (and received its present name from) the old Bethesda Presbyterian Church. It has grown from a town of about twenty families during the war to a population of over 45,000.

BIG BETHEL, Virginia—A village on the peninsula between York and the James Rivers, in Virginia. The scene of an engagement on June 10, 1861, when Union General E. W. Pierce attempted to dislodge Confederates stationed around Yorktown under Confederate General John B. Magruder.

Great censure is attached to the move, because Union forces grew so confused at one point that they fired upon their own forces by mistake. However, they did succeed in crossing Black River, but were repulsed by Magruder's forces.

BIG BLACK RIVER—A river which runs into the Mississippi at Grand Gulf, Miss. Just about fifty of its 209 miles are navigable.

It was here that Confederate General Pemberton's forces after leaving Vicksburg to attack Grant, were trapped by forces under J. A. McClernand. The Union force, fresh from victories over this same force, numbered about 10,000. Pemberton had sent the main group of his force on to Vicksburg, and only had 8,000 men with him drawn up on both sides of the river. McClernand might have completely destroyed this force had he gone about the maneuver tactfully, but, except for the impetuous Lawler, the fighting would have continued to be just what Pemberton had designed it to be—a holding action. Lawler, seeing a weak spot in the Confederate line, directed his attack there, and broke the solidarity of the Rebel force. Pemberton withdrew, nursing his wounds, to Vicksburg, the coming siege of which eventually led to the capture of the city by Grant's forces.

BIG SHANTY STATION, Georgia—A point above Marietta where Union spy James J. Andrews and his raiders stole the Confederate train the "General" with plans to move northward tearing up track and tearing down wires and burning bridges.

Captured by forces under Hood on the third of October, after Sherman had taken the entire area. This maneuver by Hood occasioned Sherman to signal to his forces, "Hold the fort for I am coming," a message that eventually became the basis for a hymn by P. P. Bliss that was used in revivals.

BIRNEY, DAVID B. (1825 – 1864)—Union. Major General. Born in Huntsville, Ala., May 29, 1825. The son of James G. Birney, outstanding philanthropist and politician of the earlier nineteenth century. Birney graduated from Andover, studied law at Cincinnati, Ohio, and set up practice in Philadelphia in 1856.

He joined the Union army when war broke out, becoming a major general of volunteers on May 5, 1863. Distinguished himself in the battles of Yorktown, Williamsburg, second Bull Run, Fredericksburg and Chancellorsville. He was in command of the Tenth Corps of the Army of the James from July, 1864. Birney died in Philadelphia, Pa., on October 18, 1864.

BLAINE, JAMES G. (1830 – 1893)— U.S. Representative. Born in West Brownsville, Pa., January 31, 1830. Renowned as an orator, and an outspoken Reconstructionist. Blaine was considered the leader of Congress. It is said that the history of Blaine from the time he entered Congress until the disclosure of the infamous "Mulligan Letters," is a history of our growth. He possessed a rare talent for political thinking.

Blaine graduated from what is now Washington and Jefferson College, in 1847. He studied law but never practiced. He taught at Western Military Institute at Georgetown, Ky., and at the Philadelphia Institute for the Blind. He edited the *Kennebec Journal* in Augusta, Me.

A strong radical Republican, but tempered in his extremism by rare logic and planning skill. He is credited with being the actual architect of the Reconstruction program.

BLAIR, FRANCIS P., JR. (1821–1875)— Union. Major General. The son of journalist and politician Blair, Sr. Born in Lexington, Ky., February 19, 1821. Blair graduated from Princeton in 1841 and studied law at Transylvania University in Lexington. He set up a practice in St. Louis, and represented Missouri in the U.S. House of Representatives in 1857–59 and 1861–63. He became a Union major general and took part in the Vicksburg campaign and Sherman's "March to the Sea."

Blair became an unsuccessful candidate for the Vice-Presidency in 1868 and later U.S. senator on the Republican ticket (1871–1873). He died in St. Louis, Mo., July 9, 1875.

BLAIR, FRANCIS P., SR. (1791–1876)— American journalist and politician born in Abingdon, Va., April 12, 1791. Founder of the Republican party. Strongly antislavery. Blair campaigned actively for Lincoln, and aided in setting up Reconstruction with Lincoln. He was driven back into the Democratic party by the radical Republicans after Lincoln's death. Blair died at Silver Springs, Md., October 18, 1876.

BLAIR, MONTGOMERY (1813–1883)— Postmaster General under Lincoln. Born in Franklin County, Ky., May 10, 1813. A graduate of West Point, 1835. Resigned from the army in 1836 and was admitted to the bar in 1837 in St. Louis, Mo. Acted as one of the counsels in the Dred Scott Case, after moving to Maryland in 1853.

Blair switched to the Republican party when the Missouri Compromise was repealed. He was president of the Maryland Republican convention in 1861, and held the favorite son post at the Republican national convention in 1860. He was given a cabinet post by Lincoln as a result of the need for a Maryland member to represent the border states in the cabinet, and a compromise made by Lincoln's manager at the convention which brought Maryland into the Lincoln camp. While in office, Blair instituted the money order system, free delivery of mail in cities, and the system of sorting mail in railroad mail cars. He died at Silver Springs, Md., July 27, 1883.

"BLUE BELLY"—A term applied to the Union soldiers by the Confederate troops, applying to the color of the uniforms worn by the federal troops. The Union soldiers usually called their opponents "Johnny Rebs" or just plain "Reb."

BONHAM, MILLEDGE LUKE (1813–1890)—Confederate. Brigadier General. Born in Edgefield, S.C., December 25, 1813. Bonham attended South Carolina College, and later studied law and was admitted to the bar in 1837. He was a state representative from 1840 to 1844, and served with the South Carolina Brigade through the Seminole War. He was with the twelfth U.S. Infantry in the Mexican War.

Bonham was elected to Congress to succeed Representative Preston S. Brooks, but left his seat on December 21, 1860 when the entire South Carolina delegation withdrew on the eve of the outbreak of war. Bonham was commissioned a brigadier general, April 19, 1861, and fought at the first Battle of Bull Run. He gave up his command on January 27, 1862 to serve in the Confederate Congress. He was governor of South Carolina from 1862 to 1864.

BOOTH, JOHN WILKES (1838–1865)—Actor. Assassin of President Abraham Lincoln. Born at Bel Air, Md., August 26, 1838. The son of Junius Brutus Booth, he sided with the Confederacy although his family generally supported the Union. He did not serve actively, but continued to perform in the North, possibly spying.

Booth devised a plan to kidnap President Lincoln. However, the war ended before the plan could be put into action. He and other accomplices mapped out a plan to kill Lincoln, Seward, and Vice-President Andrew Johnson. Booth mortally wounded Lincoln while the latter was seated in a box at the Ford Theatre in Washington on April 14, 1865. Lincoln died the next morning.

While leaping from the box to the stage of the theatre, Booth broke his leg, but managed to reach Bowling Green, Va., before being surrounded on April 26, 1865, twelve days after the assassination. It is not certain whether he was killed by a bullet from the gun of one of his captors, or whether he shot himself rather than be captured. Most believe that Booth committed suicide rather than be taken.

BOYD, BELLE (1843–1900)—Confederate spy. Born at Martinsburg, Va., May 9, 1843. She was outspoken in her sympathies for the South. In 1861, on July 4th, Belle killed a Union soldier who was molesting her mother. She was cleared of the charges of murder, but was labeled highly dangerous, and placed under guard.

Well-educated and an accomplished pianist, horsewoman and dancer, Belle was much in demand in military circles. She delivered information, garnered through these associations with Union soldiers, to both "Stonewall" Jackson and Jeb Stuart via a loyal slave. When one of her messages was intercepted, she escaped punishment by leaning once more upon her tender age, and her "ignorance of the seriousness of the offense." Belle Boyd continued her activities immediately, stealing Union arms and ammunition and delivering them to the South.

After the first Bull Run, she joined the hospital staff at Front Royal, Virginia and tended the wounded brought in from that battle. Later, she served as a courier between some of General Beauregard's forces, and also between Jackson and some of his lesser officers. She is responsible, in part, for some of Jackson's Shenandoah Valley victories.

When Front Royal fell to the Union forces in July, 1862, she was arrested, and sent to Washington for trial. She was considered so dangerous that, at times during her trip, as many as 450 cavalrymen guarded her carriage. She was imprisoned in Old Capitol Prison, where the Northern press attacked her vehemently. She was called "Secesh Cleopatra."

In August, 1862, she was officially exchanged, but was arrested just one month later and confined to Carroll Prison, Washington, for four months. While carrying letters to Confederate agents in England, the ship upon which she was travelling was boarded by a U.S. Navy ship's crew under Lieutenant Samuel Hardinge, but she persuaded him to renounce his allegiance to the Union, allow

her to go free, and eventually marry her in England. He became the first of her three husbands.

She published her memoirs in London, 1865, where she had become a prominent actress of both the British and the American stage. She retired to marry again in 1869, but need forced her back to the stage. She died of a heart attack while performing in Kilbourne, Wis. (now Wisconsin Dells), June 11, 1900.

BRADY, MATHEW B. (1823–1896)— Union. Photographer. Born in Warren County, N.Y., in 1823. Brady studied under Samuel Morse of telegraph fame, to learn how to take and develop daguerreotypes. He set up his own studio, and began to use the newly developed process of "wet plate" photography. Brady published a very valuable "Gallery of Illustrious Americans." After using a Brady photograph of himself in his political campaign, Lincoln said, "Brady and the Cooper Institute made me President."

Given official sanction and a pass to the front lines when war broke out, Brady paid his own expenses throughout the war, spending his entire fortune of over $100,000 taking 3500 wet plates of the conflict. He hired twenty-two teams of men to take pictures around the battle fronts, and covered all major battles.

Seriously injured by a horsecar after the war, and almost destitute, Brady planned a grand exhibition of his war photos to recoup his fortune, but died five days before the exhibition was due to open. By his wet plate process, he could reproduce any number of given photos.

BRADY, MATHEW B., Photographic Process of—In 1839, when Louis Daguerre, a French inventor, announced that he had discovered the daguerreotype process, few recognized the value of the discovery. Brady, however, was one of the few, and set out to familiarize himself with the process. Daguerre's method resulted in the fixing of a photographic image on a copper plate coated with silver iodide. Brady used this to set up his first studio.

However, in combat situations, and later, Brady and his crew used the "wet plate process" or the "collodion process," discovered in 1851 by the Englishman Frederick S. Archer. The difference in the two processes was that only one picture could be captured with the daguerreotype, while any number of prints could be obtained by using the "collodian process." However, the latter process was more cumbersome because of the mass of equipment needed to produce a finished plate.

To prepare a plate for his camera, Brady had to first make a solution of collodion by dissolving gun cotton in alcohol and ether; to this he added soluble iodide. When the thick, gluish liquid was ready, a glass plate was dipped into it, and covered evenly with the solution. Allowed to dry, the plate was found to be covered with a thin solution which resulted after the ether and alcohol evaporated. Next, the plate was dipped into a solution of silver nitrate which sensitized it as the silver particles stuck to the coating of emulsion. All of this was done in the dark.

To develop a plate after it had been exposed, a solution of sulfate of iron and acetic acid was used. To wash the film, a bath of cyanide of potassium was used, and this removed all excess silver particles from the image. Finally, the plate was dipped in iodized water, dried and coated with varnish.

Brady trained twenty teams of photographers to take pictures of the war. Therefore, all Brady pictures were not necessarily taken by the photographer himself.

The actual taking of the picture was almost as complicated as the process for setting up the plates. First, the plate had to be inserted, locked in, and the slide removed. Next, the lenscap had to be removed and timed so that the sun could impress the image of the subject upon the plate. When sixty seconds had elapsed, the lenscap was replaced, the protective black slide replaced, and the holder removed. The plate was then ready to be developed. A gust of wind, a slight movement, any simple distraction could necessitate the carrying out of the whole process again, for the plate would be ruined.

From the beginning of the war until 1865 some minor changes, such as increased sensitivity of the emulsions and consequently faster action plates, came about. No major changes came about, however, until well after the war.

BRAGG, BRAXTON (1817–1876)—Confederate General. Born in Warrenton, N.C., and a 1837 graduate of West Point, Bragg served in the Seminole War and the Mexican War before resigning in 1856 to become a Louisiana planter. He was rated outstanding as an artillery officer in the Mexican War.

In February, 1861, Bragg was made a brigadier general in the Confederacy. Shortly thereafter, he became a major general, and in April, 1862, became a full general. Bragg commanded a corps at Shiloh; he took over command of the Army of Tennessee in June; invaded Kentucky, but was beaten in the Battle of Perryville on October 8, 1862. He later commanded at Murfreesboro (Stone's River), Tullahoma and Chattanooga. Bragg defeated the Federal forces at Chickamauga, but was, in turn, defeated at Missionary Ridge. Joe Johnston took over his command in December of 1863. Bragg was military adviser to Jefferson Davis at points during the war.

He has been described as a rigid disciplinarian, stern, uncompromising, and a leader who usually failed to follow up his advantages. He often won minor skirmishes, but would lose the overall battle because of this fault. He died in 1876.

BRANDY STATION, Virginia, the Battle of—Actually a series of skirmishes which were waged almost continuously from August, 1862, to late 1863. Brandy Station is a village in Virginia's Culpeper County, just fifty-six miles southwest of Alexandria. It was the scene of a number of minor skirmishes, with the first large one being on August 20. Most of the engagements were cavalry battles. The skirmishes were also listed on the books under Fleetwood and Beverly's Ford.

The fiercest of these contests was that fought between the units of Union Generals John Bulford and Alfred Pleasonton against the force under Confederate raider J. E. B. Stuart on June 9, 1836. The Federal forces were badly beaten in this encounter.

BRECKINRIDGE, JOHN CABELL (1821–1875)—Confederate Secretary of War. Born near Lexington, Ky., 1821. He graduated from Centre College in 1839, and became a lawyer before joining the fight in Mexico. The son of distinguished parents, Breckinridge turned to politics and was elected to Congress in 1851. In 1856, he was nominated for Vice-President by the Democrats and was elected with James Buchanan.

When Southern Democrats bolted the party in 1860, Breckinridge became their choice for President. In a four-way race, he lost out to Lincoln, and subsequently returned to the Senate. He attempted very sincerely to avoid war. He resigned his Senate post respected and very popular. Although his talents were more in the political field than in the military, he was reasonably competent as a military leader. His battles include Shiloh, Murfreesboro, Chickamauga, Missionary Ridge, the Shenandoah Valley campaign and Cold Harbor. During these campaigns, he rose to the rank of major general. Davis recognized his talent in the political area, and made him secretary of war of the Confederacy on February 4, 1865, but this was too late to put his talent to use. When the Confederacy fell, Breckinridge fled to Cuba and then to Europe until the furor died. Returning to Lexington in 1868, he resumed his old law practice with some degree of success.

Politically, Breckinridge favored secession and non-interference by the Congress with slavery in the territories. He did not, however, feel that 1860 was the proper time for the South to secede.

He was a U.S. representative at the age of thirty; Vice-President at thirty-six; and candidate for President at forty. He died at 5:45 P.M. on May 17, 1875, at the age of fifty-four. Breckinridge was vigorously opposed to the Ku Klux Klan during Reconstruction days in Kentucky.

In 1958, a Circuit Court judge dismissed an 1862 indictment for "treason and conspiracy" against John Cabell Breckinridge and other Kentuckians—almost one hundred years after the charge had been drawn up, and eighty-three years after Breckinridge had died.

BRICE'S CROSSROADS, Mississippi— Now a national park, located in Lee County, northeastern Miss., near Baldwyn. The national park was established February 21, 1929. Here, 8,000 Union troops under General Samuel D. Sturgis, engaged the Confederate cavalry under Nathan B. Forrest, numbering about 3,500 men. After a long pursuit, Forrest turned on his pursuer and soundly defeated the Union force. The defeat was considered one of the most ignominious Union defeats of the Tennessee-Mississippi campaign, and one of Forrest's most outstanding victories.

The Union troops, originally stationed at Memphis, were forced to retreat, helter-skelter, to the safety of that base in order to escape annihilation. The battle took place on June 10, 1864.

BROUGH, JOHN (1811–1865) — Governor of Ohio (1864–1865). Born in Marietta, Ohio, September 17, 1811. Brough studied at Ohio University, and later entered journalism. He served as clerk of the Ohio senate, 1835–1837, becoming a member of the House and chairman of the committee on banking and currency, at the age of twenty-six. He was elected to the post of state auditor from 1839–1845, and bought the Cincinnati *Advertiser* and changed its name to the *Enquirer*.

Brough refused to follow Vallandigham and the Copperheads when the war broke out. He was elected governor of Ohio on the Republican ticket by an unprecedented majority of 100,009, and inaugurated January 11, 1864. However, he did not live to complete his term of office. He died at Cleveland, Ohio, August 29, 1865.

BROWN, JOHN (1800–1859) — Abolitionist. Born in Torrington, Conn., May 9, 1800. Called "Ole Osawatomie" Brown, because of his part in the massacre at Osawatomie, Kan., May 24, 1856. Some say that his raid on Harper's Ferry was to obtain arms to set up a stronghold in the hills of Virginia to which slaves could flee, and from which raids could be conducted to free others. However, these plans were never clearly outlined.

Brown used the alias of Shubel Morgan for sometime in Kansas. He was hanged long before the war broke out, but he is mentioned because of his efforts at Harper's Ferry which made him a martyr to the North during the war. Investigation during his trial disclosed frequent instances of insanity in the maternal line of his family. (See HARPER'S FERRY, JOHN BROWN'S RAID AT.) Brown was hanged at Charles Town, Va., December 2, 1859, for his part in the raid on Harper's Ferry.

BROWN, JOHN, the Courtroom Speech of—November 2, 1859. On this date, when all of the formalities of the trial of John Brown, leader of the raid on Harper's Ferry, had ended, the clerk asked the usual question, "Have you anything to say why sentence should not be pronounced against you?" John Brown, not prepared to give a reply, stood, however, and uttered words which flashed across the country before his body was cold, and became reading reference and history overnight. In his booming voice, he said:

I have, may it please the court, a few words to say.

In the first place, I deny everything but what I have all along admitted: of a design on my part to free slaves. I intended certainly to have made a clear thing of that matter, as I did last winter when I went into Missouri and took slaves without the snapping of a gun on either side, moving them through the country, and finally leaving them in Canada. I designed to have done the same thing again on a larger scale. That was all I intended. I never intended murder, or treason, or the destruction of property, or to excite or incite slaves to rebellion or to make insurrection.

I have another objection, and that is that it is unjust I should suffer such a penalty. Had I interfered in the manner which I admit has been fairly proved—for I admire the truthfullness and candor of the greater portion of the witnesses who have testified in this case—had I so interfered in behalf of the rich, the powerful, the intelligent, the so-called great, or in behalf of any of their friends, either father, mother, brother, sister, wife or children, or any of that class, and suffered and sacrificed what I have in this interference, it would have been all right. Every man in this court would have deemed it an act worthy of reward rather than punishment.

The court acknowledges too, as I suppose, the validity of the law of God. I see a book kissed, which I suppose to be the Bible, or at least the New Testament, which teaches me that all things whatsoever I would that men should do to me, I should do even so to them. It teaches me, further, to remember them that are in bonds as bound with them. I endeavored to act up to that instruction. I say I am yet too young to understand that God is any respecter of persons. I believe that to have interfered as I have done, in behalf of His despised poor, I did no wrong, but right. Now, if it is deemed necessary that I shall forfeit my life for the furtherance of the ends of justice, and mingle my blood further with the blood of my children and with the blood of millions in this slave country whose rights are disregarded by wicked, cruel, and unjust enactments, I say let it be done.

Let me say one word further. I feel entirely satisfied with the treatment I have received on my trial. Considering all the circumstances, it has been more generous than I expected. But I feel no consciousness of guilt. I have stated from the first what was my intention, and what was not. I never had any design against the liberty of any person nor any disposition to commit treason or incite slaves to rebel or make any general insurrection. I never encouraged any man to do so, but always discouraged any idea of that kind.

Let me say also, in regard to the statements made by some of those who were connected with me, I hear it has been stated by some of them that I have induced them to join me. But the contrary is true. I do not say this to injure them, but as regretting their weakness. Not one but joined me of his own accord, and the greater part at their own expense. A number of them I never saw, and never had a word of conversation with, till the day they came to me, and that was for the purpose I have stated.

Now I have done.

And thus a man whose every effort in the war against slavery had, in the final analysis, failed, said his farewell to society. He was sentenced to be hanged one month from the date of this final speech, and on December 2, 1859, the sentence was carried out.

During the fighting, the trial, the hanging, and the investigation which followed, such notable Civil War personalities as Edmund Ruffin, Robert E. Lee, J. E. B. Stuart, "Stonewall" Jackson, the Virginia Military Institute cadets, Jefferson Davis, and others were touched by John Brown.

Few, if any, of the above-named Southerners anticipated a war of the scope to follow. Little did Lee, Stuart, Jackson, and Davis realize that this same Harper's Ferry would be the place where they would wage war against the Stars and Stripes after Ruffin had allegedly fired the first shot against that flag at Fort Sumter. Little did the cadets of Virginia Military Institute realize that their followers would be defending this same Virginian soil against an invading Union army which would be rampaging down the Shenandoah Valley, in just a few short years.

BRUSH MOUNTAIN, Georgia — This location, near Kennesaw Mountain, Ga., combined with Pine Mountain and Lost Mountain to make up J. E. Johnston's Confederate lines of defense during the retreat to Atlanta.

BUCHANAN, FRANKLIN (1800–1874)— Born in Baltimore, Md. Confederate. Became a naval midshipman at the age of fifteen. He rose from this beginning to become one of the founders of the Annapolis Naval Academy and its first superintendent. In 1853, Buchanan was with Commodore Perry's expedition to Japan.

Following the Mexican War, Buchanan resigned his commission and became a captain in the Confederate navy when war broke out. At that time, the Confederate navy was an almost nonexistent thing. Buchanan made this move when Maryland threatened to secede from the Union in September of 1861.

He commanded the C.S.S. "Virginia," an ironclad constructed from the old "Merrimac." In her, he destroyed two Union vessels at Hampton Roads, Va., on March 8, 1862, but was wounded in the encounter. He was not in active command when his vessel fought the famous battle with the "Monitor," having turned over his command to Lieutenant Catesby Roger Jones. Following this encounter, Buchanan was promoted to admiral and commanded the Confederate squadron at Mobile Bay, where he challenged the entire Union navy in the ram "Tennessee." Buchanan was one of the most able of the Confederate naval officers, and an old-style navy man who believed in the new-style ways of fighting.

BUCKNER, SIMON BOLIVAR (1823–1914)—This West Point graduate (1844) became a Confederate Lieutenant General during the war as the result of his competence and high respect. He was born in the area around Mumfordville, Ky., and served in the Mexican War before resigning to become a successful businessman.

When war broke out, he was beset by both sides to accept a commission. At first, Buckner refused both forces, but when the neutrality of Kentucky was threatened, he joined the Confederate forces. When Grant attacked Fort Donelson, Buckner was forced to conduct the surrender, although only third in command at the time, because his superiors fled. As a result, he was imprisoned, but was later exchanged. He returned to active duty, commanding under Bragg in the invasion of Kentucky and East Tennessee (Chickamauga). He also saw action in Louisiana. During the course of the war, he rose steadily in rank, finally becoming a lieutenant general.

Following the war, Buckner became governor of Kentucky. He was the last of the important Confederate generals to die. Buckner was one of the pallbearers at the funeral of Grant, for whom he held deep respect and admiration. He died in 1914 at the age of 91.

BUELL, DON CARLOS (1818–1898)—Union. Of Welsh descent, Buell was born near Marietta, Ohio, but grew up in Lawrenceburg, Ind. He graduated from West Point in 1841, and served in the Seminole and Mexican Wars. At the outbreak of the Civil War, he was serving as a lieutenant colonel in the adjutant general's department. By May of 1861, he had been appointed brigadier general and had taken over the command of the Army of the Ohio by the end of that same year.

Buell moved south in support of Grant early in 1862, and occupied Nashville. He is generally given credit for saving the Battle of Pittsburg Landing (Shiloh) for the Union by his timely arrival. He was promoted to major general. During the course of his campaign in Kentucky and Tennessee, Buell's forces chased an elusive and battle-reluctant Bragg all over the area, finally cornering him at Perryville and defeating him on October 8, 1862. He was, however, removed from command for not "more effectively opposing" Bragg. Although considered an excellent desk man who was not suited for field action, Buell performed admirably under good commanders. He was noted as an organizer.

BUFFINGTON, ADELBERT RINALDO (1837–1922)—Union. Born in Wheeling, W. Va. (then Virginia), November 22, 1837, and graduated from West Point in 1861. He served no vital part in the war other than serving in ordinance depots. He was breveted major in 1865.

Buffington invented depressing carriages for heavy guns, light steel artillery and shielded machine gun carriages, novel road and recoil brakes, magazine small arms and various parts of small arms (all after the war). He died at Madison, N.J., July 10, 1922.

BUFORD, JOHN (1826–1863)—Union Major General. Born in Woodford County, Ky., March 4, 1826. Graduated from West Point in 1848, and

served in the Sioux expeditions of 1855, in Kansas (1856–57), and in the Utah Expedition (1857–58).

Buford was appointed major in the Inspector General's corps in 1861, served on Pope's staff in 1862, and made brigadier general in that same year. He commanded a cavalry brigade under Hooker in the campaign in northern Virginia and was made chief of cavalry during the Maryland campaign. He succeeded Stoneman on McClellan's staff.

Buford is credited with playing a vital part in the Battle of Gettysburg, at Round Top and Wolf's Hill. He was considered a cool-headed, competent officer, and one of the most respected on either side. He died in Washington, D.C., December 16, 1863, of disease contracted during his active duty years.

BULLOCK, JAMES DUNWOODY (1823–1901)—Confederate naval officer. Born outside of Savannah, Ga., June 25, 1823. Bullock served as an agent for the Confederate navy in England when war broke out, supervising the building and equipping of Confederate raiders including the "Florida" and the "Alabama." He later served in France in this same capacity. He settled in Liverpool when the war ended and wrote a book entitled *The Secret Service of The Confederate States In Europe* (1883). He died in Liverpool, England, January 7, 1901.

BULLOCK, RUFUS BROWN (1834–1907) —Politician. Confederate transportation specialist. Civilian. Born in Bethlehem, N.Y., March 28, 1834, Bullock graduated from Albion Academy in 1859. He set up the Southern Express Company in Augusta, Ga. Bullock served as a delegate to the convention called to set up a constitution under the Reconstruction laws. He was governor of Georgia in 1868. He courageously defended the right of Negroes to sit in the Georgia legislature, and was forced to resign in 1870, charged with corruption. He was, however, acquitted of these charges and returned to a rather prominent position as a public service official.

BULL RUN (Manassas), the First Battle of—July 21, 1861. Fought just twenty-five miles west of Washington, D.C., in northeastern Virginia. The engagement was between the forces of Union General Irvin McDowell and Confederate Generals P. G. T. Beauregard and Joseph Eggleston Johnston. At the time of this battle, General Winfield Scott was chief of the Union armies, and he ordered McDowell forward to attack Beauregard, using a second force to contain Johnston from coming to Beauregard's assistance. Johnston's forces bypassed the Union holding force and rushed to Beauregard's aid in time to turn the tide of battle and turn a Union "victory" into bitter defeat.

This, the first major battle of the war, came as the result of public clamor to take Richmond. Civilians and unengaged army forces came out from Washington in droves to watch the battle. Many brought lunches. The Federal troops, though green, fought valiantly before Johnston's force appeared. This, coupled with wild rumors of greatly superior numbers and betrayal, led to a rout which saw Union forces stream back to Washington leaving 2,900 casualties behind. The Confederacy lost 2,000. Estimated figures place the Union force at 30,000 against the combined force of 32,000 men under Beauregard and Johnston. This was one of the few important battles in which the Union forces met superior numbers.

BURNS, JOHN ("Farmer Burns")—Union. The only citizen of Gettysburg, Pa., who fought at the Battle of Gettysburg. Known as "Farmer Burns," he showed up at the battle with an old rifle and a uniform which he had worn as a soldier in the War of 1812. He fought for the whole three days, and was greatly publicized for the deed.

BURNSIDE, AMBROSE EVERETT (1824–1881)—Union. Born in Liberty, Ind., and a graduate of West Point in the class of 1847, Burnside resigned from the army in 1853 to become a gun manufacturer and later a railroad executive. He is credited with organising the first Rhode Island Regiment in April, 1861. This unit fought at the first Bull Run (Manassas). He was commissioned brigadier general, and later captured Roanoke Island (January, 1862).

In March of that year, Burnside was again promoted, and with his rank of major general, commanded the attack on South Mountain. He later served in the assault on Stone Bridge, which was holding up the Union left at Antietam. In October,

46

he received his most important (and most trying) assignment—he was appointed to succeed a vacillating McClellan as commander of the Army of the Potomac. He held the post only three months, before being relieved. By his own admission, he was not fitted for the post. His dismissal came following a December 13 defeat at Fredericksburg, where he failed in an assault. Following his relief, he defended Knoxville, and commanded the Ninth Corps, in the Wilderness. He also served at Spotsylvania, Cold Harbor, and in the Petersburg campaign.

Burnside returned to business after the war, and became a very important personage. He was elected to the governorship of Rhode Island, and later became a U.S. senator from that state. In business, he was likeable, dependable, and honest but he was definitely not to be considered a "dashing" military commander.

BUTLER, BENJAMIN FRANKLIN (1818–1893)—Union. Brigadier General. Born in Deerfield, N. H., Butler attended Waterbury College and later studied law. He gathered a highly respected group of clients, and his general practice was very successful. His investments also succeeded, and he grew rich as a young man.

The lure of politics carried him into local government before the outbreak of the war, but because of his backing of the Southern Democrats in 1860, he became the subject of great controversy when he was elected brigadier general of the Massachusetts militia.

Butler commanded New Orleans in 1862, and became known as the "Butcher" and Butler the "Beast" because of his excesses. He was removed from the post because of his harsh and high-handed methods and his illegal (never proved) speculating activities. He commanded the Army of the James after that, but was unsuccessful at both Petersburg and Fort Fisher, N.C. Consequently, he was again removed from that post.

Following the war, he became one of the radical Republicans and served with various other smaller parties thereafter. In 1882, he was elected governor of Massachusetts, and ran as a Presidential candidate on the Antimonopoly and Greenback party tickets in 1884.

Definitely a "political" general, Butler was unable to carry his brilliant and highly skilled political "know-how" over into his military service. His period as commander of New Orleans is described as "one of the saddest chapters in the Civil War history." Because of a visual defect, he was known in New England circles as "Cockeyed Ben," but his title of "The Beast" is the one by which he is most widely known.

BUTTERFIELD, DANIEL (1831–1901)—Union Major General. Born in Utica, N.Y., October 31, 1831, Butterfield entered the Civil War as a colonel of a militia regiment. He had received his education at Union College, Schenectady, N.Y., and was engaged in operating a transportation business before assuming active command of the Twelfth New York Militia.

He rose to the rank of brigadier

general of volunteers, serving under Pope, Hooker, McClellan, Sherman, and Grant. He was Meade's chief of staff at Gettysburg, and became a division commander after making major general (1865, regular army).

Butterfield was grand marshall of the Washington centennial parade in New York City, 1889. He died in Cold Springs, N.Y., July 17, 1901, and is buried in the West Point military cemetery.

C

CALDWELL, CHARLES HENRY (1828–1877)—Union naval officer. Born in Hingham, Mass., June 11, 1828, Caldwell gained fame as commander of the "Itasca," during the bombardment of Fort Jackson and St. Philip, and the Chalmette batteries. He was also active in the capture of New Orleans. After the war (1874), he was promoted to commodore. He died at Boston, Mass., November 30, 1877.

CALHOUN, JOHN CALDWELL (1782–1850)—Born in Abbeville District, S.C., Calhoun is related to the Civil War because of his "South Carolina Exposition" (1818), which he wrote in opposition to the tariff of 1828. He postulated the principles of state's rights and nullification used by the South in its fight against the overtures of the Northern politicians and abolitionists to do away with slavery and impose antislavery legislation on the South.

CAMERON, SIMON (1799–1889) — Union Secretary of War. Born in Lancaster County, Pa., March 8, 1799. A newspaperman, banker and railroad builder before the war, he served as adjutant general of Pennsylvania for a time, and commissioner to the Winnebago Indians (1838). He was accused of swindling them.

From 1845 to 1849, Cameron served as U.S. senator from Pennsylvania on the Democratic Party ticket. He joined the Republican party when it was formed, and was elected U.S. senator on its ticket in 1856. His managers switched their votes to Lincoln during the convention of 1860 in exchange for a promise of a cabinet post for Cameron in the Lincoln administration.

Cameron was an extremist. He advocated arming the slaves. Because of discontent, he resigned from the cabinet in 1862 and accepted a post as minister to Russia. He gained their support for the Union, and, in November of 1862, resigned that post to live in semi-retirement until 1866 when he was again elected to the Senate.

Cameron was America's first "political boss," and as such ruled Pennsylvania with an iron hand. Although usually deemed honest, he considered an honest politician one who "would stay bought when he was bought." Cameron died in Lancaster County, Pa., June 26, 1889.

CAMPBELL, JOHN A. (1811–1889)—Confederate Assistant Secretary of War. Campbell was a member of the Peace Commission which journeyed to Fortress Monroe to meet Lincoln and Seward.

CARROLL, SAMUEL (1832–1893)— Union. Carroll commanded the unit which had driven Jubal Early's force from Cemetery Hill at Gettysburg. He led his men in the fighting around Brock Road during the battle for the Wilderness. His unit was known simply as "Sam Carroll's Brigade."

CARTRELL, LUCIUS J.—Confederate. Brigadier General. A Georgian by birth, Cartrell studied law in the offices of Robert A. Toombs (later to become the Confederate secretary of war) prior to the war. Cartrell served in Congress from 1857 until Georgia pulled her delegation out in 1861. He organized the Seventh Georgia and became its colonel.

Elected to the Confederate Congress, he remained only one term before returning to active duty as a brigadier general. He was wounded near the end of the war.

CARR, JOSEPH B. (1828–1895)—Union Brevet Major General. Born in Albany, N.Y. Carr entered the war as a colonel of the New York Volunteers (a militia outfit). He led this unit at the battles of Big Bethel and in the Peninsular campaign, being breveted major general of volunteers for his bravery. After the war, he was prominent in politics.

CASEY, SILAS (1807–1882)—Union Major General. Born in East Greenwich, R.I., and an 1826 graduate of West Point. Casey had served in the Mexican War, and had been wounded at Chapultepec. He entered the Civil War as a colonel, but had risen to the rank of major general of volunteers by May, 1862. He assisted in the defense of Washington in that year. While there, he wrote a manual entitled *Systems of Infantry Tactics* which became known simply as "Casey's Tactics" (1862).

CEDAR CREEK, the Battle of—October 19, 1864. Following the battle of Fisher's Hill, Confederate General Jubal Early followed Union General Philip Sheridan to Cedar Creek, continuously harassing Sheridan's supply lines and his skirmishers. A number of minor skirmishes took place, and the Confederates lost heavily. At Cedar Creek, Sheridan left his command to journey to Washington, twenty miles away, to confer with military officials there. He left General H. G. Wright in command.

The Confederates hit the Union camp at Cedar Creek by surprise, on the morning of the 19th, having crossed the creek on the night before under the cover of fog and darkness. Early led approximately 18,000 men against a Union force of over 31,000.

The Confederates captured the Union guns, and turned them on Sheridan's troops with devastating and demoralizing effect. The Federals withdrew to the north and west around Middleton, Va., under heavy fire. There, although re-enforced, they were sitting (reluctant to attack) when Sheridan arrived on the scene. He had heard that fighting was taking place, and had ridden twenty miles to rally his men. He did just that, repulsing Early's attack, and launching a Union counterattack which was eventually successful, though costly.

Early's entire force fled before Sheridan's force, leaving behind the captured guns to be recaptured by the Federals. The Union lost 644 killed and 3,430 wounded. Early lost 320 killed and 1,540 wounded. In the missing or captured category, the South lost 1,050 men while Sheridan lost 1,429. Early's defeat ended another Southern invasion attempt via the Shenandoah Valley.

CEDAR MOUNTAIN, the Battle of— August 9, 1862. This battle is called variously "Cedar Run" and "Slaughter's Mountain." Cedar Mountain is located in Virginia. The battle took place between forces under Union General Nathaniel P. Banks, and Confederates under Thomas "Stonewall" Jackson.

Banks had marched from the Culpeper Courthouse to support General G. D. Bayard's cavalry being driven back by a strong force under Jackson. The Confederate force numbered nearly 24,000 and Banks was bringing up 8,000 men to re-enforce Bayard's men.

Jackson had crossed the Rapidan on the 8th, and advanced to Cedar Mountain before running into concentrated Union artillery fire. During the skirmishing, Confederate General C. S. Winder was killed by a piece of shrapnel.

The Union force under Banks attacked at five p.m., with the reserve force being called into action, and

being forced to fall back with heavy losses. Jackson then ordered a Confederate advance towards Culpeper, but was stopped by the rallying Union forces who had been re-enforced by units from James B. Rickett's division and General Franz Sigel's force. Pope arrived to assume command of the Union forces.

Jackson abandoned his position during the night of the 11th, after two days of hand-to-hand combat. He left his wounded behind, along with 1,338 dead or dying. Only 31 Confederates were reported missing. The Union lost 1,759 men killed or wounded, and 594 missing.

CHAMBERLAIN, JOSHUA (1828–1914)— Union Brigadier General. Chamberlain wanted to be a theologian, but decided to teach instead. He was teaching at Bowdoin College in Maine in 1862, when, after receiving a leave of absence to "study in Europe," he joined the army instead. He became a colonel of the Twentieth Maine Infantry.

He was seriously wounded at Petersburg on June 18, 1864, but displayed such bravery in continuing to fight and direct his men that Grant ordered him made a brigadier even before he was able to leave hospital. This was the only field promotion Grant made for gallantry in action.

Technically, it might be said that Chamberlain survived his wounds. As a tribute to his bravery, he was given command of the troops which received Lee's surrender at Appomattox. He lived until 1914, but the Petersburg wound, which never really healed, became infected, and caused his death.

CHAMBERSBURG, Pennsylvania — A borough, the seat of Franklin County, Pa. This city was used as a staging area by General Robert E. Lee in preparation for the Battle of Gettysburg. It was later burned by Confederate General Early when the townspeople refused to pay $100,000 ransom in gold which had been demanded in tribute. Early's lieutenant, General John McCausland, entered Chambersburg on July 30, 1864, with a cavalry force, and set the whole town afire. John Brown allegedly planned his raid on Harper's Ferry while living in Chambersburg in 1859.

CHAMPION'S HILL, the Battle of—May 16, 1863. Near Vicksburg, Miss. When Grant decided to cut off his supply lines and live on the Mississippi countryside, he marched across the state, captured Jackson, Miss., and turned to continue his invasion of the Southern stronghold of Vicksburg. Jackson, being an important rail center, was needed badly by the Confederates, and when Confederate commander Joe Johnston attempted to unite with Vicksburg troops under Pemberton, Grant intercepted the latter, and the Battle of Champion's Hill ensued. Pemberton, by some strategic maneuvering (and a reluctance on the part of Union General McClernand) was able to come out of the battle with no more damage done to his cause than the splitting of General Loring's force from the main Vicksburg force. Had McCler-

nand not procrastinated at Big Black River (q.v.), the entire force of Pemberton might have been smashed. At Champion's Hill (on Raymond Road) Confederate General Tighman was killed. Johnston meanwhile, was retaking Jackson, Miss.

Union generals assigned by Grant to meet Pemberton and Johnston were James B. McPherson and McClernand. Neither maneuvered with great success during the encounter. Grant had seven divisions of 32,000 men on the three roads converging on Edwards Station. Pemberton carried 17,000 men into the battle.

CHANCELLORSVILLE, the Battle of—May 1–4, 1863. Major General Joseph Hooker, after replacing Ambrose P. Burnside in command of the forces on the Potomac, split his army in an effort to pincer Lee. He sent Major General John Sedgwick toward Fredericksburg, and then crossed the Rappahannock and the Rapidan in an effort to get to the rear of Lee's force. Lee, aware that Hooker had split his force, turned to face Hooker at the little crossroads community of Chancellorsville, Va., just ten miles west of Fredericksburg. Hooker had 73,000 men compared to Lee's 43,000, but Lee was a far more strategy-minded leader, and maneuvered so adroitly that the Federal force was in retreat by May 4th, four days after the battle began.

Jackson presented the key to the victory to Lee when informed by Stuart's cavalry that the Union line ended abruptly in the woods on Hooker's right flank. Hooker, disposed to disbelieve that Lee's army had its back to the wall, allowed Lee to wiggle out of the trap by taking advantage of the open area to the flank.

Although re-enforced to bring his army up to 113,000, Hooker decided to fight on the defensive, instead of taking the offensive. This skepticism proved fatal to the victory hopes of the Union. Lee, acting upon Jackson's tip, sent Stonewall around to hit the Federals from the right. Hooker's troops watched the entire maneuver of Jackson's 26,000 men (more than half of Lee's entire army) but interpreted it as a sign of retreat instead of taking the offense. The skepticism of Hooker again (if turned in a different direction) could have turned the tide of battle. Scouts informed him of this move by Jackson, but he was inclined to disbelieve their reports.

On May 2nd, at six P.M. (suppertime), Jackson's force smashed into Hooker's right flank, catching the Fifty-fifth Ohio Regiment during its meal. Hooker still refused to credit this as more than a demonstration. Major General O. O. Howard's Eleventh Corps was hit hardest, and troops under Colonel Leopold von Gilsa started a near panic by retreating, on the run, right through the woods. This, coupled with the heavy musket fire of the advancing Rebels, under Brigadier General Robert E. Rodes, forced the Federals to move back in near rout.

Later, the Federal troops rallied, but the Confederate troops fought ruggedly, and Hooker was forced to recall his force and retreat north, making Chancellorsville another Southern victory. On the morning of the 3rd, the 55,000 men under Reynolds and Meade (in a position to pincer Jackson) had been called back towards the center, relieving the pressure from Jackson's force. Sedgewick, who had been dispatched to take Fredericksburg, barely missed annihilation at the hands of Early's force.

Also on the 3rd, the right flank of the Union force crumbled, leaving Geary's division of the Twelfth Corps and Hancock's division between Chancellor House and Lee's force—the only Union force there. The Confederates turned Geary's flank and forced his troops back to the junction of Plank Road and the Orange Turnpike.

Couch, in his account of the battle, states that a rumor of the death of Hooker, started when a ball from a Confederate artillery unit hit a post against which Hooker was leaning, added greatly to the confusion of the moment. The Fifth Maine, sent to aid Couch, suffered heavily, losing most of its non-commissioned officers, and all of its officers killed or wounded. Kirby died there—Colonel Miles fell.

Hooker, using the need to defend Washington as his excuse to withdraw, turned the army over to Couch with orders to do so. It was May 4th, and the battle was over. Lee's force of 60,000 men (if all units including hospital units be counted) had smashed Hooker's massive 124,000 (counting 11,000 men who were not even called into action —a cavalry corps, an artillery unit of 400 guns, and maintenance units). The South lost 13,000 men, but left 17,000 Federals on the field dead or wounded. However, the South lost more than it could ever replace, for the valuable Thomas "Stonewall" Jackson was killed there. His loss was one of the South's greatest.

To again quote Couch concerning the battle : "In looking for the cause of the loss of Chancellorsville, the primary ones were that Hooker expected Lee to fall back without a battle. Finding himself mistaken, he assumed the defensive, and was outgeneraled . . . by the superior tactical boldness of the enemy."

CHANDLER, ZACHARIAH (1813–1879)— Statesman. Former Mayor of Detroit. Chandler succeeded General Lewis Cass in the U.S. Senate in 1857, on a Republican ticket after having helped organize the party in 1854. He was the author of the "Blood Letter" in which he held that "without a little blood-letting, the Union will not . . . be worth a rush."

Chandler opposed the admission of Kansas under the LeCompton Constitution. He was a friend of Lincoln's but much more radical than the President. He was, in fact, one of the leaders of the radical Republicans. Chandler led the attack on Jefferson Davis after the war. He served as secretary of the interior under Grant.

CHANTILLY, Virginia, the Battle of— September 1–2, 1861. About three miles west of Fairfax Courthouse, Va., Lee formed his troops after the second Battle of Bull Run (Man-

assas), interposing his forces between those of the Union General Pope and the city of Washington. The main position was held by Jackson's force.

When Pope learned of this maneuver, he assigned General Issac L. Stevens the task of clearing the Rebels out of the position at Ox Hill (Jackson's force). Stevens proceeded with 3,000 men, to advance on the entrenched Confederates. In the battle which followed, neither side gained an appreciable foot of ground after a full day (and most of the night) of fighting, and Pope fell back to Washington to be fired, while Lee leisurely marched his tired troops across the Potomac to Maryland. The Union lost about 800 men; the Confederates lost 700. The battle ended in darkness but scattered skirmishes took place until a severe rainstorm ended all action for the muzzle-loading soldiers. During the fighting, five color bearers of the leading Seventy-ninth New York went down in rapid succession. The Twenty-first Massachusetts suffered heavy losses also.

CHARLESTON, South Carolina—The second largest city in South Carolina. The scene of the passing of the Nullification Ordinance of November 24, 1832, and the first Ordinance of Secession, December 20, 1860. The first act of war occurred in Charleston Harbor when Fort Sumter's supply ship the "Star of the West" was fired upon, January 9, 1861. Fort Sumter itself was fired upon and captured, April 12–14, 1861, and Federal troops occupied the city in 1863.

53

Here too, in the harbor, the first submarine to sink an enemy ship in time of war (see "HUNLEY") performed its deed against a Union vessel in February, 1864. The city was under Federal blockade from May, 1861, until February 17, 1865. It was partly destroyed by fire by troops under Confederate General Hardee to prevent use of its facilities by Federal forces advancing on the city in February, 1865.

CHATTANOOGA, Tennessee, the Battle of—November 23–25. Hooker occupied Lookout Mountain; Sherman had a force of three divisions concealed behind the hills above Chattanooga; and the Army of the Cumberland (with the Eleventh Corps in support) was on a line directly above the city. All in all, Grant's force totaled about 60,000 men against the Confederates' 40,000, and this was the situation on November 23, when the Battle of Chattanooga began.

Grant planned to have Hooker hold Lookout Mountain against Bragg's left, while Sherman crossed the Tennessee River and mounted Missionary Ridge to proceed South. General Thomas, and his Army of the Cumberland, was to connect with Sherman on the left and clear the ridge and valley. After three days of fighting, Bragg had been swept back into lower Tennessee and the Union forces were in complete control of the area around Chattanooga. Union losses totaled 753 killed; 4,722 wounded; and 349 missing. The South lost 361 killed; 2,180 wounded; and 4,146 missing.

CHASE, SALMON PORTLAND (1808–1873)—Union Secretary of the Treasury. Born in Cornish, N.H., and a graduate of Dartmouth. Prior to the war, Chase was very active as an anti-slavery politician and an abolitionist. He often defended fugitive slaves in his law practice in Cincinnati.

Chase was one of the organizers of the Liberal Party in 1841, and founded the Free-Soil Party in that year also. He served in the U.S. Senate from 1849 to 1855, when he resigned to become governor of Ohio. In 1860, he was re-elected to the Senate after an unsuccessful attempt to get the Republican nomination for President. He never got over this defeat.

When Lincoln was elected, he appointed Chase secretary of the treasury, against the wishes of Secretary of State Seward. Both Seward and Chase handed in their resignations when they heard that the other had been appointed also. Lincoln refused to honor either of the resignations.

Chase was in constant conflict with Seward, and in general opposition to Lincoln with regard to the handling of the slavery question. His strong will and ambition offset many of his outstanding contributions which included the National Banking Act, 1863, and his reorganization of the Federal court system in later years.

Chase submitted four resignations to Lincoln before Lincoln finally accepted one (an act which surprised Chase). Strangely enough (and substantiating the belief that Chase held strange power over the President) six months after his resignation, Chase was made chief justice of the U.S. Supreme Court by Lincoln. No reason was given for this move. Chase presided over the trial of Jefferson Davis, and recommended that the indictment of treason be dropped (1867). He also presided over the impeachment proceedings against President Andrew Johnson (1868).

Along with Seward, Chase is referred to as the most moving political entity in the Lincoln cabinet. He was moody, violently antislavery, and a dedicated radical Republican. He has been described as "jealous of the President," "overly ambitious," "capable." It was at his insistence that Lincoln added the words "invoking the favor of Almighty God" to the Emancipation Proclamation. He also insisted that the phrase which originally read :

> The executive Government of the United States, including the Military and the Naval authority, will recognize and maintain the freedom of such persons. . . .

be changed to read :

> . . and will do no act or acts to repress such persons or any of them in any effort they may make for their actual freedom.

Chase also wished the language stronger in reference to arming the Negroes, but conceded the point when Montgomery Blair stated that such a move would alienate the border states in the coming election.

Lincoln's personal secretary, John Nicolay, wrote, "There is enough in Chase's letters abusing Lincoln behind his back for quite a scorcher."

A group of discontented Unionists sounded Chase out as a possible Presidential candidate. He was mentioned in the circular which became known as the "Pomeroy Circular" as the logical candidate to succeed Lincoln (written by Senator Pomeroy of Kansas). The paper, circulated secretly, fell into the hands of the press, and was published in one of Washington's most powerful newspapers. Chase was cleared of any personal responsibility or knowledge of the paper.

His resignation from the cabinet was accepted by Lincoln in a note which stated :

> Of all I have said in commendation of your ability and fidelity, I have nothing to unsay; and yet, you and I have reached a point of mutual embarassment in our official relations which it seems cannot be overcome or longer sustained consistently with the public service.

And six months later, he made Chase chief justice of the Supreme Court. Chase's diary indicates that he would have remained in the cabinet if prevailed upon strongly enough by Lincoln (as on the three other occasions).

Chase was an admirable Supreme Court leader, and was extremely capable as secretary of the treasury. His only fault was his seeming inability to keep personalities outside of his office.

CHEVAUX DE FRISE—Armed beams of square timber or strong material, used to defend fronts of camps, trenches or beaches. They were usually about 15 to 18 feet long, connected with chains or strong wire. In the original form, the *Chevaux de Frise* was a hedge of spikes or spears designed to impail a man who was charging the barricade. It received its name from a siege in the Netherlands (Friesland) in 1658. The name actually means, "horses of Friesland."

CHICAGO BOARD OF TRADE PETITION— In the latter stages of the war, the news of life in prison camps began to filter out, and civilians on both sides grew indignant. Andersonville prison in Georgia was one which stirred the wrath of most Northerners during this period. The president and secretary of the Chicago Board of Trade wrote to President Lincoln, listing scores of horrible evils which were being inflicted upon Union troops.

They suggested that Lincoln take "retaliatory measures" against the South by setting aside an equal number of Confederate prisoners and subjecting them to the same treatment being accorded Northern soldiers in Andersonville. "We are aware," they wrote, "that this, our petition, savors of cruelty." Lincoln did not heed the letter.

CHICKAMAUGA, the Battle of—September 19–20, 1863. Chickamauga, just fifteen miles south of Chattanooga, Tenn., across the Georgia border, was the scene of a fierce battle between the forces of Union General Rosecrans and Confederate General Braxton Bragg. Rosecrans, after chasing Bragg back into the city of Chattanooga, decided to split his army into three parts, encircle the city, and set up siege operations.

Bragg, seeing the danger, hit the divided army of Rosecrans, driving it back to a place called West Chickamauga Creek in northwest Georgia. There, the Federals regrouped before Bragg could do any extensive damage, and prepared to hit back.

On the night of the 19th, reenforced by fresh troops under Longstreet, Bragg attacked Rosecrans. He successfully carried one of the Federal flanks, forcing the major part of the Union army to fall back to Chattanooga. General George Thomas, however, refused to draw his troops back until late on the night of the 20th, allowing Rosecrans to withdraw all vital equipment and supplies. He earned the sobriquet "the Rock of Chickamauga" for this feat. The Union lost 16,000 men; Bragg lost 18,000 This was decidely a Southern tactical victory, but the loss of 18,000 men sapped the Southern strength dangerously. Thomas replaced Rosecrans as commander of the troops around Chattanooga after this engagement.

CHICKASAW BLUFFS, Mississippi, the Battle of—December 29, 1862. Also called the Battle of Chickasaw Bayou. This was one of the few Union defeats during the Vicksburg campaign under Grant, and was not really necessary.

Sherman, commanding four divisions under Morgan, A. J. Smith, Steele and M. L. Smith, attempted to storm the Chickasaw Bluffs enroute to taking Vicksburg. The bluffs overlooked the river and Chickasaw Bayou, and were heavily fortified by troops of Vaugh, Gregg, and S. D.

Lee under Pemberton. Rifle pits were in place, and batteries had been set up by engineer Lee. In addition, the Confederates were on the firm footing of the bluffs while Sherman's force had to land and attack in marshy, thick bottom land, densely wooded.

Against the advice of his subordinate commanders, Sherman ordered the assault. He is alleged to have said, "We will lose 5,000 men before we take Vicksburg, and may as well lose them here as anywhere else."

After clearing a path through the vegetation, troops under DeCourcy, Blair and Thayer succeeded in establishing a lodgement on the mesa between the marsh and the bluffs. The Confederates had earlier abandoned these fortifications. The main body pushed up the slope under heavy fire, and were met at the top of the hill by a murderous crossfire from the rifle pits and the batteries set up by Lee. The Union troops fell back, leaving 1,500 killed, wounded or captured at the top of the bluffs. Under cover of darkness, Sherman withdrew his forces to a point just out of gunfire range.

The next morning, Sherman planned to resume the attack, but when daylight broke, he thought better of the action, loaded his men back aboard the transports furnished by Admiral David Porter, and moved on down river. Porter was supposed to have supported the Union attack, but a heavy fog made it impossible for him to move his ships into attack position. Union losses totaled 1,776 (most of them at the top of the bluffs). The Confederates, behind strong entrenchments, lost a mere 177 killed or wounded, with 10 missing. This was a deserved tribute to the strength of the position laid out by S. D. Lee.

CITY POINT — Union supply base. From this point, Grant's quartermaster corps ran 18 trains each day to the Union troops at the front, over a 21-mile long railroad which they had built (see CITY POINT RAILROAD). City Point was a seaport town. Before the war, it had been a sleepy riverside hamlet, with few commercial facilities. During the war years, it became one of the greatest seaports in the world at that time. The Union engineers built wharves which extended for over one mile.

Two steam engines were set up to pump in a water supply daily, and an average of 40–50 steamboats docked there every day, along with 70–75 sailboats and 100–110 barges.

There was an army hospital there which covered 200 acres, and had a patient capability of as many as 10,000 at a time. The city was a maze of warehouses, shops, barracks, and civilian quarters. The quartermaster there boasted that he could supply an army of 500,000 if called upon to do so. Four passenger steamers plied daily between City Point and Washington.

The wealth of supplies at City Point was often mentioned by the supply-short Confederates in their camps. In its entirety, City Point was a purely military city after it became a supply depot for the eastern armies.

CITY POINT RAILROAD—The government built a 21-mile long railroad to connect City Point with the area of the front lines. The nucleus of this network of track, yards, roundhouses, and repair shops was the railroad which had originally been built to connect City Point with Petersburg. The track itself, however, had been destroyed, and only the right-of-way remained when the Union began its work. The railroad serviced all of the front line to Appomattox. It was used to supply, re-enforce, and bring back the wounded. The line operated a maximum of 18 trains a day, with from 15–24 cars in each train. Passengers of a non-military nature were sometimes carried.

CIVIL RIGHTS IN THE CONFEDERACY—Contrary to popular Northern belief, the South expressed great concern over civil rights during the period between 1860 and 1865. On the military scene, it is a known fact that democracy played a greater part in the Southern army than in the Northern force (particularly in the east) — to the detriment of the Southern cause.

Jefferson Davis was continuousuly expounding the civil rights theories found in the Constitution, mainly, freedom of speech, freedom of the press, and freedom from arbitrary arrest. Persons abusing the Davis administration were allowed to continue to do so, as long as they did not openly express Union sympathies or preach revolt.

In the North, a tighter rein was kept on public utterances. True, the Lincoln administration drew its share of condemnations, but when these became too vocal, or "tinted" with Southern ideas, the government clamped down. Note the suspension of the writ of habeas corpus in many instances. Clement Laird Vallandigham, a peace "Copperhead," was actually expelled from the Union because of his views.

The results of the two rather conflicting attitudes were these : (1) The disloyal elements in the South (disloyal to the Confederacy) had free and unrestricted movement to meet, organize and express their views; (2) This freedom of movement allowed them to form organizations such as the Peace Societies, to grow, and to foster the peace ideas of others. If caught, they were subject to civil law rather than military law as in the Union.

In the North, treasonable orders were promptly stamped out, and arrested persons were subject to military trial. Armed troops were used to quell riots (i.e., draft, food rationing, etc.).

By granting a greater amount of civil rights during wartime, the Davis administration actually helped in its own downfall. As Charles H. Wesley says in his *Collapse of the Confederacy,* the people of the South lost the war because the home front actually became disenchanted with the privations and the news of losses on the battlefield.

"Peacemongers" circulated among the homefolks, suggesting that they write to their relatives at the front telling them to lay down their guns and come home. Desertion in the

Confederate army reached atrocious proportions in the latter stages of the war.

Dr. Wesley contends that letters from home and the attitude conveyed to soldiers home on leave caused the men at the front to lose interest in the war. Had the Davis administration been more strict, loose talk such as this would have been squelched before it reached the fighting force.

Basically then, the Confederacy would have done better had it been more rigid instead of more civil rights conscious. It is to be noted also that the term civil rights as expressed in 1861 did not carry the same connotation as today. It referred to only one segment of the population, dealing in the rights of the white resident, and excluding the Negro entirely. When the term "all people" was used, in Confederate communications, it was done with the thought in mind that the Negro (whether free or slave) was not a person in the Southerner's eyesight.

In the book, *Why the North Won the Civil War,* edited by David Donald, the South is described as having "died of democracy." It describes the North's action, however, in a different light. Donald states that "the Lincoln government handles disloyalty and sedition with the same grim efficiency which was shown during the later Woodrow Wilson and Franklin D. Roosevelt administrations."

CLEBURNE, PATRICK RONAYNE (1828–1864)—Confederate major general. Born in Cork, Ireland. Cleburne served in the British army before coming to the United States in 1849. He settled in Helena, Arkansas, and became both a druggist and a lawyer.

In 1860, Cleburne organized a group of sharpshooters known as the Yell Rifles, and, upon secession of Arkansas, became a captain and later a colonel of the Confederate infantry. By early 1862, he had risen to brigadier general, and had served at Shiloh, Richmond, Kentucky and Perrysville. He was promoted to major general in December, 1862, and fought at Murfreesboro, Chickamauga and Missionary Ridge with that rank.

Cleburne constantly urged the Confederacy to free the slaves during the war, but his opinion only served to keep him from rising higher militarily. In the battle around Atlanta, he served under both Johnston and Hood. He was mortally wounded while with Hood's advancing army at the Battle of Franklin. Among his fellow officers he was known as the "Stonewall Jackson of the West." He was greatly respected by both sides.

COLD HARBOR, the Battle of, Virginia —June 1–12, 1864. After moving around a well-entrenched group of Lee's troops at North Anna River, Grant marched towards Mechanicsville. There he found Lee in force, and rather than risk further losses for an unimportant location, Grant bypassed Lee for the fourth time of the campaign. His move, however, was countered by Lee, and the Federal forces came face-to-face with the fast-moving Confederates at Cold Harbor.

The Union army was only ten

miles northeast of Richmond, and Grant had been re-enforced during his march (bringing his force to approximately 108,000). Lee, with additional troops from Richmond, had been able to bring his army to 59,000. Not having accurate reconnaissance reports of the enemy disposition and strength, Grant threw three charges at the Confederate front. Each was stopped by heavy musket fire and artillery, forcing Grant to settle down to trench warfare.

Two other corps attacked Confederate Ewell's position at Bethesda Church, and this caused the attack of the 2nd to fail for the Union when Burnside and Warren were unable to coordinate their attacks. On the 3rd, the area which became famous (or infamous) as the "Bloody Angle" played an important part. There, over 800 men fell before the concentrated Southern firepower.

Grant was defeated here also, but the size and power of his army forced Lee to allow him to bypass and reach Richmond. Union casualties totaled 7,000. Lee lost 1,500.

COLORED SOLDIERS (see NEGRO TROOPS).

COLUMBIA, South Carolina, the Fall of—February 17, 1865. Columbia is the state capital of South Carolina, and the seat of Richland County. The city fell on February 17, 1865, when troops under Union General Sherman marched into the city following a formal surrender.

Sherman had bombarded the city from a position across the Congaree River. After the surrender, a large portion of the city was destroyed by fire, with both sides denying blame for setting the city ablaze.

COLUMBUS, Mississippi—The Confederate government maintained an arsenal there during the war. The city, located on the Tombigbee River about seven miles from the Alabama border, was a communications center and the scene of minor skirmishes between cavalry units during the war.

CONFEDERATE STATES OF AMERICA, the Military Leaders of the (1861–1865)—The top echelon of the Confederacy varied very little during the war except in the post of secretary of war. Prior to 1865, there was no general-in-chief. The government military leaders for the period of the Confederacy's existence were:

President and Commander-in-Chief:
    Jefferson Davis
    (Feb. 18, 1861–May 10, 1865).

Secretary of War:
    LeRoy P. Walker
    (Feb. 21, 1861–Sept. 16, 1861).
    Judah P. Benjamin
    (Sept. 17, 1861–March 22, 1862).
    George W. Randolph
    (Mar. 22, 1862–Nov. 17, 1862).
    Gustavus W. Smith, Maj. Gen. (Nov. 17, 1862–Nov. 20, 1862).
    James A. Seddon
    (Nov. 21, 1862–Feb. 4, 1865).

John C. Breckinridge, Maj. Gen. (Feb. 4, 1865–May 10, 1865).

General-in-Chief :

(This post created for Lee by the Confederate Congress.)

Robert E. Lee
(Feb. 6, 1865–April 24, 1865).

CONFISCATION ACT, the—This act provided that the property of persons in rebellion against the government could be siezed and held by the Federal forces in the area. It meant the appropriation of this property by the state and national government without compensation. In the latter years of the war, slaves were declared "contraband" and were subject to the Confiscation Act's provisions.

During the early nineteenth century, the tendency had been to exempt the property of enemies in that belligerent's own territory. However, during the Civil War, the U. S. Congress authorized seizure of cotton, slaves, and other properties used for insurrectionary purposes.

CONSCRIPTION ACT OF 1863—Union. March 3, 1863. This was the first major conscription act in U.S. history. It was remarkably unsuccessful. The act called for all males between the ages of twenty and forty-five to be declared eligible for military service. The announcement of the draft levies brought about riots in many cities (see DRAFT RIOTS), and actually resulted in the necessity of drawing troops from the front lines to restore order.

CONSCRIPTION ACT OF 1862—Confed-erate. April 16, 1862. This act was adopted by the Confederacy to bolster the front line strength. There were no major demonstrations against the act.

CONTRABAND—A term referring to goods destined for the enemy which a belligerent may lawfully seize and confiscate. The contesting forces during the war intercepted each other's property, and interpreted the term to mean any property that might aid the enemy in the prosecution of the war.

The North declared Negro slaves contraband in 1863 (because of their potential as labor manpower). Usually, however, the term applied to goods seized in the possession of neutrals but destined for a belligerent.

COOPER, SAMUEL (1789–1876)—Confederate General. Born in Hackensack, N.J., and a West Point graduate. Cooper became a regular army officer upon graduation, and settled down to an army career. He married a Virginia woman, and consequently resigned his post at the outbreak of war (he was adjutant general) to accept a similar post under his friend Jefferson Davis, with the rank of full general. Until February 6, 1865, he was the highest ranking officer in the Confederate army by virtue of his seniority in rank.

He is seldom mentioned by historians in connection with the war, because he saw no active duty, and performed rather inconspicuously. He was 87 when he died.

CORDUROYING—The method of laying log roads along marshy or swampy paths in order to move heavy equipment and supplies. It was in this manner that the war was pursued during the spring and fall of the war years, when roads in many sectors were normally impassable. Prior to the introduction of this system, the two seasons were combined with winter to recoup and rest troops. Only late spring, summer and early fall were used for fighting.

CORSE, JOHN M. (1835–1917)—Union Brevet Major General. Born in Pittsburgh, Pa. Corse attended West Point for two years, but resigned to practice law. He commanded at Allatoona, Ga., and near Cartersville and around Adairsville, Ga., during the Atlanta Campaign.

It was to him that Sherman sent the now famous heliograph message, "Hold the fort, for I am coming," which is said to have inspired Philip P. Bliss to compose the hymn "Hold the Fort." Corse held the fort. He accompanied Sherman on his "March to the Sea," and was with him in North Carolina. Corse became an internal revenue collector in Chicago after the war, and later postmaster of Boston.

COUCH, DARIUS N. (1822–1897)—Union Major General. Born in southeast Putnam County, N.Y., and a graduate of West Point in 1846. In 1861, Couch was commissioned a brigadier general, and became a major general in May of that year. He served at Williamsburg, Fair Oaks, Malvern Hill, Fredericksburg, Chancellorsville, Nashville, and in North Carolina.

Couch commanded the Second Corps during most of his army career, as a major general. He is responsible for organizing the Pennsylvania Militia to resist Lee's invasion in 1863, and is generally referred to as having been a good officer. He served as port collector of Boston after the war, and later became adjutant general of the state of Connecticut.

COX, JACOB DOLSON (1828–1900)—Union Major General. Born in Montreal, Canada, and a graduate of Oberlin College, 1851. Cox taught school before the war, and practiced law. He became a brigadier general of Ohio volunteers when war broke out. By 1862, he had risen to major general. He commanded a division at Nashville.

After the war, Cox wrote a number of books on the Civil War, including *Atlanta, The March to the Sea, Franklin and Nashville,* and *The Battle of Franklin.* His most noted work is his *Military Reminiscences of the Civil War.* Cox was elected governor of Ohio after the war, but spoke out so strongly against Negro suffrage that he lost favor with his party. He became secretary of the interior under Grant in 1870.

CRATER, the Petersburg—Just 130 yards from the Confederate trenches at Petersburg, the Forty-eighth Pennsylvania under Colonel Henry Pleasants, began to dig a tunnel towards the Confederate lines. The unit, made up mainly of coal miners, was directed to serve under Pleasants, a mining engineer, when the idea was presented to the commanding officers by the young colonel.

It took about twenty-eight days to dig the tunnel, and four tons of powder were laid. During the digging operations, the Confederates, aware of some type of tunneling project, dug numerous counter tunnels, hoping to either break through or cave in the Union tunnel. Their efforts failed, and on July 30, 1864, at 4:45 A.M., the charge was exploded.

Due to ineffective preparations for the attack through the tunnel, disaster struck the Union attacking force. The charge, as planned, ripped a gaping hole 500 yards wide in the very center of Lee's line. The explosion was accompanied by a heavy Union artillery barrage. Although fresh Negro troops were standing by to lead the assault, the high command felt that there would be some repercussions if the move failed and the Negroes were slaughtered, so they sent battle-weary whites into the tunnel.

In addition to this fiasco, no scaling ladders had been provided for the troops, and the crater walls were inaccessible. The parapet walls could not even be scaled without ladders, and thus the Confederates were given time to rally from the initial shock of the explosion and slaughter the Union forces in the deep crater.

Quick-thinking Rebel general William Mahone is credited with rallying the Southerners and attacking the break. It became a "cauldron of hell" for Federal troops. By one P.M., the Confederates had plugged the hole by killing great numbers of Union troops. Grant termed the maneuver by the Federals "a stupendous failure."

CRITTENDEN COMPROMISE—Proposed in 1860–1861 as a Constitutional amendment by Kentucky Senator John Jordan Crittenden. He proposed that the line between free and slave states be drawn to conform with the line of the Missouri Compromise, and that Federal powers agree to support slavery in areas where it already existed and fight it where it did not already exist. He strongly supported the Fugitive Slave Act.

The legislatures of New Jersey, Virginia, Kentucky and Tennessee ordered their delegates to the Peace Conference to support the Crittenden proposals. It lost in the House 113 to 80 (January 14, 1861), and in the Senate, 20 to 19 (March 2, 1861). Had it been voted on prior to December, 1860, it might have passed in the Senate. The passage of the compromise would have put off the war for a few years, and stopped the rash of secessions. However, it would not have ended the threat of war entirely.

CRITTENDEN, GEORGE BIBB (1812–1880)—Confederate Brigadier General. Born in Russellville, Ky., and an 1832 West Point graduate. Crittenden suffered ignominious defeat at Mills Springs, Ky., in 1862, and was arrested for his failure to perform his duties properly. He remained under guard until he resigned his commission. Later, he joined the army as a volunteer. This Crittenden served the state of Kentucky as librarian from 1867 to 1871.

CRITTENDEN, JOHN JORDAN (1787–1863)—Politician. Born in Woodford County, Ky. This Crittenden, the father of the abortive Crittenden Compromise, was also the father of two generals—one on each side of the war. He graduated from William and Mary College in 1807, and was prominent in politics from 1816 through 1863 when he died. He was a vital cog in the move to keep the state of Kentucky neutral, and later, loyal to the Union.

CRITTENDEN, THOMAS LEONIDAS (1819–1893) — Union Major General. Born in Russellville, Ky., and served as state attorney for Kentucky before the war. This Crittenden was the brother of Confederate General George Bibbs Crittenden. He served as consul at Liverpool in 1849, and became a brigadier general of volunteers when the Civil War broke out. By 1862, he had become a major general.

Crittenden, although considered by some to have been a "political general," distinguished himself at Shiloh, Stone's, and Chickamauga. He retired from the army in 1881.

CROOK, GEORGE (1829–1890)—Union Major General. Born near Dayton, Ohio, and an 1852 graduate of West Point. Crook served in the Pacific Northwest prior to the war. He distinguished himself during the Civil War at South Mountain, Antietam, Chickamauga, and at Appomattox. He resigned his commission after the war, but not before campaigning against the Sioux in 1866. He was considered an extremely capable officer.

CULP, WESLEY (d. 1863)—Confederate Private. Born near Gettysburg, Pa. Culp died on Culp's Hill, a piece of property owned by his family. He fought against his own brother there (as did many others); and at Winchester, Va. The young private was allegedly trying to carry a message to a Miss Jennie Wade (who was killed before he could deliver the message). She was the only civilian casualty of the Battle of Gettysburg.

CUMBERLAND, the Army of the—Union. When Major General Don Carlos Buell took over the command of the Department of the Ohio on November 15, 1861, the name of the army was changed to the Army of the Ohio. Following the invasion of Tennessee, the name became official. When Rosecrans replaced Buell following the Battle of Perrysville, the name of the army was again changed—this time to the Army of the Cumberland (October, 1862).

This army was a combination of the old Army of the Tennessee and the spit and polish Army of the Potomac, as far as character and make-up were concerned. Its officers were usually formal, but its men were typical Midwesterners. This was the main army in the Midwest and the West.

CUSHING, WILLIAM B. (1842–1874)—
Union Lieutenant Commander. Born
in Delafield, Wis. Cushing attended
the U.S. Naval Academy, but resigned before graduating. He was on
blockade duty off the North Carolina
coast during most of the war. On
October 27, 1864, he torpedoed the
Confederate ram "Albemarle," and
was promoted to lieutenant commander for the feat. He was at Fort
Fisher in 1865. After the war, Cushing became a full commander (1872).
(See "ALBEMARLE.")

CUSTER, GEORGE ARMSTRONG (1839–
1876)—Union Major General. Born
in New Rumley, Ohio, and a graduate of West Point (at the bottom of
his class of thirty-four students). Custer served at the first Bull Run battle,
and, following that battle, became
aide to McClellan with the rank of
captain in June, 1862. After charging
almost blindly into a mass of Confederate troops at Aldie, Va., Custer
was promoted to the rank of brigadier general of volunteers (June 27,
1863). He served through the Gettysburg battle and the Virginia campaign. He was commended for his
pursuit of Lee from Richmond.

Although his West Point record
had shown demerits for "visiting out
of hours," "room unswept," "sitting
down on sentry duty," and "table-
cloth dirty," Custer allowed none of
his troops to be guilty of these types
of infractions. He was a harsh disciplinarian. His uniform was one of
the most irregular in the entire
Union army—black velveteen jacket,
trousers of the same color and
material, scarlet tie, blue shirt, and
gold braid at every conceivable
point. Yet, at West Point, he had
been described as the "most slovenly
dressed male at the Point." Because
of his harsh methods, he never won
the love of his troops, but he did earn
their respect by his feats of daring
in battle. He received General Longstreet's flag of truce at Appomattox.

When the war ended, the daring
major general was only twenty-five
years old. At Little Big Horn, in the
Montata territory, Cuter led 264
men to their deaths in a rash move.
He became lastingly famous for
doing so. He was a hard-hitting
cavalryman who had little use for
desk work.

D

DAHLGREN, JOHN A. (1809–1870)—
Union Rear Admiral. Dahlgren
served as Ordnance Bureau chief
prior to the war, but left this post,
soon after the hostilities began, to
take command of the South Atlantic
blockading squadron. He had been
with the Ordnance Bureau for ten
years before war broke out, and had
perfected the famous Dahlgren Gun
which bears his name. The weapon
became a standard naval piece during the war.

DANA, CHARLES ANDERSON (1819–
1897)—Union newsman. Born in
Hinsdale, N.H., and a student at
Harvard University before the war.
Dana served as city editor of the New
York *Tribune* under Horace Greeley,
and while there, contrived the war

cry "On to Richmond" which put so much public pressure on McClellan. He broke with Greeley in March, 1862, and entered the War Department to serve as the "eyes and ears of Stanton."

In mid-1863, he returned to journalism as owner of the New York *Sun,* and set up in competition with Greeley. Like Greeley, he broke with Grant (an old friend) but remained politically independent throughout the war, and throughout his entire career. Dana traveled with Grant during much of the western campaign, but was unable to maintain continuous coverage of the armies of the eastern sector when Grant moved east.

DANVILLE, Virginia—This was the last capital of the Confederacy (1865). The city is located in Pittsylvania County on the Dan river, southwest of Richmond (about 150 miles). The Confederate Memorial Mansion is located there. It was used as the government building of the Confederacy after the fall of Richmond in 1865.

DAVIS, JEFFERSON FINIS (1808–1889)—President of the Confederacy. Born in Christian County (now Todd), Ky., and a graduate of both Transylvania University and West Point (1828). Davis was reared in Wilkinson County, Miss. There is a striking resemblance between him and Lincoln which has prompted many unfounded rumors that the two were related. This, added to their near-common birthplaces,

caused much talk during the 1860's.

Davis gathered what little military experience he had during the Blackhawk and the Mexican War. He was wounded at Buena Vista in the latter war, while in command of the "Mississippi Rifles." These two experiences are perhaps the reason he over-evaluated himself as a military leader. His West Point record was "spotty" as far as conduct was concerned. His record there was far less than ideal.

Throughout his life, Davis allowed himself to be influenced by others. His brother exerted great influence over him as did his wife, Sarah Knox Taylor, daughter of General Zachary Taylor. She died in 1835, before Davis assumed an important role in politics. Yet, his second wife, Varina Howell, seemed to have had more influence than even his first wife Sarah.

Davis served as senator from Mississippi from 1847 to 1851. He was defeated in a bid for the governorship of the state, but became secretary of war under Pierce from 1853 to 1857. Even his position there did not do much to instill sound leadership qualities of a military nature in Davis. He returned to the Senate in 1857 where he remained until it was announced that Lincoln had won election.

Davis did not actively seek the presidency of the Confederacy. His main ambition was to take over a military command. He showed his leaning towards the military side throughout his tenure as president of the Confederacy, being inclined to delve too deeply into military affairs, alienating his commanders, and hampering the war effort.

On February 18, 1861, he became provisional president of the Confederacy officially. He had been selected on February 9th. The temporary election was made final on November 9, 1861, when he was elected by popular vote. He never personally gave up the fight for the Confederacy until captured outside of Irwinville, Ga., on May 10, 1865, although he admitted the collapse of the Confederacy on April 24, 1865.

He was inaugurated at Richmond, Va., on February 22, 1862, and held the Confederate states together for four long years.

Davis spent two years in prison while the public clamored for his death as a traitor. Strangely enough, it was radical Republican Salmon P. Chase who strongly opposed the treason charge. Davis was released in May, 1867, and entered business. He retired to Biloxi, Miss., to write his defense of the Confederacy and the South which was entitled *The Rise and Fall of the Confederacy*.

Davis was a forceful orator, and an outright defender of state's rights. He was, however, rather overbearing and aristocratic in his manner, and this did not do much to win him the loyalty of all of his generals. Most of his postwar years were wasted showing resentment over the "unjust" criticism heaped upon him by both the North and the South.

DAVIS, JEFFERSON COLUMBUS (1828–1879)—Union Brevet Brigadier General. Born in Clark County, Ind. Davis was garrisoned at Fort Sumter, S.C., when the fort was bombarded, starting the war. He was serving as a first lieutenant at the time. Because of distinguished combat service during the war, Davis was breveted brigadier general of volunteers with a regular army colonelcy. After the war, he became the first U.S. officer to hold command in Alaska, newly purchased by Secretary of State Seward for the United States. Port Davis was named after him in 1900.

DAVIS, SAMUEL (1842–1863)— Confederate spy. Davis was captured near Pulaski, Tenn., by Kansas Jayhawkers under General Grenville Dodge. On his person and in his saddlebags were found amazingly accurate maps and information concerning the disposition of Union troops. Also found were papers (including a pass) signed by Confederate General Braxton Bragg's Chief Scout, "Captain E. Coleman." The name, a ficticious one used by Captain Henry Shaw, was well-known to the Union. Shaw, at that time, was in the same jail with Davis, but Davis refused to divulge this information. Dodge offered to spare Davis' life if the spy would give the information about "Coleman," but Davis refused to speak. While Shaw watched from his jail window, Davis was hanged for spying, on November 27, 1863, the day after Thanksgiving.

DECLARATION OF CAUSES—December 24, 1860. When the South Carolina convention of December 20, 1860, declared the South Carolina legislature ready to "dissolve the Union between the State of South Carolina and the other States united with her under the compact entitled 'the Constitution of the United States,' " a declaration of causes was drawn up immediately to explain the act of secession. In a lengthy document, the delegates attempted to justify their move. The document became one of the most highly valued pieces in American history.

Declaration of Causes
December 24, 1860.

The people of the State of South Carolina in convention assembled on the second day of April, A.D., 1852, declared that the frequent violations of the Constitution of the United States by the Federal government, and its encroachments upon the reserved rights of the states, fully justified this state in their withdrawal from the Federal union, but in deference to the opinions and wishes of the other slaveholding states, she forebore, at that time, to exercise this right. Since that time, these encroachments have continued to increase, and further forebearance ceases to be a virtue.

And now, the State of South Carolina, having resumed her separate and equal place among nations, deems it due to herself, to the remaining United States of America, and to the nations of the world, that she should declare the immediate causes which have led to this act.

In the year 1765, that portion of the British Empire embracing Great Britain undertook to make laws for the government of that portion composed of the thirteen American colonies. A struggle for the right of self-government ensued, which resulted, on the fourth of July, 1776, in a declaration, by the colonies, "that they are, and of right ought to be, *free and independent states;* and that, as free and independent states, they have full power to levy war, conclude peace, contract alliances, establish commerce, and to do all other acts and things which independent states may of right do."

They further solemnly declared that whenever any "form of government becomes destructive of the ends for which it was established, it is the right of the people to alter or abolish it, and to institute a new government." Deeming the government of Great Britain to have become destructive of these ends, they declared that the colonies "are absolved from all allegiance to the British Crown, and that all political connections between them and the state of Great Britain is, and ought to be, totally dissolved."

In pursuance of this Declaration of Independence, each of the thirteen states proceeded to exercise its separate sovereignty; adopted for itself a constitution, and appointed officers for the administration of government in all its departments—legislative, executive, and judicial. For the purposes of defense, they united their arms and their counsels; and, in 1778, they entered into a league known as the Articles of Confederation, whereby they agreed to entrust the administration of their external relations to a common agent, known as the Congress of the United States, expressly declaring, in the first article, "that each state retains its sovereignty, freedom, and independence, and every power, jurisdiction and right which is not, by this Confederation, expressely delegated to the United States in Congress assembled."

Under this Confederation, the War of the Revolution was carried on; and on the third of September, 1873, the contest ended, and a definite treaty was signed by Great Britain, in which she acknowledged the independence of the colonies . . .

Thus were established the two great principles asserted by the colonies, namely, the right of a state to govern itself; and the right of a people to abolish a government when it becomes destructive of the ends for which it was instituted. And, concurrent with the establishment of these principles, was the fact that each colony became and was recognized by the mother country as a *free, sovereign, and independent state.*

In 1787, deputies were appointed by the states to revise the Articles of Confederation; and on (the) seventeenth of September, 1787, these deputies recommended for the adoption of the states, the articles of union known as the Constitution of the United States. . . .

By this Constitution, certain duties were imposed upon the several states, and the exercise of certain of their powers was restrained, which necessarily impelled their continued existence as sovereign states. But, to remove all doubt, an amendment was added, which declared that the powers not delegated to the United States by the Constitution, nor prohibited by it to the states, are reserved to the states respectively, or to the people. On the twenty-third (of) May, 1788, South Carolina, by a convention of her people, passed an ordinance assenting to this Constitution, and afterward altered her own Constitution to conform herself to the obligations she had undertaken.

Thus was established by compact between the states, a government with defined objects, and powers, limited to the express words of the grant. This limitation left the whole remaining mass of power subject to the clause reserving it to the states or the people, and rendering unnecessary any specification of reserved rights. . . .

The text of the Declaration goes on for some great number of words, and may be found in almost any work on American documents. Although the facts listed were basically correct, Northerners took the stand that the pact between the states bound each state to conform to the rulings of the majority, unless it infringed upon some specific right not covered by the Constitution. The questions which had caused the Southerners to draw up the Declaration of Causes were not considered outside of Federal jurisdiction by the Northerners.

DELANY, MARTIN R.—Union major, and a graduate of Harvard Medical School. Delany became the first

Negro to take a field command after the United States had authorized the use of the Negro as a soldier. He is one of the few Negroes who is known to have made a conscientious effort to trace his lineage back through the African line. He led the fight for equal pay for Negro troops in 1865.

DEVIL'S DEN—Located at the foot of Little Round Top, Gettysburg, Pa. The location served as protection for sharpshooters of both sides.

"DICTATOR," THE—A mortar. This was a giant mortar mounted on a flatcar, and used against Petersburg, Va., during the siege of that city by Union forces.

DINWIDDIE COURT HOUSE, the Battle of—March 30–31, 1865. This battle is also known as the Battle of White Oak Road, and took place just prior to Appomattox, when Grant's forces had the Confederate Army of Northern Virginia in retreat below Richmond, Va. Union forces under Griffin defeated Lee's force at Boydton Road, and forced that section of the army to retreat to White Oak Road. The Confederate forces launched a counter-attack against the pursuing Second and Fifth Corps, but were repulsed on both the 30th and the 31st in what is known as the Battle of Dinwiddie Courthouse.

Major General Philip Sheridan arrived at nearby Dinwiddie Courthouse with a strong cavalry and artillery re-enforcement for the embattled Union forces in time to rout the Confederate forces under Major

General George E. Pickett of Gettysburg fame, just in time to save the battle for the Union. The Confederates retired to Five Forks. The battle was really a series of engagements (as were most in these last days of the eastern campaign), and was part of the running battle which occurred between the two armies until April 9, 1865, when Lee finally surrendered.

The Union forces lost 2,198 of their 42,000. The Confederates lost an undetermined number. Union missing totaled 538. The totals deal with the Dinwiddie Courthouse action, and minor skirmishes and engagements surrounding the area.

DISABLED VETERANS, the Corps of—Union. Union officials, concerned over the great loss of manpower resulting from the discharge of all wounded veterans, decided to organize the "walking wounded" into a body for light duties around the camp, such as guarding prison camps, arsenal duty, hospital orderlies and guards, etc. The original name of the corps was the "Invalid Corps" and wounded men enlisted voluntarily. The name was not the most desirable, and so it was officially changed to the Veteran Reserve Corps, and the men were given regular army uniforms upon enlisting.

The corps was broken down into battalions, with the first battalion being the most able men; and the second battalion being composed of those who were unable to carry muskets or pull guard duty. This latter battalion furnished a regiment (the

Eighteenth) to pull guard duty at Belle Plain, although they were not supposed to be able to carry muskets because of their infirmities. They also served at Port Royal when the Belle Plain base was moved.

The Veterans Reserve Corps combined their limited talents to ward off an attack by Wade Hampton at Port Royal, assisting the handful of able bodied men to repel the attack. After a medical board checked the condition of some of the men, the Veteran Reserve Corps was sent back to Washington to serve in its original capacity.

DIX, DOROTHEA (1802–1887)—Union Superintendent of Nurses. Miss Dix was sixty years old when she was appointed superintendent of nurses by Secretary of War Simon Cameron. The social reformer had been vitally concerned with the treatment being accorded the mentally ill during that time, and had established hospitals around the country to aid them. She was appointed primarily to quell the growing disturbance over the appointment of women nurses. She instituted the Dix Plan for Nurses (see below) which caused another stir, and gave rise to the "old woman" cry which prevailed throughout the war.

At the age of fourteen, Miss Dix (she never married) became a school teacher. She had written her first book at the age of twenty-two and was engrossed in the business of obtaining reforms in the mental health picture when appointed by Stanton. In many instances, she had to pay the nurses out of her own pocket, because the government had made no provision for payment to the ladies.

Accounts of her actions appear throughout most diaries of women who served in the war in any way.

DIX PLAN FOR NURSES, THE—Formulated by Dorothea Dix when she was appointed superintendent of nurses for the Union army. The plan was not popular with the younger ladies of the time who felt that they would like to take part in the treatment of the wounded. It called for the following stipulations :

1. No women under thirty were to be accepted for service.
2. All nurses were required to be "plain-looking women."
3. All dresses must be brown or black without adornment.
4. No hoop skirts were allowed.

In the beginning, the plan called for nurses to administer aid only in hospitals far to the rear. Later in the war, however, Miss Dix consented to allow some of the "older, more plain" nurses to go to the front lines. She insisted that nurses be "women who can afford to give their services and time and meet part of their expenses or the whole, who will associate themselves by twos to be ready for duty at any hour of day or night—those who are sober, earnest, self-sacrificing, and self-sustained."

She described her ideal nurse as being : "(one) who can bear the presence of suffering and exercise entire self-control, of speech and manner; who can be calm, gentle, quiet, active, and steadfast in duty, also who (is) willing to take and to execute the directions of the surgeons of the divisions in which she is stationed."

"DIXIE"—This name is generally applied to the section of the country below the Mason-Dixon line. It is held by many to be derived from Mr. Dixon's name. However, this is refuted in a number of quarters.

Daniel Decatur Emmet (1815–1904) wrote the song, which was originally referred to as "Walking Around," for a minstrel show in 1859. It was first used as a song by the Confederates at the inauguration of Jefferson Davis in Richmond. Later, General Albert Pike worked out another pro-Southern version of the song, and T. M. Cooley wrote in a pro-Northern version.

Actually, the song was centered around the name of a mythical Manhattan Island plantation owner named Dixie, who was (as legend tells) so kind-hearted to his slaves that his plantation was looked upon as a paradise for the slave. Those who were forced away from "Dixie's" for one reason or another, allegedly pined for it so much that they sang about it.

It is said that when slavery moved southward, the ideal of "Dixie's" was carried in the songs of the slaves who had formerly been on his plantation. The song became so widespread that the origin of the word became lost, and Southern slaveholders (ironically)

took up the chant as their rallying call. The term generally encompassed the Southern states, and is still used in that context today.

DOCTOR'S CREEK, Kentucky—This creek is near Perrysville, Ky. A skirmish took place here on October 8, 1862, when Union forces under Philip Sheridan met Confederate forces under Braxton Bragg in a fight for the water supply afforded by the creek. This was during a severe drought in Kentucky, and the creek was the only suitable available water in the area. The skirmish resulted in Union control of the creek.

DODGE, GRENVILLE MELLEN (1831–1916)—Union Major General. Born in Danvers, Mass., and a graduate of the University of Norwich, Vt., 1850. Dodge worked as a railroad engineer in Illinois and Iowa before the Civil War. He joined the Union army, and was promoted to brigadier general for gallantry at Pea Ridge, Ark., 1862, where he was wounded.

He commanded the Sixteenth Army Corps at Atlanta as a major general, and was given command of the Missouri Department after the Atlanta campaign, but resigned from the army in 1866 to become chief engineer of the Union Pacific railroad and later the Texas and Pacific. Dodge published two books on the Civil War.

DONEHOGAWA (1818–1895) — Union Brigadier General. Born in Genesee County, N.Y., on a reservation. He is best known as Ely Samuel Parker, his "whiteman's name." Donehogawa was the highest ranking Indian in the Union army, and was a Sachem of the Senecas. He represented his tribe in Washington, D.C., for twenty years, studying law while there. He was well-educated but the government denied him permission to practice before the bar of the United States because he was "not a United States citizen." He returned to his studies (this time at Rensselaer Polytechnic Institute) where he learned civil engineering. As a result, he became superintendent of a government project near Galena, Ill., where he met U. S. Grant. He was given the Galena position because all other qualified engineers refused to take it.

Donehogawa was refused a commission in both the New York Militia and the U.S. Army. His greatest foe in Washington was Stanton. Nevertheless, he eventually received a commission as captain of engineers in 1863, when things were going rather badly for the North, engineers were in demand, and most school-trained engineers had been elevated to field-grade ranks. He became Grant's military secretary, and was raised to the rank of Lieutenant Colonel.

Often mistaken for a Negro because of his swarthy complexion, he was known simply as "The Indian" by Grant's army. He is credited with saving Grant's life at Spotsylvania. Legend has it that Lee, when he first met Donehogawa at the surrender meeting, stared at him quite a while, and then took his hand saying, "I am glad to see one real American here."

Donehogawa, by his own statement, is reputed to have said in reply, "Now we are *all* Americans." He transcribed the entire proceedings of the sessions from his own penciled draft to the legible and recordable documents which have existed to this date.

He was promoted to brigadier general with the commission dating from Appomattox. After Grant became President, Donehogawa became the first Indian to be appointed United States Indian Commissioner. Although a brigadier general, Donehogawa was not the highest ranking Indian in the war. Confederate Brigadier General Stand Watie outranked him on a seniority basis.

DOUBLEDAY, ABNER (1819–1893)—Union Major General. Born in Ballston Spa, N.Y., and educated as an engineer, at West Point, 1842. Doubleday is more famous for his development of the game of baseball at Cooperstown, N.Y., than he is as a Civil War figure. However, he served admirably in the war.

In February, 1862, Doubleday was appointed a brigadier general of volunteers, after having served at Fort Sumter as a captain when the fort was fired upon in 1861. He commanded at second Bull Run, South Mountain, Antietam, and Fredericksburg before being promoted to major general in November of 1862. He subsequently served at Chancellorsville and Gettysburg, temporarily commanding General Reynolds' forces when the general was killed in action. Doubleday ended the war in Washington, but went into the regular army and served with the rank of colonel.

DOUGLASS, FREDERICK (1817–1895)— Union abolitionist. Born near Tuckahoe, Md., in slavery. Douglass had no formal education. He was born officially Frederick Augustus Washington Bailey, but took the name of Douglass after escaping to freedom from Baltimore, Maryland, on September 3, 1838. He had learned to read and write while a house servant in Baltimore.

This son of a Negro slave and her white owner became one of the world's most renowned abolitionists, after being touted in Massachusetts after a strong and moving speech against slavery before the Massachusetts Anti-slavery Society Convention at Nantucket in 1841. He was forced to flee to England and later to Ireland to escape possible re-enslavement, and remained there from 1845 to 1847. While abroad, he wrote a frank account of his life called the *Narrative of the Life of Frederick Douglass*.

When abroad, Douglass collected enough money to buy his freedom upon his return to the United States. He founded the *North Star* (an abolitionist newspaper in Rochester, N.Y.) and supported industrial education for Negroes, and woman's suffrage.

As a result of his friendship and advice extended to John Brown prior to Harper's Ferry, Douglass was again forced to flee from the United States, going this time to Canada and the British Isles. Upon his return, he continued to agitate for Negro regiments during the early years of the war. Following the war, he served in many government posts, among which was that of United States consul general in Haiti (1889–1891). He died in Washington, D.C., on February 20, 1895.

DOUGLAS, STEPHEN ARNOLD (1813–1861)—Union legislator. Born in Brandon, Vt. Douglas attended Canadaigua Academy in New Yerk before settling in Jackson, Ill., in 1833. There he began to study law while teaching school, and was licensed to practice in 1834. He became the state's attorney general just one year later. Douglas entered the state legislature in 1835, and was there for a year. He became the secretary of state for Illinois in 1840, and was appointed to the state Supreme Court bench in 1841. Thus, after just seven years as a licensed lawyer, Douglas was seated on the Supreme Court of the state.

In 1843, he began a two-year term in the U.S. House, where he became prominent as a spokesman for the squatter sovereignty group. In 1847, he entered the Senate, and remained there until his death in 1861. He was known as the "Little Giant," and became famous for his debates with Lincoln in which he expounded the theory that the state had a right to determine whether or not it would be slave or free.

He was unsuccessful as a candidate for the Democratic Presidential nomination in 1852 and 1856. He supported Lincoln after the election, and was a likely candidate for a cabinet post in the Lincoln administration had he lived.

DOWD, W. C.—Confederate Captain. Along with a Major E. Hollis, Dowd is supposed to have uncovered facts leading to the discovery of the existence of a peace society in middle Alabama in 1864. (See PEACE SOCIETIES.)

DRAFT RIOTS, the New York—July 12–16, 1863. On July 12, 1863, the names of the first draftees in New York were published. For four days, a mob of 50,000 people ranged the city's streets in bitter defiance to the call. They attacked and lynched helpless Negroes, using lampposts, trees, and windows to do the job. The bodies of burned Negroes were to be seen in the streets. Known abolitionists were attacked, beaten, and their property destroyed. Troops returning from Gettysburg were called in to quell the riots, and were forced to fire upon the mob which had turned to looting and pillaging.

In the four national draft calls from 1863 through 1864, 776,829 names were drawn, but only 46,347 men were called in as draftees, (and most of these were "substitutes"). Yet, after each call, there were major disturbances over the selections. The draft did, however, result in a larger number of men volunteering in order to obtain bounty for doing so.

DRAYTON, PERCIVAL (1812–1865)— Confederate steamer captain. Drayton commanded one of the three Confederate steamers which went out to meet and engage Du Pont's 12,000-man amphibious force at Port Royal on November 7, 1861. The Confederates surrendered in less than four hours.

DREWERY'S BLUFF, the Battle of— may 12–16, 1864. General Benjamin F. Butler advanced from his position at the Bermuda Hundred towards Richmond, Va., but was blocked by a strong Confederate entrenchment at Drewery's Bluff over the James River, just nine miles below the Confederate capital. Confederate General P. G. T. Beauregard's forces defeated Butler's troops and forced them to retreat to their base at the Bermuda Hundred after four days of seesaw battle which only resulted in the loss of 2,500 Confederates and 3,012 Union troops. The defeat allowed the Southern forces to re-establish communications and supply lines west of Richmond, and delayed Grant's action against Richmond.

DUNKER CHURCH (see ANTIETAM)

DU PONT, HENRY (1812–1889)—Major general, Delaware Militia. Born in Eleutherian Mills, Del. Du Pont was a member of the famous family of du Pont de Nemours which settled near Wilmington, Del. He headed the vital E. I. du Pont de Nemours and Company in the Civil War period, and his firm supplied the Army, during both the Mexican War and the Civil War, with gunpowder.

Du Pont was also of political importance, being the leader of the Delaware Republican party, and a presidential elector in the years following the war from 1868 to 1888. He was appointed major general of the Delaware militia in 1861, by Governor William Burton. He ran into trouble, however, when he demanded that each militia man take the oath of allegiance to the Union or turn in his weapons. His order was suspended by the governor of the border state, but Du Pont appealed to the commander of the Federal troops in the area, General John A. Dix at Baltimore, and an armed unit was sent in to assure that Delaware remained loyal to the Union.

DU PONT, HENRY ALGERNON (1838–1926)—Union Captain. Congressional Medal of Honor awardee. Born in Eleutherian Mills, Del., and an 1861 graduate of West Point (head of his class). A member of the family of du Pont de Nemours which settled near Wilmington, Del. He was the eldest son of industrialist Henry Du Pont. Following his graduation from West Point, he was assigned to duty in Washington. He did not see active combat duty until 1863, as a first lieutenant. In 1864, he was promoted to captain. His most important assignment was as chief of artillery of the Department of West Virginia. He was awarded the Congressional Medal of Honor for services at Cedar Creek, Va., October 19, 1864.

Du Pont stayed in the army until 1875, and became president of the Wilmington & Norfolk Railroad Company in 1877.

DU PONT, SAMUEL F. (1803–1865)—Union Rear Admiral. Born in Bergen Point, N.J. A member of the family of du Pont de Nemours which settled near Wilmington, Del. He was appointed a midshipman by President James Madison in 1815, when he was twelve. He was a naval commander by 1842, and was instrumental in the setting up of the Naval Academy at Annapolis.

Du Pont served prominently in the Mexican War, as commander of the U.S.S. "Cyane." When the Civil War broke out, he was appointed flag officer, and was placed in command of the South Atlantic blockading squadron. He assisted in the capture of Port Royal, S.C., while supporting Sherman's forces, November, 1861. He also set up a chain of blockade stations along the coast which was very effective.

By 1862, he had risen to rear admiral. He attacked Charleston, S.C., on April 7, 1863, but was repulsed with heavy losses. He was relieved of his command July 5, 1863, and retired from active duty. He died two years later.

DURHAM STATION, North Carolina—Sherman and Joseph E. Johnston met there to determine surrender terms for the Confederate army under Johnston, on April 18, 1865. Also present was Confederate Secretary of War John C. Breckinridge. Sherman offered terms which not only covered Johnston's army of 40,000 men, but also covered all of the men under Breckinridge's command—the entire remaining Confederate army and navy. (see SURRENDER TERMS, THE DURHAM STATION) The terms offered by Sherman were even more lenient than those offered Lee by Grant. However, the government ruled that Sherman had no right to offer such terms, and refused to ratify what was, in essence, a peace treaty.

E

EARLY, JUBAL ANDERSON (1816–1894) —Confederate Major General. Born in Franklin County, Va., and an 1837 graduate of West Point. Early had military experience from the Seminole and the Mexican Wars behind him when he entered the Civil War as a colonel in the Confederate army. He was opposed to secession. In 1862, he became a division commander, and by 1864, had risen to corps commander.

Early was at his best when working under a capable commanding general who knew enough to give him a free hand. From June, 1864, to the end of the war, he was an independent commander in the Shenandoah Valley. On July 11 and 12 of that year, his forces entered the outskirts of Washington, forcing the military to detach troops from front line duty to repel him. He was driven back into Virginia under heavy fire.

Early's only major defeats came at the hands of Sherman and Sheridan. Sherman defeated him at Winchester and at Fisher's Hill; Sheridan arrived just in time to turn the tide at Cedar Creek (October 12, 1864) and defeated Early soundly. (See CEDAR CREEK.) This latter was Early's most discouraging loss during the war.

Early was not "popular" in the social sense of the word, but was a capable leader under usually outstandingly trying conditions. His name was hated and feared in Maryland and Pennsylvania after he invaded those states, levied a tax of $200,000 on Frederic, Md., and burned two-thirds of Chambersburg, Pa., when the people refused to pay a levy of $500,000. His raids stirred consternation in the hearts of the people of the border states of the Union.

ELLSWORTH, ELMER EPHRAIM (1837– 1861)—Union Colonel. Born in New York City, Ellsworth studied law under Abraham Lincoln, and offered his services to the President when the war broke out. He led a regiment of New York firemen to Washington to defend the city. As a result, he was dispatched across the Potomac to Alexandria, Va., to seize the city.

Upon entering the town, Ellsworth noticed a Confederate flag flying over the town hotel. He and one of his troopers rushed into the hotel and proceeded to rip the flag down. On their way down from the roof, the two encountered the irate owner of the hotel, Jesse Jackson, who fired point-blank at Ellsworth. The trooper, Corporal Francis E. Brownell, fired upon the owner and mortally wounded him. Ellsworth, however, was dead, and became the first officer to die in the civil war.

EMANCIPATION PROCLAMATION—January 1, 1863. Early in September,

1862, President Abraham Lincoln announced to his cabinet that he intended to issue a proclamation freeing the slaves, in order to save the Union. At the suggestion of Secretary of State Seward, the President put off the announcement until, as Seward put it, "you can give it to the country supported by military success, instead of issuing it, as would be the case now, upon the greatest disasters of the war."

On September 17, 1862, McClellan scored a rare victory over Lee's Army of Northern Virginia at Antietam Creek, pushing the invading Southerners back into Virginia and leaving Maryland free of the threat of invasion for a while. This was the first major Northern victory of the war, and Lincoln pounced upon the occasion to serve notice of the emancipation.

On September 22, 1862, the Emancipation Proclamation was made public, to become effective on January 1, 1863. The measure was, for all practical purposes, to effect only the slaves in those states still in rebellion against the Union, and the military force was directed to enforce the edict. (See CHASE, SALMON PORTLAND.) Actually, the proclamation had no power to end slavery in the states concerned, for the Union was not even in control of those states. Only as the Union forces took control of Rebel states could the edict become effective.

It did, however, keep many foreign nations from recognizing the Confederacy, for fear of the stigma which would be attached to the support of a fight to extend and protect slavery. The proclamation laid the groundwork for the vital Thirteenth Amendment which did legally free the slaves.

ERICSSON, JOHN (1803–1889)—Union. Builder of the "Monitor." Born in Wermland, Sweden. Ericsson served in the Swedish Army from 1820 to 1826, but resigned to become one of the best known inventors of his time.

In 1839, he supplied the engines and screws for the first steam vessel to cross the Atlantic. He came to the United States in that same year, and two years later built the warship "Princeton," the first vessel to have her engines and boilers below the waterline. In 1861, Ericsson, under a patent granted by the U.S. Government to Theodore R. Timby, constructed the "Monitor." Timby invented the revolving turret. (See "MONITOR.")

Ericsson was interested in torpedoes and solar energy. A statue of him stands in Battery Park, N.Y., and in Worcester, Mass. There is also a memorial erected in Stockholm, Sweden.

EVANS, NATHAN G. (1824–1868)— Confederate Major. Evans was known affectionately as "Shanks" by his fellow officers because of his knock-knees. He fought in the Indian Wars in the West prior to the Civil War. He was adjutant of the South Carolina forces when Sumter was fired upon.

Evans fought in the first Battle of Bull Run, and correctly interpreted a flanking move by McDowell, promptly stopping the

Federal move to encircle the Confederate force.

EWELL, RICHARD STODDERT (1817–1872)—Confederate Lieutenant General. Born in Georgetown, D.C., and an 1840 graduate of West Point. Ewell gained military experience in the Mexican War, and entered the Confederate army in May, 1861. By the first Battle of Bull Run, he had risen to brigadier general, and was a major general by January of 1862.

Ewell took Jackson's place as one of Lee's top lieutenants after Chancellorsville. His campaigns included service in the Shenandoah Valley under Jackson, the Seven Days Campaign, Groveton (where he lost a leg), Gettysburg (where he failed on the Confederate left flank), at the Wilderness and at Spotsylvania. He also commanded at Sailor's Creek, and at Richmond. His forces surrendered at Sailor's Creek.

Ewell is considered one of the "blood and guts" generals of the war, who thoroughly enjoyed a good fight. His tactics were amazingly similar to Grant's—hard, dogmatic, relentless fighting. Unfortunately, he did not have the manpower at his disposal to make this type of battling pay off.

EWING, HUGH BOYLE (1826–1905)—Union Brevet Major General. Born in Lancaster, Ohio. Ewing left West Point to join the Gold Rush to California in 1849. He returned in 1852 to practice law in Washington and in St. Louis, Mo. The young lawyer was the foster brother of William Tecumseh Sherman, and a law partner in the firm of Thomas Ewing, Sherman, Dan McCook and others.

He joined the Union army in 1861, and served with McClellan in western Virginia. In 1861 he also became a colonel of the Thirtieth Ohio Infantry. After fighting at South Mountain and Antietam, Ewing was promoted to brigadier general. His other major commands include a brigade at Vicksburg; divisions at Chickamauga and Missionary Ridge and North Carolina. After the war, he served as minister to Holland (1866–1870).

EWING, THOMAS, JR. (1829–1896)—Union Brigadier General. Born in Lancaster, Ohio. This Ewing was the younger brother of General Hugh Ewing. (See EWING, HUGH BOYLE.) He was chosen chief justice of the Kansas Supreme Court in 1861, but resigned in 1862 to recruit the Eleventh Kansas Volunteer unit. He became a colonel of that unit but was promoted to brigadier general in 1863, and commanded the border district of Kansas and Missouri (and later the St. Louis district).

Ewing was active in the defense of St. Louis in 1864, and in engagements at Fort Davidson and Fort Harrison. He resigned his commission in 1865, and was breveted major general of volunteers. After the war, he served as congressman from Lancaster from 1877 to 1881. His father, Thomas, Sr., was the first Secretary of the Interior of the United States.

EZRA CHURCH, the Battle of—July 28, 1864. Part of the battle for

79

Atlanta. In fact, the scene of the battle is now part of the Westside district of Atlanta, well within the confines of the city limits.

This was an engagement between the forces under Confederate General John B. Hood, and the Army of the Tennessee under Sherman. In a move to encircle Atlanta and cut off its communications to the west and south, Sherman moved the Army of the Tennessee from the far left to the extreme right of the battle line. Hood moved the greater part of his force to this point, during the night of July 27, and the fighting began early on the morning of the 28th. It lasted until late afternoon. Hood was forced to withdraw his forces to the inner confines of the works surrounding the city. Union losses : approximately 600 killed, wounded and missing. Confederate losses : approximated 2,800 killed, wounded and missing. The Union force numbered about 13,000, while Hood commanded over 18,000.

F

FARMSVILLE, Virginia—A small hamlet on the path followed by Lee's troops during the retreat from Richmond towards Appomattox in 1865. Lee turned his troops through this hamlet when he found that the federal troops had blocked his route to Danville, Va. The Confederate troops made their move towards Farmsville on April 4, 1865, placing the force under Sherman on their left, and the remainder of the Union force behind them. As a result of this move, a series of continuous skirmishes ensued on April 5th.

FARNSWORTH, ELON JOHN (1837–1863) — Union Brigadier General. This University of Michigan student joined the Eighth Illinois cavalry at the outbreak of the war as a first lieutenant, and was promoted to captain by December of 1861. He participated in over forty battles and skirmishes in less than two years, and became aide-de-camp to General Alfred Pleasonton in 1863. He was promoted to brigadier general of the U. S. volunteers in that year

During an assault on the enemy right flank at Gettysburg, Farnsworth was killed, and almost one fourth of his brigade lost. However, the unit forced the Confederates to retreat. He was found to have been hit by five bullets—any one of which could have been fatal. He was considered a daring and competent officer.

FARRAGUT, DAVID GLASGOW (1801–1870)—Union Vice-Admiral. Farragut went to sea under the sponsorship of David Porter, after being taken to New Orleans and entering the navy. His first duty was on the "Essex" as a midshipman under his sponsor. By 1825, he had risen to the rank of lieutenant, and by 1841, he had become a commander and served in the Mexican War with this rank.

His subsequent naval record prior to the war lists ordinance duty in 1850's, promotion to captain in 1855, and the establishment of Mare Island Navy Yards in California. When war broke out, he had served forty-nine years in the navy.

During the war, his fleet ranged the southern coast of the Confederacy, and figured prominently in most of the major sea battles in that area. Farragut commanded at the capture of New Orleans, and was instrumental during the Vicksburg campaign on the Mississippi. In July, 1862, he was commissioned rear admiral. Perhaps his best remembered battle is the Battle of Mobile Bay where he is credited with having said, "Damn the torpedoes, full speed ahead."

He became vice-admiral (a rank created for him) in December, 1864. His painstakingly exact methods of fighting paid off for him time and time again, and he was made a full admiral (another post created for him) in 1866. Grant, knowing the independent nature of the man, recommended that Farragut be given a free hand. Farragut, consequently, became one of the most successful naval figures in the war.

FARRAND, EBENEZER — Confederate commodore. Farrand was in command of a tiny fleet of gunboats in the battle of Mobile Bay. His force controlled the upper bay for a major portion of the time consumed by the battle, but was pinned in due to the fact that the Union fleet and army had complete control of the lower bay and the forts controlling the mouth of the bay. (See MOBILE BAY, the battle of.)

FINEGAN, JOSEPH—Confederate Brig-adier General. Finegan's greatest moment during the war was at the Battle of Olustee in Florida. The Confederate forces under Finegan (mainly troops from Georgia) defeated Union General Seymour's force on February 20, 1864, repelling the Federal force with heavy losses, and ending the Union invasion of interior Florida. The North did not attempt to take this territory for the duration of the war.

FISHING CREEK, the Battle of—January 19, 1862. Fought in central Kentucky in a victory push by Union General George H. Thomas against the forces under Zollicoffer. This victory forced the Confederates into withdrawing from Tennessee. Confederate leader Felix K. Zollicoffer was killed in this battle, which alternately has been referred to as the "Battle of Logan's Crossroads," "Somerset," "Mill Springs," and "Fishing Creek." Crittenden was co-commander of the Confederate force.

FIVE FORKS, the Battle of—March 31–April 1, 1865. Five Forks was mainly a holding action by the Confederates. First, the junction was important to Lee's supply line to Petersburg. Secondly, it was the key to the Confederate's last supply line. Thirdly, the Petersburg lines were so weakened that an action of this type was necessary to slow down the Union assault long enough for the faltering Southerners to strengthen the city's defenses.

Sheridan circled westward but was met by Pickett and stopped until

81

Warren attacked the Confederate rear. Pickett, after hours of delaying tactics, was routed and Union forces nearly encircled Petersburg. During the fighting, the Union forced the Southerns to come out of their trenches in an effort to hold their supply lines, and the statistics of the battle show the results : Union losses, 1,000; Confederate losses, 4,500 captured (the dead were unlisted).

FLORIDA, the Secession of—January 10, 1861. The secession convention voted to secede from the Union by a 62-7 margin, making Florida the third state (behind South Carolina and Mississippi) to proceed into the Confederacy and out of the Union.

FLOYD, JOHN BUCHANAN (1806–1863)—Confederate Brigadier General. Floyd was the Union Secretary of War until Lincoln took office. An avowed Southerner (born in Smithfield, Virginia), he was accused of transferring arms to Southern arsenals before the outbreak of war, in order to allow the Confederates to seize them when war became a reality. Floyd was indicted by a Washington grand jury, but was never found guilty. He returned north to answer the charges brought against him. He resigned his post as secretary of war, because of Anderson's occupation of Fort Sumter. On March 7, 1861, the government entered a nolle prosequi, returning the bail which he had put up when he returned north. He was accused of leaving Fort Donelson with his brigade when Grant attacked (leaving Buckner to command and negoti-

ate the surrender). For this action, Davis removed him from command. He later became a major general in the army of the state of Virginia.

FOOTE, ANDREW HULL (1806–1863)—Union Rear Admiral. Foote entered the navy in 1822 as a midshipman, and was active in the surpression of the slave trade, and in the retaliatory actions in China. He was in charge of the Brooklyn Navy Yard before the war, and commanded the naval expedition against Forts Henry and Donelson in 1861 on the Tennessee and Cumberland Rivers. In 1862, Foote was promoted to rear admiral and commander of the Charleston Fleet, succeeding Admiral Du Pont who was relieved from his command. He died, however, before assuming this post.

FORREST, NATHAN BEDFORD (1821–1877)—Confederate Major General. Though not highly educated, he grew wealthy by shrewdness in land purchases and the slave trade in Memphis, Tenn. After beginning his army career as a Confederate private, Forrest decided to equip a mounted battalion at his own expense and head it with higher rank. As a lieutenant colonel, he served at Fort Donelson, and made good his escape when Grant's forces attacked. He fought at Shiloh as a colonel, and in July, 1862, was made a brigadier general.

Soon after, Forrest began his career of cavalry raids which made him one of the most feared and respected figures in the war. He was seldom defeated because of his ability to hit hard and run until a battle site more favorable to his force could be found. After being promoted to major general, Forrest was given independent command, and seldom served under any other general for the remainder of the war.

He is accused of having slaughtered many Negroes at Fort Pillow, in April, 1864, and (considering his violent temper and his postwar activities as founder and leader of the Ku Klux Klan) this rumor takes on significance. Numerous diaries and reports accuse Forrest of ordering the "no quarter" type of fighting which led to the infamous Fort Pillow Massacre. A number of Confederate soldiers report in their diaries that they hid rather than carry out the instructions to bayonet any Negro soldier found within the confines of the fort.

One of his most brilliant victories was at Brice's Crossroads (q.v.). In February of 1865, he was made lieutenant general, following the Battle of Nashville. His courage was unquestionable, and his military ability has been described as "bordering on genius"; however, his shady background in his dealings with the Negro soldiers who opposed him and the freed Negroes after the war, takes a great deal of honor away from one of the smartest soldiers of the Civil War. He is credited with uttering the statement, "The one who gets there first with the most is usually victorious." (See FORT PILLOW.)

FORT DONELSON—Following the fall of Fort Henry, Grant moved his forces overland to Fort Donelson and forced its surrender on February 11, 1862. The fall of this fort broke the Confederate hold on two rivers of great importance to Union plans, the Tennessee and the Cumberland. Totals in both engagements : Union, 2,800; and the Confederacy, 2,000. In addition, the Confederacy had 11,500 men captured when the forts surrendered.

FORT FISHER—In New Hanover County, N.C. Built by the Confederates to defend the entrance to the South's most formidable southeastern shipping area—Wilmington port and the Cape Fear River. Built to withstand naval bombardment and heavy artillery, this fort was considered one of the strongest on the East coast. Under the command of Colonel William Lamb in 1864, this fort was assaulted by a combined land and sea force under Butler and Porter which totaled 150 vessels and 3,000 men. Lamb commanded just 1,400 Confederates.

Because of the failure of Porter's guns to dent the 25-foot thick parapets of the fort, Butler deemed it unwise to attack, and withdrew his force. In this first effort, the Union lost 83 men and the Confederacy reported 58 killed or wounded.

On January 15, 1865, the combined land and sea force of General Alfred H. Terry and Porter succeeded in landing 1,600 sailors and 400 marines (who were repulsed) near the fort. Over 8,000 soldiers complimented this force, and the fort fell. This closed the port of Wilmington and resulted in the fall of that city soon after. In this latter engagement, Union losses totaled 266 killed, 1,008 wounded, and 57 missing; Confederates lost 500 killed or wounded. There are no figures on the number captured.

FORT HENRY, the Attack on—Heavily supported by Foote's gunboats, Grant steamed up the Tennessee River to a point approximately seventy miles northwest of Nashville, and hit vulnerable Fort Henry. Grant's force of 25,000 men had little to do, for the seven accompanying gunboats battered the fort into submission from the water. Confederate General Lloyd Tilghman, having only 5,000 men, surrendered on February 6, 1862. (See FORT DONELSON for casualty figures.)

FORT HINDMAN, the Battle of—January 10–11, 1863 (Arkansas Post). Grant directed General John McClernand north from Vicksburg to attack Fort Hindman at the little village of Arkansas Post on the Arkansas River. The fort, commanded by General Thomas J. Churchill, had 5,000 men. McClernand commanded 29,000.

On January 10, 1863, Admiral Porter's fleet began to bombard the little fort, and on the 11th, McClernand's artillery opened up also. Outnumbered six to one, and penned in, Churchill was unable to prevent his force from being overrun. However, the Confederates fought valiantly, killing and wounding over 1,000 Union soldiers while losing only 140 themselves. The remainder of the garrison force was either captured,

or was able to slip away during the confusion. Because the fort did not add to the Union control of the Mississippi, McClernand burned it and returned to Vicksburg.

FORT PICKENS, Florida — On the Santa Rosa Island, commanding the entrance to Pensacola Harbor along with Forts Barrancas and McRee. During the early part of 1861, the fort's commander, Lieutenant A. J. Slemmer, transferred all of the garrison of Barrancas to Pickens, allowing the Confederates to seize the other two forts. Federal re-enforcements arrived, preventing the Confederates from taking Pickens, and the fort remained in Union hands throughout the remainder of the war.

FORT PILLOW, Tennessee—Built by the Confederates on the Mississippi north of Memphis. Abandoned on June 4, 1862, and occupied the next day by a small Union force. On April 12, 1864, Confederate forces under General Nathan B. Forrest attacked the garrison killing or wounding more than half of the force. A large number of Negro troops there were slain in what is termed the "Fort Pillow Massacre." It was here that the practice of "no quarter" to Negro troops was supposed to have reached its most disgusting height. A number of the Confederate cavalry men are said to have hidden in the woods rather than to carry out the orders to slaughter the Negroes.

Among Negroes, Forrest is referred

to as the "Butcher of Fort Pillow." (See FORREST, NATHAN BEDFORD.)

FORT PULASKI, Georgia—On Cockspur Island. Seized by Georgia troops January 3, 1861, and attacked by Union General Q. A. Gillmore in January, 1862, in an attempt to recapture the fort. By February 10th, siege guns were in place, and the firing began in earnest. At two P.M., the fort surrendered its 385 officers and men. The Union loss was one man killed. The fall of Fort Pulaski closed the Savannah River to blockade-runners.

FOSTER, JOHN G. (1836–1917) — Union officer. Born in Pike County, Ind., March 2, 1836. Died in Washington, D.C., Nov. 15, 1917. A graduate of Indiana University, 1855, Foster received the M.A. degree in 1858 from Harvard Law School. He served in the Union army and was promoted for gallantry at Fort Donelson and Shiloh. After the war, he served as minister to Russia, secretary of state, and U.S. agent in the Bering Sea controversy.

FOX, GUSTAVUS VASA (1821–1883)— Union naval officer. Assistant Secretary of the Navy. Born in Saugus, Mass. A graduate of Annapolis, 1841. Fox served in the Mexican War handling troop transportation. He was reassigned in 1856, and was consulted when the problem of relieving Fort Sumter came up in 1861.

In May of that year, he became chief clerk of the Navy Department in Washington, and in August of that same year, the post of assistant secretary of the navy was created for him. He is credited with aiding in the development of the Union navy to a degree of high efficiency during the war.

When the word reached Washington that the former Union warship "Merrimac" (renamed the "Virginia") was being converted into an ironclad, Fox promoted the development of the "Monitor." He is considered one of the top administrators in U.S. naval history, and, because of his ability and tact, was sent to Russia on a diplomatic mission following the war.

FRANKLIN, the Battle of—A Union victory. This battle was fought at the Tennessee town of Franklin during the struggle for the state in 1864. Hood had bypassed an opportunity to smash the forces under Schofield at Spring Hill and Duck River, and was determined to destroy the Federals by direct frontal assault on the Franklin trenches. Schofield had 30,000 men.

Six Confederate generals, including Pat Cleburne, died in this assault. The attack was a fruitless, suicidal attempt to dislodge strongly entrenched forces, and resulted in a statistic sheet which backs up this statement. The Union lost 189 killed, 1,033 wounded; Confederate losses totaled 1,750 killed and 3,800 wounded.

FRANKLIN, WILLIAM B. (1823–1903)— Union Major General. Born in York, Pa., Feb. 27, 1823. Died in Hartford, Conn., Mar. 8, 1903. Franklin, a West Point graduate (1843, at the head of his class), was a classmate of U. S. Grant's. He participated in the Battle of South Mountain, but was blocked from taking a major part by the holding actions of Confederate General Lafayette Laws. He also fought at Manassas and Fredericksburg. He held commands in the Peninsular campaign, in Maryland, and in the Department of the Gulf. Severely criticized for his actions at Fredericksburg, he resigned his commission under fire. However, he returned to the army in mid-1863, and was seriously wounded at Sabine Crossroads, April 8, 1864.

Franklin was not conspicuously successful after his return to active duty in 1863. He was captured by the Confederates on July 11, 1864, but escaped that same night. In March, 1865, he was brevetted major general, but resigned to engage in business in 1866. He served as U.S. commissioner general to Paris for the Exposition in 1900. He was made grand officer of the Legion of Honor before he died in 1903.

FRAYSER'S FARM, the Battle of — June 30, 1862. The area is often referred to as Glendale. Here, in the sector known as "White Oak Swamp," forces under McClellan held off Confederates under Lee, and executed a brilliant retreat to Malvern Hill north of the James River.

FREDERICKSBURG, the Battle of— December 13, 1862. Burnside was successful in breaching one wing of the Confederate line during this battle, but the main line of Lee's 72,500 troops repulsed the invading Federals. Burnside had intended to move on Richmond by way of Fredericksburg, a key Virginia railroad junction just forty-five miles north of the Confederate capital. Lee, however, selected his defensive position with care and built his line around the almost impregnable Marye's Heights which kept the Union line under fire during the entire battle. This area. so steeply elevated that Union charges could be broken up, developed into the center of action. Burnside wasted countless numbers of men in fruitless charges against this height.

That night, the Federal forces retired across the river in frustrated disgust. The Union losses almost tripled those of the Confederacy, but, against the background of a lack of reserves, the loss of 5,300 men posed a severe strain on Lee's dwindling force. Burnside lost 12,000 of his massive force of 106,000. Hooker replaced Burnside after this campaign, and continued the assault on Fredericksburg.

FREEDMENS BUREAU—Established by the Congress of the United States in 1865 to handle the problems of the Negro, "newly placed in society without background, skill, or friendly hand."

FREMONT, JOHN CHARLES (1813–1890)—Union Major General. Born in Richmond, Va., 1813. Fremont served briefly in the navy and then in the topographical corps. He began his career of western exploration which made him famous. He was one of the first major generals appointed by Lincoln. Some historians list his birthplace as Savannah, Ga. He was expelled from college in Charleston, S.C., for "continuous disregard of discipline."

Fremont took command of the St. Louis arsenal in 1861, and promptly drew criticism for his lavish headquarters set up (the $6,000 rental of which went to one of his wife's relatives). In 1845, he had been tried and found guilty of mutiny (and a number of other charges) in a case involving statehood for California. These old facts came back to haunt him, as the partisan St. Louisians opposed him. Fremont kept an elite guard of Hungarians and Garibaldian troops around him and his headquarters. He was perhaps the most renowned (and least active) of all of the generals in the West, but was well liked by the abolitionist elements of New England.

On August 30, 1861, he issued the controversial "Fremont's Emancipation Proclamation," which assumed far-reaching authority as far as his office was concerned, and promptly brought the administration in Washington down upon him. After being asked by Lincoln to change certain sections of the proclamation or to rescind it entirely (and refusing to do so), Fremont was removed from office on October 24, 1861, and replaced by General Hunter. He did not receive the order from Lincoln relieving him from office until November 2, 1861, due to the fact that he had given orders that no courier from Washington was to be admitted to his headquarters.

His release almost caused riots in some parts of the country. He was nominated for President on the radical Republican ticket in 1864, but refused to run. High tempered, Fremont lacked the ability to control large numbers of men effectively. He could manage an exploration of 200–300 men superbly, but was "in deep water" when it came to administering an entire department. He played no really important role in the war, except that he nearly alienated the border states, and caused the abolitionists to side against Lincoln. (See FREMONT'S EMANCIPATION PROCLAMATION.)

FREMONT'S EMANCIPATION PROCLAMATION—This was considered part of the proclamation sent out by General John C. Fremont in Missouri, August 30, 1861. It stated basically the same things that Lincoln's later proclamation stated concerning the slaves of owners who were in rebellion against the Union. It stated that these slaves were automatically "freemen." Fremont even issued papers of manumission to Missouri Negroes. (See FREMONT, JOHN CHARLES.)

FRENCH, SAMUEL G. — Confederate Major General. Born in New Jersey. A West Point graduate, 1843, but resigned his commission in 1856 to become a Mississippi planter as a result of an inheritance received by his wife. He aligned with the South when war broke out, and became a brigadier general in the fall of 1861. By 1862, he had been made a major general.

French became the central figure

in a controversy between J. E. Johnston and Longstreet when the latter (dissatisfied with French) transferred him to Johnston's command. Johnston's troops had been complaining that too many Northern-born generals were being sent to the army in Mississippi, and this stirred up the controversy.

French commanded a division of the Army of Tennessee, but was not with the army in North Carolina when the Union forces smashed it. He was commanding a unit when the army was defeated in the area around Nashville.

FRITCHIE, BARBARA (*ca.* 1766)—Union sympathizer. A resident of Frederick, Md., who allegedly dared the wrath of Stonewall Jackson's troops by hurling her defiance at them from an upstairs window as they paraded through her town. For this act, she was immortalized in a poem, but there is no valid authentication that she ever waved a Union flag or that she ever hurled taunts at Jackson himself. Chroniclers differ on this subject. One history of the Maryland invasion describes her as "Dame Fritchie who was nearly a hundred years old and remembered 1776." Most agree that she did live in Frederick's residential section at the time of the invasion. Few agree, however, as to the street, or the incident. Generally, it is accepted that the heroic deeds of this elderly lady are mainly figments of a poet's mind, and designed to increase the patriotism of a tired nation.

FRONT ROYAL, Virginia, the Engagement at—May 23, 1862; May 30, 1862. Colonel John R. Kenly, with nine companies of the First Maryland, two companies of the Twenty-ninth Pennsylvania, and one company from the Twenty-eighth New York—about 900 men in all—was holding the town when Stonewall Jackson's force pushed through in an attempt to cut off Banks. The main fighting took place outside of the town, in a running battle which ended in the disintegration of Kenly's force, and the capture of most of them. The Union lost 18 killed, 58 wounded, and 718 captured. Jackson lost only 11 killed and 15 wounded.

Jackson pushed after Banks, leaving the Twelfth Georgia with a battery at Front Royal. However, on the 30th, the advance unit of McDowell's Corps surprised Confederate Colonel David Conner and his force there, capturing 156 officers and men, and one gun. Front Royal was back in Union hands.

This town was the key to Luray Valley, sitting as it did, just twelve miles east of Strasburg at the head of the valley.

FROST, "MISSOURI" — Confederate sympathizer. Union General. Frost was in command of the Missouri Militia outside of St. Louis, Mo., when Captain Nathaniel Lyon and his troops attacked in early May of 1861. Lyon captured most of Frost's men and paraded them through the streets of St. Louis with disastrous results.

During the march, angry citizens mobbed the prisoners, killing one and

88

injuring many. A total of twenty-eight spectators and members of the mob were killed when a German unit under Lyon was forced to fire into the rioting mass to restore order. Frost commanded only a small force when overrun by Lyon, and his unit was officially flying the United States flag when attacked. Lyon and Francis P. Blair (governor of the state), however, felt that the camp was "a fearful menace . . ." and "a hotbed of secessionists." Forces under Union General William S. Harney entered St. Louis and restored order after the riot was quelled.

FUGITIVE SLAVE ACT, the repeal of the—June 28, 1864. The 1850 law, which had done so much to stir up prewar enmity between the Republicans and the Democrats, was repealed on June 28, 1864. In the hustle and bustle of the war, it had almost been forgotten.

In January, 1861, the House of Representatives had received a committee report that this act be strenuously enforced, and that the personal liberty laws be repealed. The same committee (thoroughly infiltrated by Southerners) recommended an amendment to the Constitution which would protect slave states from interference with slavery.

The amendment was adopted, but was not ratified. Once the Southern senators and representatives had withdrawn from Congress the Fugitive Slave Act, instead of being strengthened, was repealed. Antislavery legislation was strengthened.

FULLER J. F. C. (b. 1878)—English

soldier and historian. Born in Sussex, England, September 1, 1878. He wrote extensively on the war, and his *Decisive Battles of the U.S.A.* (1939–1940) is considered one of the best dealing with many of the major engagements of the Civil War.

G

GAINES MILL, the Battle of—The second of the Seven Days' Battles, and a Confederate victory. On June 27, 1862, over 35,000 Union troops under General Fitz-John Porter engaged 55,000 Confederates under General Robert E. Lee at Gaines Mill just eight miles northeast of Richmond, Virginia.

The Union victory at Mechanicsville on June 26 had given Porter's force a chance to entrench along the north bank of the winding Chickahominy River near Cold Harbor. After preliminary skirmishing with Confederates under A. P. Hill (coming in from Mechanicsville), Porter was hit hard by Lee's main force at about two P.M. Lee's two main lieutenants (Longstreet and Jackson) were on his right and left flanks respectively.

After a full day of hard battle, the Union center collapsed and was forced to retreat. During the night, the remainder of the Federal force crossed the Chicahominy River and joined McClellan's army in retreat to Harrison's Landing on the James River. The Union losses were 6,837 killed, wounded, or missing. Lee lost 8,000 killed, wounded, or missing.

GALVESTON, TEXAS, the Battle of—
On New Years Day, 1863, a Confederate party under General John Magruder launched a combined land and sea attack upon the Union forces in Galveston and on the bay. Union Admiral Farragut had previously ordered the coast of Texas blockaded (summer, 1862), and had forced the Confederate military unit to abandon the city and surrender to U.S. Naval Commander Renshaw (October 8, 1862). Magruder's force captured the Union force left to hold the city, and succeeded in capturing the "Harriet Jane," a member of the blockading squadron. Union sailors blew up the "Westfield" to prevent her capture.

After a sea engagement between the "Hatteras" and the Confederate raider "Alabama," Farragut was able to restore the blockade in the bay, but the city remained in the hands of the Confederates until the end of the war.

As a result of this "joint" possession of the area, a number of sea and land engagements took place in the Galveston Bay area.

GARNETT, ROBERT S. (1819–1861)— Confederate commander in West Virginia against McClellan. Garnett executed a brilliant rear guard action while escaping from McClellan after the "Philippi Races" from Philippi, (W.) Va., thirty miles south of Grafton.

He was killed at Carrick's Ford during the rear guard action described above, becoming the first general officer to die in battle in the war. Ephraim Ellsworth was the first officer to fall (*q.v.*) but his rank at the time was that of colonel. Garnett was killed while attempting to set an example for his "green" troops in the art of retreating under fire without becoming excited. He was killed by a sharpshooter's bullet on July 13, 1861.

GARRISON, WILLIAM LLOYD (1805– 1879)—Union abolitionist and editor. Garrison was mentioned in the plot preceding the raid on Harper's Ferry. Aside from his constant demand for abolition, and his editorial support of Lincoln after the issuance of the Emancipation Proclamation, Garrison is more important in the areas concerned with the causes of the war, and the era preceding its eruption.

GATLING GUN, the—Used very seldom by the Union because of its late appearance upon the military scene. It was avoided by many commanders as a "gadget." The gun had a 350-round-per-minute firing power, but could not fire for long periods of time because of cooling deficiencies.

GEARY, JOHN WHITE (1819–1873)— Union Brigadier General. Political. The Mount Pleasant, Pa., native was the first postmaster of San Francisco prior to the war. He joined the war as a volunteer, and rose to brigadier general of volunteers by April 25, 1862. He commanded a division at Chancellorsville, after fighting at Cedar Mountain. He also commanded divisions at Gettysburg and

Lookout Mountain. While governor of Kansas prior to the war, he won acclaim for restoring order in that territory (1856–1857). He was elected governor of Pennsylvania in 1867.

GERMANNA FORD—On the Rapidan southwest of Fredericksburg. It was used frequently during the fight for Richmond. The Germanna Plank Road begins at the ford, and runs southwest to cross the turnpike at the Old Wilderness Tavern.

GERMANNA PLANK ROAD—Begins at Germanna Ford, Va., southwest of Fredericksburg, and runs to Wilderness Tavern and Orange Turnpike. Here, the road changes names and becomes the Brock Road as far as Spotsylvania Court House and Richmond, Va.

"GENERAL," the—(see ANDREWS RAID, the)

GENERAL ORDER, NUMBER ELEVEN— Issued December 17, 1862. Anti-Jewish regulation. This order was issued by Assistant Adjutant General John A. Rawlins under the signature of Major General U. S. Grant, commander along the Mississippi and of the Department of the Tennessee.

The order is considered to be perhaps the most generalized anti-Semetic regulation of the war, and possibly in U.S. history. It was issued by Grant after the profiteering in his sector had reached a stage where it was hurting the war effort. His mistake was in assuming that, because a large portion of the Jews in the area were merchants or traders, they must be the sole source of this violation of the law. In fact, Jesse Grant, the general's father, was accused of obtaining trading permits for certain merchants through his son. Lincoln is reputed to have said, "The army itself is diverted from fighting the rebels to speculating in cotton."

The general order was wired from Grant's headquarters in Holly Springs, Miss., on December 17, and read :

> The Jews, as a class violating every regulation of trade established by the Treasury Department and also department orders, are hereby expelled from the department within twenty-four hours from the receipt of this order.
>
> Post commanders will see that all of this class of people be furnished passes and required to leave, and anyone returning after such notification will be arrested and held in confinement until an opportunity occurs of sending them out as prisoners, unless furnished with permit from headquarters.
>
> No passes will be given these people to visit headquarters for the purpose of making personal application for trade permits.
>
> By order of Major General
> U. S. Grant
> John A. Rawlins
> Assistant Adjutant General

The order resulted in an hurried and mass exodus of Jews from the department of the Tennessee, with many forced to leave behind valuable property. The order was carried out with particular effectiveness in Paducah, Kentucky, Holly Springs, Miss., and Oxford, Miss. Ironically, in the latter two towns Jewish soldiers were stationed as members of Grant's army.

When the Jews carried their protest directly to President Lincoln through Paducah, Ky., residents Cesar Kaskel, his brother J. W. Kaskel, and one D. Wolff, Lincoln immediately sent a letter to the General-in-chief, Henry W. Halleck, directing him to telegraph instructions for the cancellation of General Order No. 11. Halleck, who had no prior knowledge of the order, immediately forwarded a wire to Grant which read: "A paper purporting to be General Order No. 11 issued by you December 17, has been presented here. By its terms, it expels all Jews from your department. *If such an order has been issued,* it will be immediately revoked."

Three days later, Grant's office transmitted the order of recall, taking pains to state that it was, "by direction of General-in-chief of the army, at Washington." Grant failed to defend his actions, and Halleck subsequently sent the following wire to Grant:

General. It may be proper to give some explanation of the revocation of your order expelling all Jews from your department. The President has no objection to your expelling traitors and Jew peddlers, which, I suppose, was the object of your order; but as it in terms proscribed an entire religious class, some of whom are fighting in our ranks, the President deemed it necessary to revoke it.

Like Halleck, most of the officials were indifferent to the effect of the General Order No. 11. Had not Lincoln intervened, it is doubtful that the order would have been rescinded.

GEORGIA, the Army of—Union. This army consisted mainly of two corps under Sherman during the march from Atlanta to Savannah and the sea. The army was directed by Major General Henry W. Slocum as part of Sherman's general command.

GETTY, GEORGE WASHINGTON (1819–1901)—Union Brigadier General. A native of Georgetown, D.C., and a West Point graduate in the class of 1840, Getty served under Winfield Scott in the Mexican War, and fought in the Seminole War. He entered the Civil War with the rank of Lieutenant Colonel, and served in the battles of Caines Mill, Malvern Hill, South Mountain, Antietam and in the Peninsular campaign. Getty commanded a brigade of volunteers at Fredericksburg, and distinguished himself in the siege of Norfolk, Va. He commanded a division at the Wilderness and Petersburg.

In 1864, when Early was threatening Washington, Getty was sent to Washington with his division to intercept the Confederate force. He was used in pursuit a great deal by both Sheridan and Grant.

GETTYSBURG ADDRESS, the—November 19, 1863. A commission, undertaking to establish a cemetery where the dead of the Battle of Gettysburg might be buried, invited President Abraham Lincoln to "say a few appropriate remarks" at the dedication following the main address by Edward Everett, one of the nation's greatest orators. The invitation was extended at a very late date, but President Lincoln accepted with no obvious distraction at the breach of etiquette. He prepared his speech ten days in advance and arrived at Gettysburg on November 18, 1863, a full day ahead of time. On the day of the dedication, a procession composed of troops, a band, dignitaries, and the President astride a horse (with his gangling legs hanging almost to the ground) started for the cemetery.

It is noteworthy to statesmen of today that Lincoln rose (after Everett had delivered a two-hour long oration) delivered his speech, and was gone through the crowd before most of them even realized that he had spoken. Actually, the speech gained fame as a result of the widespread press coverage of the dedicatory ceremony. Most of the people there might never have remembered Lincoln's speech had they not read its contents in their newspapers. Most of them, in fact, did not even hear Lincoln speak.

The President said from the platform :

Fourscore and seven years ago, our fathers brought forth on this continent, a new nation, conceived in liberty, and dedicated to the proposition that all men are created equal.

Now, we are engaged in a great civil war, testing whether that nation, or any nation so conceived and so dedicated can long endure. We are met on a great battlefield of that war. We have come to dedicate a portion of that field, as a final resting place for those who here gave their lives that that nation might live. It is altogether fitting and proper that we should do this.

But, in a larger sense, we cannot dedicate—we cannot consecrate—we cannot hallow this ground. The brave men, living and dead, who struggled here, have consecrated it far above our poor power to add or detract. The world will little note, nor long remember what we say here, but it can never forget what they did here. It is for us the living, rather, to be dedicated here to the unfinished work which they who fought here have thus far so nobly advanced. It is rather for us to be here dedicated to the great task remaining before us—that from these honored dead we take increased devotion to that cause for which they gave the last full measure of devotion—that we here highly resolve that those dead shall not have died in vain—that this nation, under God, shall have a new birth of freedom—and that government of the people, by the people for the people, shall not perish from the earth.

With little fanfare, and very little attention from his restless audience, the sixteenth President of the United States delivered one of the shortest—

yet greatest—speeches in American history. His statement, "The world will little note, nor long remember what we say here," can go down in history as the greatest misstatement ever uttered.

GETTYSBURG, the Battle of—July 1–3, 1863. While Grant was preparing to accept the surrender of Vicksburg, Lee had made up his mind to devote his forces to an all-out effort to carry the fight to the North.

The battle at Gettysburg was not a planned one. Federal cavalry made contact with the Confederate forces when a Southern foraging detail was discovered near the town of Gettysburg. In the running fight which ensued, the Confederates forced the Union troops back to the town. The Federals called for help, and the stage was set for the fight, as both sides moved up re-enforcements.

Fresh on the heels of two major victories at Fredericksburg and Chancellorsville, the Southerners were in high spirits. They had a particular interest in the invasion of Pennsylvania because of the fertile resources of the lower countryside of that state.

The encounter came on June 30, and by July 1st the Confederates were in the Gettysburg vicinity in force. The first Federal line of defense was northwest of the town, but, as the Confederate strength grew, the Union forces were forced back through the town to Cemetery Ridge to the south, where they made their final stand.

Lee's reorganized army was in three corps of three divisions each, under his top commanders. Backed by the Confederacy's best cavalry under J. E. B. Stuart, and a newly organized artillery group under Pendleton consisting of 69 batteries and 287 guns, the Southerners were in good fighting strength.

On the other hand, Meade had newly assumed command of the Union Army of the Potomac (June 28). He, like Lee, had no intention of fighting at Gettysburg, having planned an encounter around the Pipe Creek area. Had not Pettigrew's force from Lee's army forced the battle during the chance encounter, it is likely that the battle would have taken place when and where Meade originally planned.

The Union force had been paralleling Lee's Army of Northern Virginia since Chancellorsville, and Stuart had been keeping Lee informed of Federal movements. However, on this occasion, Stuart was off on another of his "jaunts" around the Federal army, and the Southerners were left without their "probing finger." As a result, they went into the battle at Gettysburg without full knowledge of the Union strength or disposition.

The battle which began on July 1st, raged from northwest of Gettysburg to a ridge dominated by the Lutheran Seminary (Seminary Ridge) to a second commanding spot, Cemetery Ridge (or Hill). Meade threw 88,000 men against Lee's 75,000 invaders, in a battle which saw the Confederates attempt four times to take Cemetery Hill on the second day of battle.

On July 3rd, Lee threw 4,800 men under George Pickett in a head-on assault which failed (and exhausted Lee's supply of fresh troops). This charge hit the Union center at Cemetery Ridge, but was halted by a withering fire from the Federal force there which broke the back of the Confederate attack (see PICKETT'S CHARGE). Lee retreated southward.

As was to happen throughout the war, the Union commander failed to take advantage of the situation by following and soundly scattering Lee's army. Meade, happy with the respite from battle, allowed the whipped Confederates to escape across the Virginia line unopposed. Lee pulled his army back on the night of July 4th, the day that Vicksburg was being entered by Grant's troops in the West.

Although heavy losses were sustained by both sides at Gettysburg, Lee's losses seriously sapped the South's fighting strength. The Confederates lost 28,000 men against 23,000 lost by the Union. These figures do not accurately give an estimate of how sorely the 28,000 lost by Lee were to be missed in future campaigns.

GIBBON, JOHN (1827–1896)—Union Major General. Gibbon was appointed to West Point from North Carolina, although he was born in Holmsburg, Pa. He graduated from the Point in 1847, and served in

Florida before returning to the Academy to teach.

During the war, he served under McDowell, and was considered an outstanding molder of volunteer troops. He prepared the artillery manual used by the Union forces, and served as brigade, division and corps commander. Gibbon led the famous "Iron Brigade" at Manassas, South Mountain, Antietam, and in other engagements. At Fredericksburg, he was in command of a division when wounded. At Gettysburg, he commanded the Second Corps until wounded again. He returned to duty in time to command a division at the Wilderness (1864) and at Spotsylvania.

Gibbon had three brothers in the Confederate army. He was promoted to major general in June, 1864, and took over the newly organized Twenty-fourth Corps which he headed for the remainder of the war. At Appomattox, he was one of the three men selected by Grant to serve on the commission to accept Lee's surrender. He was considered to have been one of the best organizers of troops on either side. After the war, he served in the West as a colonel.

GLENDALE, the Battle of—(see FRAYSER'S FARM)

GLORIETTA, the Battle of—Fought on Pigeon's Ranch in New Mexico, and at a place called Glorietta Pass about half a mile west of the actual ranch proper. Glorietta Pass was a rough gorge which made way for the Santa

Fe Trail. Here, six companies of Union troops from Colorado, a company of New Mexico volunteers, and two detachments of cavalry met a superior Confederate force in one of the most decisive battles of the Southwest. The Union force was accompanied by two batteries of artillery and a supply train of over 100 wagons with guards.

The Union force, outnumbered and on the defensive most of the time, won the battle (this will be disputed by many historians) by snapping the confederate supply line and destroying the supply base. The Federals, already suitably mounted, killed almost 500 mules and horses by bayoneting them, in order to prevent their recapture or re-use by Rebel forces. This supply train, mules, horses, ammunition and clothing of the Confederate force (mainly Texans) was destroyed, stopping Confederate attempt to take over all of the Southwest. Some consider the battle at Glorietta a minor skirmish, but when viewed with regard to the damage which would have been done had the Confederates been able to take over all of the Southwest, this battle is (as many refer to it) a "western Gettysburg."

Both sides claimed the victory, but the fact remains that the Confederate troops were forced to retreat to Pigeon's Ranch to recuperate, minus vital supplies and the animals with which to haul any others that they might be able to forage. The Union lost 100 men, and the Confederacy lost 36 killed and 60 wounded. Some writers list Confederate losses as high as 581, with the Union losses just below 100. There are no actual authentic records from this battle, but due to the fact that the Union force was dug in on the defensively suitable position in the pass, logic would dictate that the attacking force would lose more men. The Santa Fe Weekly Gazette wrote, "We have frequently heard the remark made by military men after a successful battle that they could not stand another such victory, but now we have an instance in which one claimed victory has proved the destruction of an army and rendered it necessary for them to attempt to evacuate the Territory which they had invaded." (April 26, 1862). This reference to the Confederate "victory" seems to bear out the surmise that the Union forces were justified in claiming the victory.

Regardless of the victor, it is generally conceded that the Battle of Glorietta Pass was the most decisive battle of the far western phase of the war. It resulted in an end to the Confederate attempt to take Texas, Colorado, New Mexico, and Arizona into its fold, and eventually resulted in the complete Union takeover of the territory concerned.

GOLDSBOROUGH, LOUIS MALESHERBES (1805–1877)—Union Rear Admiral. Goldsborough retired from the navy in 1833, and commanded a company of volunteer cavalry in the Seminole Wars in Florida. He returned to the navy in 1841 as a commander. In 1849, he served as a member of the joint Army-Navy Commission in California.

When war broke out, he was made a flag officer and rear admiral, commanding the North Atlantic blockading fleet. Prior to this, he had served as superintendent of the Naval Academy at Annapolis (1853–1857). After the war, he was in command of the European squadron for two years, and commandant of the Mare Island Navy Yards for over six years.

GORDON, JOHN BROWN (1832–1904)— Confederate Lieutenant General. A graduate of the University of Georgia, and a lawyer before the outbreak of war, Gordon had no prior military experience when he entered the service. He served as a minor officer until November, 1862, when he was made a brigadier general.

He was elevated to major general in May, 1864, and later rose to lieutenant general. His service campaigns include Seven Bays, Antietam, Chancellorsville, Gettysburg, the Wilderness, Spontsylvania, and the Petersburg - Appomattox campaign. His army career was not exceptionally outstanding, but he did perform in a steady, dependable fashion.

Following the war, Gordon became governor of Georgia, and later a U.S. senator from that state, serving three terms. He served as commander of the United Confederate Veterans from the outset of 1890 until his death in 1904. He was accused of bargaining and political corruption while in office after the war, but these charges were denied and never proved. He was vitally interested in Reconstruction, and was one of Georgia's most honored citizens.

GOSS, WARREN LEE (1835–1925)— Union private. A graduate of Harvard who served inconspicuously in the war, but who was afterwards president of the National Union of Ex-prisoners of War. He was highly placed in the Grand Army of the Republic. Active as an author and editor, he wrote a number of Civil War books for children and *The Soldier's Story of Captivity at Andersonville*, in addition to *Recollections of a Private*.

GRANGER, GORDON (1822–1876) — Union Brevet Major General. Granger graduated from West Point in 1845, served in the Mexican War, and as commander of the Army of Kentucky during the war between the states. He was instrumental in the capture of Forts Gaines and Morgan. After the war, he served as commander of the district of New Mexico.

GRANT, HIRAM ULYSSES (1822–1885)—Union Lieutenant General of the Armies. (Full General following the war, 1866.) Born in Mount Pleasant, Ohio, but raised in Georgetown, Ohio, Grant was of a middle class family, and was well liked as a boy. He acquired the name "Ulysses Simpson Grant" through a mistake made during the processing of his request for admission to West Point. His sponsoring state senator could only remember Grant's middle name and his mother's maiden name (Simpson), so he told the registrar that Grant's name was Ulysses Simpson Grant—a misnomer which stayed with him throughout the remainder of his life, and down through posterity.

Grant graduated from West Point with an undistinguished record—his only superior marks being in horsemanship—in 1843. He married Julia Dent in 1848, after serving in the Mexican War as a quartermaster. He resigned from the service under pressure after numerous charges of heavy drinking reached the Department of the Army. This record— accurate or not — followed Grant throughout his subsequent career. He was a captain when he resigned in 1854.

Grant received a commission as colonel of the unruly Twenty-first Illinois, June, 1861, and (as a result of a spectacular job of making soldiers out of the mob) was appointed brigadier general in August of the same year, and took charge of his troops in Cairo, Ill. From that point, he led a raid on Belmont, Mo., in November, 1861.

Grant acquired the title "Unconditional Surrender" as a result of the terms given at Fort Donelson by him. The demands caught the fancy of President Lincoln, and Grant's rise to fame began. He was made a major general, but, following a defeat at Shiloh, the cloud of suspicion built upon the old rumor of drunkenness arose. He promptly dispelled the fears of the public by laying siege to Vicksburg, deep in the heart of the Confederacy. Following the city's surrender on July 4, 1862, Grant was named commander of the West, and proceeded to clear the Tennessee River area of Confederate opposition.

In March, 1864, the rank of lieutenant general of the armies was revived for him, and he went to Washington to assume command of all Union armies. Grant led Meade's Army of the Potomac to victory in Virginia in 1864–65, although his total losses were staggering in most of the campaigns. He was known in the North to many of his enemies as "Butcher Grant." However, his dogged style of persistently weakening the enemy until the Confederates were forced to surrender at Appomattox probably saved countless numbers of lives in the long run.

He was made a full general in 1866, following the war, and became involved in a political hassle between Secretary Stanton and President Johnson, coming out of the fight as the unanimous choice of the Republican Party for the Presidential nomination. He was easily elected to two consecutive terms (1869–1876), but failed in business after his second term. He became a writer for Samuel L. Clemens (Mark Twain), who published Grant's memoirs. Grant finished the work shortly before his death from cancer in 1885.

Grant was an exceptional soldier with all of the strategy and military know-how to pursue the Confederate army to its final surrender. Throughout his life, he gave every indication of being aware of his shortcomings—

some he overcame, others he ignored. He was never successful in any business endeavor into which he went. His *Personal Memoirs*, however, earned nearly $500,000.

GRAPEVINE BRIDGE — Across the Chickahominy River below Mechanicsville Bridge. This bridge was used frequently during the war to cross the river during strategic engagements in the fight for Richmond.

GREAT SEAL OF THE CONFEDERACY, THE—The official seal of the Confederacy had an equestrian statue of George Washington surrounded by a wreath composed of the Confederacy's principal agricultural products : corn, wheat, rice and sugar cane. In the margin were the words, "The Confederate States of America," stamped with the date, February, 1862, and the motto, "Deo Vindice," completing the circle.

The seal was made of silver and ivory, and was designed by a London sculptor and brought to Richmond via Wilmington, N.C., in late 1864. Due to the fact that the press by which the seal was to be stamped upon documents was lost at sea, the seal was never used.

The Great Seal was authorized by the Confederate House in a Resolution No. 13, on April 30, 1863, and was designed to portray the importance of agriculture to the Confederate States of America. It was also to denote the degree to which the Confederate States of America were supposed to be adhering to the principles of the founding father of the United States, George Washington.

GREENE, GEORGE SEARS (1801–1899) —Union officer. A graduate of West Point, 1823. He served as professor there. Greene designed and constructed the reservoir at Central Park in New York City. When war broke out, he assumed command of the Sixtieth New York Volunteers, and later took command of a brigade at Cedar Mountain. At Antietam, Greene led a division. In 1863, at Chattanooga, he was severely wounded. After the war, he served as chief engineer of public works in Washington, D.C., and planned the sewer system of the nation's capital.

GREELEY, HORACE (1811–1872) — Northern newspaper editor. Greeley, a native of Amherst, N.H., was active in Whig politics. He was the person who coined the phrase, "Let the erring sisters go," with reference to the seceding Southern states.

Described as "wishy-washy" because of his constant political changing during the war, Greeley was actually one of America's greatest editors. He opposed Lincoln's re-election in 1864, but attempted to make reconciliation following the election. He was badly beaten by Grant in the Presidential race in 1872, and died a broken man following the death of his wife and his defeat at the polls. Just before his death, he lost control of his beloved (and powerful) New York *Tribune*.

GREENE, S. DANA (1840–1884)—Union

naval officer. A graduate of the Naval Academy in 1859, Greene volunteered to serve as executive of the untried "Monitor" in 1862. He actually commanded the vessel when an accident befell the commander, Captain J. L. Worden, during the engagement with the Confederate ram, "Merrimac." He served as a pursuer of blockade runners during the war, and taught at the Naval Academy for ten years after the war ended.

GRIERSON, BENJAMIN HENRY (1826–1911)—Union cavalry raider. A native of Pittsburgh, Pa., Grierson was educated in Youngstown, Ohio. He took up teaching in Jacksonville, Ill., but set up business as a merchant in Meredosia, Ill. All of which shows his constant desire for activity and movement. Engaging in a number of cavalry raids following the outbreak of war, Grierson rose rapidly from major to colonel.

His most famous cavalry raid was made through Tennessee, Mississippi, and parts of Louisiana, and is known in history as "Grierson's Raid." The Union troops left La Grange, Tenn., on April 17, 1863, and moved through Mississippi and Louisiana for sixteen days destroying railroads and public property. His 1,700 men caused great destruction and consternation in those states (supposedly safe deep in the heart of the Confederacy), and served as a means of pulling troops away from the Vicksburg area which was facing attack by Grant. On May 2, 1863, after having been of almost terrifying assistance to Grant's campaign, Grierson and his men emerged at Baton Rouge, La. He was promoted to brigadier general of volunteers and continued making raids—but none as spectacular as his ride through the heart of Dixie.

In the spring of 1865, Grierson was promoted to major general. Strangely enough, this daring cavalry raider was said to have a dislike for horses. He was considered one of the most valuable and competent officers in both the war and postwar years.

GRIFFIN, CHARLES (1825–1867) — Union Brevet Major General. A graduate of West Point (1847), and an instructor there after the outbreak of war, Griffin was considered an artillery expert. He, however, committed the "unpardonable sin" at the first Bull Run, by allowing a group of Confederates, mistakenly identified as Federal troops, to approach his battery without opposition. The battery was nearly wiped out. Griffin, however, escaped blame, and rose rapidly in the ranks.

At the time of the surrender at Appomattox, he was a brevet major general, commanding the Fifth Corps. His fellow officers described him as "controversial," "arrogant," and "hard to get along with." But, all rated him as an excellent officer.

The battery which was nearly annihilated at Bull Run was a battery of enlisted men from West Point which Griffin had trained.

GRIFFIN, SIMON GOODELL (1824–

1902)—Union Major General of volunteers. A New Hampshire lawyer, teacher and legislator before the war, Griffin helped to organize the Second New Hampshire Infantry Regiment, and was made a captain of the unit. Later he rose to colonel of that unit. During most of the war, he served in Virginia, and was considered a good soldier and leader. After the war, he re-entered politics for three terms in the New Hampshire legislature, serving as its speaker during his last two years there.

GUINEA'S STATION—On the railroad from Fredericksburg to Richmond, Va. It was near here, at Chandler house, that Thomas "Stonewall" Jackson died following the battle of Chancellorsville. The railroad passing through Guinea's Station was the Richmond-Fredericksburg railroad.

GULF, THE ARMY AND DEPARTMENT OF THE—Union. Commanded by Major General Benjamin F. Butler from February, 1862 (when it officially came into existence), until Major General N. P. Banks assumed command late in 1862. Other commanders included S. A. Hurlbut and E. R. S. Canby. This army unsuccessfully campaigned in the Red River expedition in 1864, and fought around Mobile late in the war.

H

HALLECK, HENRY WAGNER (1815–1872)—Union Chief of Staff. Halleck, a graduate of West Point (1839), was a very high scholar at the Military Academy. An engineer, he studied and wrote on military science, and was a noted scholar and student of the philosophy of Jomini. He was also active in mining, and wrote on the subject.

At the outbreak of war, he received a commission as a major general (August, 1861) in the regular army. He succeeded Fremont in command of St. Louis, and was Grant's superior when Forts Henry and Donelson were captured. Afraid that Halleck would order him *not* to go, Grant commenced his move on Vicksburg *before* wiring Halleck that the move was to be made. His fears were justified, because after the campaign was well underway, Grant received a wire from Halleck ordering him *not* to undertake the move. Halleck was Pope's commander during the capture of Island No. 10, and commanded the whole West after May, 1862, until Grant took over. He took to the field after Shiloh, for the first and only time in his career.

Overcautious, and a leader who believed in fighting the war by the book, Halleck often failed to follow up his victories, and was better suited to desk work. In March, 1864, he became chief of staff, and had little to do with the actual prosecution of the war thereafter except from a desk in Washington.

HAMPTON, WADE, III (1818–1902)—Confederate Major General. Hampton was born in Charleston, S.C., of distinguished parents, and graduated from South Carolina College (now the University of South Carolina) in

101

1836. He became a planter, but gave up this to enter the state legislature in 1860 where he was listed as one of those who opposed secession. When war broke out, however, he volunteered (with his personally outfitted "Hampton's Legion") and fought at Manassas.

In the Peninsular Campaign, he commanded a brigade after being promoted to brigadier general in May of 1862. Although he conducted raids on his own, he was actually under J. E. B. Stuart's command. In August, 1863, he was made commander of the cavalry corps of the Army of Northern Virginia, and subsequently was promoted to major general to warrant the command.

HAMPTON ROADS, THE CONFERENCE AT —February 3, 1865. During the war, Hampton Roads was the staging-out and rendezvous area for numerous expeditions. It was here that the "Monitor" and the "Merrimac" met in the first naval battle of ironclads. Therefore, it was a natural spot for the informal conference between President Lincoln, Secretary of State William H. Seward, and the Confederate representatives, Vice-President Alexander H. Stephens, Senator Robert M. T. Hunter, and Assistant Secretary of War, John A. Campbell.

The meeting took place near Fort Monroe, aboard the "River Queen," and its objective was to negotiate a peace between the North and the South. Lincoln held that peace could only be negotiated in this manner between *nations,* and the Confederacy was not (in his opinion) in this category. Therefore, although the conference lasted four hours, nothing concrete came of it.

HANCOCK, WINFIELD SCOTT (1824–1886)—Union Major General. A graduate of West Point (1844) and a veteran of the Mexican War, the Florida campaigns, and the Indian fighting in the West when the Civil War broke out. He was, consequently, experienced in the handling of troops and was made a brigadier general in charge of volunteers in September, 1861.

His major campaigns early in the war included the Peninsular campaign, South Mountain, and Antietam. In November, 1862, he was elevated to major general and headed a division at Fredericksburg and Chancellorsville afterwards. Hancock won commendation for his second and third day fighting at Gettysburg as commander of the famous Second Corps.

After the war, he remained in the army and led an expedition in the West. Barely defeated in the Presidential race in 1880 against Republican opponent Garfield, Hancock is described by historians as aggressive, yet careful, steady and capable. He was well liked by his men.

HANOVER COURTHOUSE, VIRGINIA, the Engagement near—May 27, 1862. This was a Union victory in an engagement designed to protect the communications lines of General G. B. McClellan during a move on the part of the Federals to destroy Confederate communications in and around the Shenandoah Valley. It was a running engagement fought by a number of small units as each tried to destroy the other's communications lines. The Union lost 255 killed, wounded or missing. The Confederates lost 265 killed or wounded, and 730 captured. Of those captured, 150 were also wounded.

HARDEE, WILLIAM JOSEPH (1815–1873)—Confederate Lieutenant General. Hardee, a native of Camden County, Ga., graduated from West Point in 1838, and was a captain by 1844. He fought in Mexico, and later wrote a book on tactics (*Hardee's Tactics*) which became the byword in the field. The book, officially entitled *Rifle and Light Infantry Tactics* (1855) was known more commonly as *Hardee's Tactics*.

By the outbreak of the Civil War, he was a lieutenant colonel, but resigned his Union army post to become a brigadier general in the Confederate army. By the fall of the year, he had risen to major general. His major campaigns included Arkansas, Kentucky, Shiloh, Perrysville, Murfreesboro, Missionary Ridge, and Atlanta. By October, 1862, he had been promoted to lieutenant general, which he remained until the end of the war. After the fall of Atlanta, he commanded in South Carolina, Georgia, and Florida. Most of his latter commands fought against Sherman. Hardee had the respect of men of both sides.

HARPER'S FERRY, JOHN BROWN'S RAID AT—October 16, 1859. This pre-Civil War engagement was so significant that many of the principals involved took definite sides. As a result, its effect upon the thinking of the times was tremendous.

After extensive preparation and support-gaining, John Brown gathered together a group of twenty-one men, including five Negroes, at the farmhouse of the widow of a man named Adam Kennedy. The Kennedy farmhouse was located just inside the Maryland line, five miles from Harper's Ferry. In addition to Brown, the group included:

Jeremiah G. Anderson
Osborn P. Anderson
Oliver Brown
Owen Brown
Watson Brown
John E. Cook
John A. Copeland, Jr.
Barclay Coppoc
Edwin Coppoc
Shield "the Emperor" Green
Albert Hazlett
John H. Kagi
Lewis Sheridan Leary
William H. Leeman
Francis J. Meriam
Dangerfield Newby
Aaron D. Stevens
Stewart Taylor Dauphin Thompson
William Thompson
Charles P. Tidd

At the time of the raid, the town was slightly over 3,000, and was a vital Federal arsenal location. It was also a railtown. During the raid Brown's men successfully captured the arsenal, the rifle works, the railroad bridge, and points between without the town knowing that a raid was taking place.

A detail of men captured Colonel Lewis Washington, great-grand-nephew of George Washington, who

103

lived about five miles away, forcing him to hand over a sword reputedly given to him by Frederick the Great. Osborn Anderson, a free Canadian Negro accepted the sword. Brown reportedly wanted this sword brought to him by a Negro so that he might "use it to strike the first blow in the new war for freedom." On the way back to Harper's Ferry, the party freed slaves along the route and captured an eighteen-year-old boy along with almost thirty older prisoners.

Watchman Patrick Higgins of the railroad became the first man to be wounded in the raid when he came on duty to relieve the captured William Williams (the other watchman). For some reason, he refused to obey the raiders' order to halt, and was shot. However, he kept running and gave the alarm. It was not until seven A.M., however, that the U.S. Government knew of the raid on one of its arsenals—a full nine hours after the raid began on Harper's Ferry.

Hayward Shepherd, a free Negro, came out of the station to investigate the noise, and was killed by the raiders, becoming the first casualty of the raid. He lived for twelve hours in intense agony before dying. Ironically the first man to die in what was actually the first engagement between pro and anti-slavery forces turned out to be a free Negro. He was shot by Oliver Brown and Stewart Taylor.

Meanwhile, the warning had been sent to Charles Town and to Shepherdstown that a raid was in progress. Despite warnings from his men, Brown lingered at the arsenal.

At one point during the raid, he even sent to the Wager House for breakfast for forty-five men. The breakfast was served. Due to his lingering, the raiders were captured when a militia unit under the direction of Colonel Robert E. Lee arrived and stormed the arsenal. The first of Brown's men to die was Dangerfield Newby, a free Negro. During the firing, Mayor Fontaine Beckham of the town was killed by raider Edwin Coppoc. Brown's son Oliver fell mortally wounded, and one by one, the raiders were picked off. A charge led by young Lieutenant Israel Greene carried the arsenal barricade and captured the remaining seven raiders. Eleven prisoners were set free. Anderson, Cook, and those left at the farmhouse in Maryland escaped capture.

During the fighting, such future Civil War notables as J. E. B. Stuart, Lee, Greene and a number of others took part. Stonewall Jackson and Edmund Ruffin attended the hanging of Brown.

A Congressional committee was set up to investigate Brown's backers, but nothing was ever proved. Among those listed as sponsors of Brown were: Gerrit Smith, George L. Stearns, Frederick Douglass, Samuel Gridley Howe, Franklin B. Sanborn, Theodore Parker, and Thomas W. Higginson. One of the Congressional investigators was Jefferson Davis.

Of Brown, Douglass said: "His defeat was already assuming the form and pressure of victory, and his death was giving new life to the principles of justice and liberty . . .

What he had lost by the sword, he had more than gained by the truth."

Strangely enough, one year and a half later, in April, 1861, the former governor of Virginia, Henry A. Wise, seized the arsenal in exactly the same manner, with the intention of using its supplies for an armed rebellion against the United States. He did so without bloodshed, for his neighbors (approving of the move) did not resist.

The town is now a national monument, with a monument to Hayward Shepherd, the first man to fall in the war against slavery; the engine house is now referred to as "Brown's Fort"; and the Kennedy farmhouse has become a national monument also. The engine house, destroyed during the Civil War, has been rebuilt on the campus of nearby Storer College for Negroes, which stands on a hill overlooking the town.

HARRISONBURG, the engagement near—June 8–9, 1862. Harrisonburg, Va., located on the Great Valley Turnpike just twenty-two miles north of Staunton and 122 miles northwest of Richmond, was the scene of skirmishes during the war.

It was occupied by Banks in April, 1862, reoccupied by Jackson after he had chased Banks down the Shenandoah Valley in May, 1862, captured again by Union forces when McDowell and Fremont forced Jackson out of the main valley, and fought over for much of the early part of the war. The town was situated in territory which is generally referred to as "Stonewall" Jackson's "stomping grounds."

When Union forces forced Jackson out of Harrisonburg, Confederate Ashby Turner (serving as Jackson's rear guard) defeated a Union force southeast of the town, but was forced to fall back and call for infantry support southeast of his victory point, when General G. D. Bayard reenforced the embattled Federal troops.

Jackson sent J. E. B. Stuart's brigade to Ashby's rescue, but during the fighting, Ashby was killed, and the Confederates were forced to withdraw towards Fort Republic. The Union force then occupied Harrisonburg. In that particular engagement, Union losses were 65 killed, wounded or missing. Confederate losses were 18 killed, 50 wounded, and 3 missing. The vital fact here was that Ashby had been killed.

HENRY HOUSE HILL—The command site during the first Battle of Bull Run. This house was owned by eighty-five year old widow, Mrs. Judith Henry, whose husband had served under Truxton on the "Constellation" in the U.S. Navy fifty years prior to the Battle of Manassas.

Brigadier General B. E. Bee, who is alleged to have given Jackson the name of "Stonewall," was killed on this hill. It was to this rise that the Confederates retreated in the early stages of the battle to rally around Jackson's Virginians and turn the tide of battle.

Mrs. Henry was bedridden and helpless during the engagements at Bull Run around her now-famous hill. The only other house on the hill belonged to a free Negro named Robinson.

HEROES OF AMERICA, THE ORDER OF THE—A secret peace society designed to overthrow the Confederate government, end the war, and return the Southern states to the Union. This organization was not discovered by Confederate agents until 1864. The Raleigh *Standard* accused state auditor Henderson Adams of being one of the founders of the organization in North Carolina, allegedly the birthplace of the order.

General John Echols, assigned to investigate the organization for the Confederacy, reported to Jefferson Davis that the organization had its headquarters behind Union lines; however, Henry Questine, a member of the order in Montgomery County, Virginia, testified that a Horace Dean of North Carolina had organized the order in late 1863.

Union authorities, allegedly, offered immunity to Confederates who would join the organization. Southerners accused both Lincoln and Grant of being members. The order had a "grip, a password, signs, obligations, and an oath," writes Dr. Georgia Tatum, a North Carolina historian. (SEE PEACE SOCIETIES)

"HOMESPUN DRESS," THE—A Southern war song which praised southern womanhood for bearing up under the hardships of war. It ended, "Three cheers for the homespun dress the Southern ladies wear."

"HORNET'S NEST," THE—The Union strong point at the battle of Shiloh. Here, for more than four hours, troops under W. H. L. Wallace, Hurlbut, and Prentiss held off the Confederate advance. Here, Confederate General A. S. Johnston received a mortal wound (see JOHNSTON, ALBERT S.). The time gained by the vicious defense of the "Hornet's Nest" made it possible for J. D. Webster to mount artillery along the ridge of the Landing and dig in for a lasting defense that eventually saved the day. The pocket of resistance called the "Hornet's Nest" was finally taken late in the day by troops under Ammen of Nelson's division of the Confederate army. However, the defense there had given the Union time to set up a second line of defense. Union losses totaled 239 dead, wounded or missing; Confederate losses were 1,636 dead, wounded or missing.

HERRON, FRANCIS JAY (1837–1902)— Union Major General. Congressional Medal of Honor. Herron, born in Pittsburgh and a student of the University of Pittsburgh and Western University of Pennsylvania (the name of the University of Pittsburgh at that time), was in the banking business in Dubuque, Iowa, when war broke out. He organized the Governor's Grays, a militia group which later became part of the First Iowa Regiment.

Herron served as a lieutenant colonel of the Ninth Iowa Regiment, and received a promotion to brigadier general and a Congressional Medal of Honor for his gallantry at Pea Ridge, Ark. (March, 1862). The medal was awarded in 1863. He became the youngest major general in the Union army, after an important victory at Prairie Grove, Ark., in late 1862. He practiced law in the South after the war, until connecting himself with a manufacturing firm in New York.

HETH, HENRY (1825–1899)—Confederate Major General. Heth graduated from West Point in 1847, and fought in the Mexican War becoming a captain in 1855. He joined the Confederacy as a colonel, and fought throughout the West Virginia campaign. On January 6, 1862, he became a brigadier general. Wounded at Chancellorsville, he was made a major general May 24, 1863.

Heth commanded a division of Hill's Third Corps in Lee's invasion of Pennsylvania. It was his force that met Buford's unexpectedly at Gettysburg, bringing on that vital battle. Heth was wounded in the engagement with Buford's force at Gettysburg, and his division was taken over by Pettigrew. It led the way during the famous charge by Pickett. Heth served well at Bristoe Station and in numerous other engagements. He was with Lee at Appomattox on April 9, 1865. After the war, he engaged in the insurance business, and later became special agent for the office of Indian Affairs.

HEWETT, EDWARD—An official British observer.

HIGGINSON, THOMAS WENTWORTH STORROW (1823–1911) — Union Colonel. A graduate of Harvard Divinity School, 1847. He was forced to resign his pastorate of the Unitarian Church in Newsburyport, Mass., because of his antislavery views. He was prominent in antislavery, women's suffrage and temperance movements before the war. He allegedly backed John Brown's raid on Harper's Ferry. He was the only alleged backer to come to the aid of the widow Brown after the raider had been hanged.

Higginson became the colonel of the First South Carolina Volunteers in 1862, the first regiment of freed slaves in U.S. Army history.

HILL, AMBROSE POWELL (1825–1863)—Confederate Lieutenant General. Known to his close friends as "Powell Hill," but to most historians as "A. P. Hill," the Culpeper, Va., native graduated from West Point in 1847. He resigned his colonelcy in the U.S. Army when war broke out, and became a brigadier general in the Confederate army (February, 1862). By May of that year, he had been promoted to major general.

He commanded the Confederate left at Sevens Days. His unit was known as "Hill's Light Division" in this campaign. At the second Bull Run, his troops performed admirably, and at Antietam, they stemmed the tide of the Federal advance. Hill commanded units at Fredericksburg and Chancellorsville as a lieutenant general, with his rank dating from May, 1863, as commander of a corps. He also fought well at Gettysburg, the Wilderness and the siege of Petersburg. He was killed at Petersburg during the retreat on April 2, 1865. This officer was one of the most brilliant commanders on either side, and liked by all. He is best known as A. P. Hill.

HILL, DANIEL HARVEY (1821–1889)—Confederate Lieutenant General. This native of the York district of South Carolina was no relation to A. P. Hill, although he did attend West Point, and entered the Civil War as a colonel. From July, 1861, he rose from brigadier to major general (March, 1862).

Hill led a division during the Seven Days battle and commanded at South Mountain. In the spring of 1863, he was given the job of defending Richmond. By July, 1863, he had been promoted to lieutenant general and was sent to the Army of Tennessee. There, he had difficulty with both Bragg and Jeff Davis, and lost his command. He commanded no more until Bentonville. Following the war, Hill became a writer and educator. A strict disciplinarian and a deeply religious man, he had trouble throughout his military years with his superiors, and this kept him from rising higher.

HILTON HEAD, South Carolina—An island. One of the Sea Islands, lying south of Port Royal Sound, seventeen miles northeast of Savannah, Georgia. It is part of Beaufort County. The island was captured by a Union fleet under Captain Samuel F. Du Pont, November 7, 1861. It was the site of Fort Walker, a Confederate fortification, and is just 12 miles long and about one fourth of a mile wide. Hilton Head Village is on the west shore of the island.

HOBART - HAMPDEN, AUGUSTUS CHARLES (1822–1886)—Known as "Hobart Pasha." English naval officer and Confederate blockade-runner. Ironically, Hobert-Hampden was engaged in several expeditions against slave traders off the coast of South America while in the British navy. In 1863, he resigned the rank of captain to become a blockade-runner for the Confederate States of America. As such, he used many aliases, among which were : Hewitt, Ridge, Gulick, and A. Roberts. His first blockade-running vessel was the "Don."

After the war, he published a book entitled *Never Caught,* which describes (with much embellishment) his adventures as a blockade-runner. He resumed his naval career, but resigned again to accept command of the entire Turkish navy during the Turkish War with Russia. He gained fame as "Hobart Pasha" and eventually became admiral of the Sultan's navy.

HOKE, ROBERT FREDERICK (1837–1912)—Confederate Major General. A graduate of Kentucky Military Institute, Hoke enlisted in the Confederate army as a private. He became a colonel after taking part in the fighting around Richmond, Va., in the early part of the war. On January 17, 1863, he was promoted to brigadier general.

Hoke was wounded at Chancellorsville, but recuperated in time to lead the capture of Plymouth, N.C., for which he was promoted to major general on April 20, 1864. He commanded a division of the Army of Northern Virginia, and fought in front of Richmond, from May to December, 1864. He served with particular distinction at Cold Harbor, where his unit withstood the full force of the Union attack. He took over a division of J. E. Johnston's army in North Carolina, and fought his last battle at Bentonville. Hoke surrendered at Durham Station, N.C., April 26, 1865.

After the war, he engaged in the iron business, and later became president of the Seaboard Air Line System. He died in 1912.

HOLMES, THEOPHILUS H. (1804–1880)—Confederate Lieutenant General. Commander of the Trans-Mississippi area. A classmate of Jefferson Davis at West Point, Holmes was commissioned a brigadier general by Davis at the outbreak of the war. He was promoted to division commander after the Seven Days battles, and received the rank of lieutenant general although his record did not warrant the move. Next, still in defiance of his record, Holmes received command of the entire Trans-Mississippi Department, but, at his own request, was relieved and re-turned to field command. He failed there also, and was placed in charge of the North Carolina Militia, in which command he ended the war.

His rapid rise in rank was due to his personal friendship with Davis. As a military leader, he possessed no outstanding quality to warrant general officer rank.

HOOD, JOHN BELL (1831–1879)—Confederate full General. Hood graduated from West Point in 1853, and received his early military experience in the Indian wars. He began his Confederate army career as a lieutenant, but rose so rapidly that by 1864 he had become a full general.

When his native Kentucky refused to secede, Hood became a Texan. He received a crippling arm injury at Gettysburg and lost a leg at Chickamauga. His commands included the Texas Brigade, which fought at Gaines Hill, second Bull Run and Antietam; a division at Gettysburg where he was wounded; a division at Chickamauga where he lost an arm; and another division at other times. He served as a corps commander under Johnson at Atlanta, as commander of the Army of Tennessee (replacing Johnston), and he fought at Spring Hill, Franklin, and Nashville.

Following the war, Hood entered business. He is best described as a man of great ability, but an over-eager nature. "He fought too much and too often," it was commented.

HOOKER, JOSEPH (1814–1879) — Union. Commander of the Army of the Potomac. This Hadley, Mass., native was graduated from West Point in 1837, and gathered experience in the Mexican War prior to the outbreak of civil strife. He returned to duty as a brigadier of volunteers in May of 1861, and was made a major general following the Peninsula fighting, in which he led a division.

Hooker is best known by the misnomer "Fighting Joe Hooker." True, he fought well at the beginning of the war, but following major defeats at Fredericksburg (which he blamed on Burnside's actions in battle), and at the hands of Lee and Jackson at Chancellorsville (May, 1863), he seemed to lose his normal drive. In January, 1863, he assumed command of the Army of the Potomac, and in this post, he suffered the defeats from Lee and Jackson. His army followed Lee's into Pennsylvania, but took little action. On June 28, 1863, just three days before the battle of Gettysburg, he was relieved from command and replaced by Meade. Hooker subsequently took two corps to the West. At Lookout Mountain and around Atlanta, he fought well, but was bypassed for a command by Sherman, when McPherson died. As a result, he asked to be allowed to retire.

After the war, he commanded a number of varying army departments. Intensely ambitious, and very capable, but his temperamental nature aroused distrust and antagonism in his superiors, and kept him from advancing further. At one point during the war, Lincoln had to caution Hooker for taking rash steps as commander of the Army of the Potomac.

HOMER WINSLOW (1836–1910) — Reporter-Painter. This artist attended night school classes in and around New York to add to his natural talents. He served as an illustrator for *Harper's Weekly* during the war, and covered the Lincoln inauguration in Washington, D.C. He was used as an artist-reporter on numerous occasions during the war, especially with the Army of the Potomac while McClellan commanded. His paintings generally reflect life on the front, but outside of the realm of fighting. His painting, "Prisoners from the Front," made him famous.

HOTCHKISS, JEDEDIAH—Confederate Major. Hotchkiss was a topographical corps major assigned to Stonewall Jackson because of his knowledge of the terrain in the Shenandoah Valley. He drew maps of the valley from Lexington to Harper's Ferry, which enabled Jackson's forces to perform such amazing feats of forced marching to and from major battle areas in the dark of night. He is given credit for making Jackson's "Foot Cavalry" as effective as it was. Like Jackson, he was nicknamed "the Professor."

In 1864, Hotchkiss opened a topographical office in Staunton, Virginia, with two assistants, but continued to aid Jubal Early, whom he had joined after the death of Jackson, in 1862. Of the 2,202 Confederate maps among the Official Records Atlas, 1,006, over half, were drawn by Hotchkiss. Most of the others were done by topographers who had studied under him during the war.

HOUGH, DANIEL—(see HOWE, DANIEL)

HOVEY, ALVIN PETERSON (1821–1891)—Union Major General. Hovey was a teacher and a lawyer before the war. He served as a circuit judge, judge of the supreme court of Indiana, and U.S. district attorney before entering the Civil War as colonel of the Twenty-fourth Indiana Volunteers. Hovey had served in the Mexican War, but saw no action.

He was very highly rated by Grant following the Vicksburg campaign, and was made a major general later in his career partly on the strength of this commendation (1864). With the promotion to major general, Hovey was appointed commander of Indiana.

After the war, he was elected governor of the state (1889–1891), and later served in other capacities. Prior to being elected governor, he had served as Congressman (1887) and minister to Peru (1865–1870).

HOWARD, OLIVER OTIS (1830–1909)—Union Lieutenant General. Born in Leeds, Me., Howard graduated from West Point in the Class of 1854. He rose to the rank of major general just one year after the outbreak of war, and drew public notice as a result of his valor at first Bull Run (where he lost an arm), South Mountain, Antietam, Fredericksburg, Chancellorsville, and Gettysburg.

As a corps commander, he received criticism for allowing Jackson to surprise him at Chancellorsville. He was again criticized for his first day tactics at Gettysburg, but offered no excuse. For these "mistakes," Howard was shifted to the West, September, 1863, where he blossomed into one of the better corps commanders in the campaign between Chattanooga and Atlanta. In July, 1864, he assumed command of the Army of Tennessee. His military ability was neither exceptional nor poor, but there is an indication that desk work would have been more to his liking.

Howard's main fame came after the war when he became very active in the work of the Freedman's Bureau which he headed. He established Howard University for Negroes in Washington, D.C., and helped start Lincoln Memorial University. It is alleged that, when leaving Atlanta in 1866, he asked a group of Negroes what they wished him to tell the people up North about them, and he received this reply from ten-year-old Richard R. Wright, "Tell them we are rising." Howard was so impressed by this boy's statement that he became one of the leading exponents of education for the freed slaves. The first school he established for Negroes in Georgia was in a boxcar in the Atlanta freight yards.

HOWE, ALBION PARRIS (1818–1897)—Union Brigadier General. A member of the 1841 class at West Point, Howe returned to the academy in 1843 to teach mathematics. He left again in 1846 to serve on active duty in the Mexican War.

Howe was appointed chief of artillery under McClellan when the war broke out, and was promoted to brigadier general in 1862. He served under Darius N. Couch also. From 1864 to 1866, he commanded the artillery depot at Washington, and was one of the honor guards over Lincoln's coffin after the assassination. He was a member of the commission at the trial of the conspirators. He retired from the army in 1882.

HOWE, DANIEL (?–1861) — Union Private. His name is often misspelled "Hough." This New Yorker was allegedly the first man killed in actual combat during the Civil War. He died at Fort Sumter in 1861, as a result of the premature discharging of a gun.

HOWITZER-TYPE CANNON—A short-barreled decidedly short - ranged weapon which fired a heavy twelve-pound shot, using a very heavy powder load. This gun often exploded during the firing and caused more injuries to its handlers than to the enemy.

HUMPHREYS, ANDREW A. (1810–1883)—Union Brevet Major General. A West Point graduate in the class of 1831, Humphreys was the grandson of Joshua Humphreys, the "Father of the American Navy." He worked as a civil engineer for a while, and re-entered the army as a member of the newly formed topographical engineering corps, and supervised the construction of railroad routes to the Pacific.

Humphreys was made chief topographical engineer for the Army of the Potomac when war broke out, and was promoted to brigadier general in 1862. He commanded divisions at Gettysburg, after having commanded the Fifth Corps at Fredericksburg and Chancellorsville. He was chief of staff to Meade from 1863 to 1864, and served as commander of the Second Corps of the Army of the Potomac in the campaign which led to Lee's surrender at Appomattox. After the battle of Sailor's Creek, he was brevetted regular army major general. After the war, he served as chief of the Corps of Engineers with the regular rank of brigadier general. He retired in 1879.

"HUNLEY," THE C.S.S.—Confederate submarine. The first submarine to sink an enemy warship in combat, the "Hunley" was an iron-cylinder about thirty feet long, and four feet in diameter (very similar to the two-man submarines used by the Japanese in World War II). It had adjustable planes along the sides and a propeller at the stern which was turned by a crank handle operated by the eight-man crew inside.

The sub had no periscope, and had to be either sailed blindly, or submerged just below the surface with its hatch above water so that the captain could stick his head out and direct the action (just as early tanks were forced to do). This maneuver usually resulted in the craft being swamped if the sea was heavy. In her four trial runs, the "Hunley" sank each time, killing her crews.

The submarine was designed to drag a mine at the end of a long tow line, dive under the enemy craft, rising on the other side, and continuing on until the mine struck the enemy ship. Because of the submerging fatalities, the plan was changed, and a long spar was attached to the bow, and a torpedo attached to the spar.

The submarine, under the command of Lieutenant George Dixon of the Twenty-first Alabama Artillery, with a nine-man crew, sent the sloop "Howsatonic" to the bottom, but sank also while doing it. All hands were drowned.

HUNT, HENRY JACKSON (1819–1889)—Union Brigadier General. Hunt, a member of the 1839 West Point class, took part in quelling the Canadian Rebellion (1837–1839), and also served in the Mexican War. In 1856, he was placed on the board to revise light artillery tactics. When war broke out, he was stationed at Fort Pickens, Fla. He commanded the artillery at the Battle of Bull Run, and in the defense of Washington. He later commanded the reserve artillery of the Army of the Potomac for a short time.

Hunt took part in the battles of Malvern Hill and South Mountain.

He was commissioned brevet brigadier general of volunteers in 1862, and took part in the battles of Antietam, Fredericksburg, Chancellorsville, Gettysburg, and in the Wilderness Campaign.

After the war, he received the rank of colonel in the regular army, and became governor of the National Soldier's Home in Washington. Among his writings are *Instruction for Field Artillery* (1860), and *Battles and Leaders of the Civil War* (1887).

HUNTER, DAVID (1802–1886)—Union Major General of Volunteers. Hunter graduated from West Point in 1822, but resigned his commission in 1836. He re-entered the service in 1842 as paymaster with the rank of major, and was appointed brigadier general of volunteers when war broke out. A few months later, he was made a major general.

Hunter recruited and organized the first Negro regiment in the Union army, from freed slaves in North Carolina (see HIGGINSON, T. W.). In 1863, his manumission of slaves in Florida, Georgia and South Carolina was annulled by the President.

Hunter defeated the Confederates at Piedmont, June 5, 1864, and (after the war) served as chairman of the commission which tried the conspirators involved in the assassination of President Lincoln. He was breveted major general in the regular army in 1865. He retired in 1866.

HUNTER, ROBERT MERCER TALIAFERRO (1809–1887)—Confederate Secretary of State. A graduate of the University of Virginia, and a lawyer and politician before the war. He served in the U.S. Senate from 1847 to 1861, after having been in and out of the U.S. House of Representatives between 1837 and 1847.

Hunter became Confederate secretary of state after leaving the Senate in 1861. In 1862, he became a senator from Virginia, and served in this capacity in the Confederate Congress until 1865. In 1865, he was one of the members of the Conference at Hampton Roads, Va., seeking peace between the Union and the Confederacy. Hunter served as treasurer of the state of Virginia from 1877 to 1880, retiring from public life in 1880, except for a term as port collector of Tappahannock, Va., after 1885.

I

IMBODEN, JOHN D. (1823–1895) Confederate Captain. Later in the war, Imboden was assigned the task of commanding cavalry, but his greatest moment was at the Battle of Bull Run where he commanded the artillery unit that emplaced at Henry House Hill and was instrumental in stopping the Federal advance.

INAUGURAL ADDRESS, Jefferson Davis' —February 22, 1862, Richmond, Virginia. On Washington's birthday, in a steady drizzle, President Jefferson Davis of the newly formed Confederate States of America stepped forward to deliver his inaugural address. In 1861, Davis had been made provisional president of the Confederacy, but this was his first address as elected president of the rebellious states. With his hand on a Bible which had been printed somewhere in the Confederacy, Davis took the oath of office for a term of six years, and stepped forward to address the assembled thousands :

Fellow-citizens : On this the birthday of the man most identified with the establishment of American independence, and beneath the monument erected to commemorate his heroic virtues and those of his compatriots, we have assembled to usher into existence the permanent government of the Confederate States. Through this instrumentality, under the favor of Divine Providence, we hope to perpetuate the principles of our Revolutionary fathers. The day, the memory, and the purpose seem fitly associated.

It is with mingled feelings of humility and pride that I appear to take, in the presence of the people and before High Heaven, the oath prescribed as a qualification for the exalted station to which the unanimous voice of the people has called me. Deeply sensible of all that is implied by this manifestation of the people's confidence, I am yet more profoundly impressed by the vast responsibility of the office, and humbly feel my own unworthiness.

In return for their kindness, I can offer assurances of the gratitude with which it is received, and can but pledge a zealous devotion of every faculty to the service of those who have chosen me as their chief magistrate.

When a long course of class legislation, directed not to the general welfare but to the aggrandizement of the Northern section of the Union, culminated in a warfare on the domestic institutions of the Southern States —when the dogmas of a sectional party, substituted for the provisions of the constitutional compact, threatened to destroy the sovereign rights of the states—six of those states, withdrawing from the Union, confederated together to exercise the right and perform the duty of instituting a government which would better secure the liberties for the preservation of which that Union was established.

Whatever of hope some may have entertained that a returning sense of justice would remove the danger with which our rights were threatened and render it possible to preserve the Union of the Constitution, must have been dispelled by the malignity and barbarity of the Northern States in the prosecution of the existing war. The confidence of the most hopeful among us must have been destroyed by the disregard they have recently exhibited for all the time-honored bulwarks of civil and religious liberty.

Bastilles filled with prisoners, arrested without civil process or indictment duly found; the writ of habeas corpus suspended by executive mandate; a state legislature controlled by the imprisonment of members whose avowed principles suggested to the federal executive that there might be another added to the list of seceded states; elections held under threats of a military power; civil officers, peaceful citizens, and gentlewomen incarcerated for opinions sake—(all) proclaimed the incapacity of our late associates to administer a government as free, liberal, and humane as that established for our common use.

For proof of the sincerity of our purpose to maintain our ancient institutions, we may point to the Constitution of the Confederacy and the laws enacted unter it, as well as to the fact that through all the necessities of an unequal struggle there has been no act on our part to impair personal liberty or freedom of speech, of thought, or of the press. The courts have been open, the judicial functions fully executed, and every right of the peaceful citizen maintained as securely as if a war of invasion had not disturbed the land.

The people of the states now confederated became convinced that the government of the United States had fallen into the hands of a sectional majority, who would pervert that most sacred of all trusts to the destruction of the rights which it was pledged to protect. They believed that to remain longer in the Union would subject them to a continuance of disparaging discrimination, submission to which would be inconsistent with their welfare and intolerable to a proud people. They therefore determined to sever its bonds and establish a new confederacy for themselves.

The experiment instituted by our Revolutionary fathers, of a voluntary union of sovereign states for purposes specified in a solemn compact, had been perverted by those who, feeling power and forgetting right, were determined to respect no law but their own will. The government ceased to answer the ends for which it was ordained and established. To save ourselves from a revolution which, in its silent but rapid progress, was about to place us under the despotism of numbers, and to preserve in spirit, as well as in form, a system of government we believed to be peculiarly fitted to our condition, and full of promise for mankind, we determined to make a new association, composed of states homogeneous in interest, in policy, and in feeling.

True to our traditions of peace and our love of justice, we send commissioners to the United States to propose a fair and amicable settlement of all questions of public debt or property which might be in dispute. But Washington, denying our right to self government, refused even to listen to any proposals for a peaceful separation. Nothing was then left to do but to prepare for war.

The first year in our history has been the most eventful in the annals of this continent. A new government has been established, and its machinery put in operation over an area exceeding seven hundred thousand square miles. The great principles upon which we have been willing to hazard everything that is dear to man have made conquests for us which could never have been achieved by the sword. Our Confederacy has grown from six to thirteen states; and Maryland, already united to us by hallowed memories and material interest will, I believe, when able to speak with unstifled voice, connect her destiny with the South.

Our people have rallied with unexampled unanimity to the support of the great principles of constitutional government, with firm resolve to perpetuate by arms the right which they could not peacefully secure. A million of men, it is estimated, are now standing in hostile array and waging war along a frontier of thousands of miles. Battles have been fought, sieges have been conducted, and although the contest is not ended, and the tide for the moment is against us, the final result in our favor is not doubtful.

The period is near at hand when our foes must sink under the immense load of debt which they have incurred, a debt which in their effort to subjugate us has already attained such fearful dimensions as will subject them to burthens which must continue to oppress them for generations to come.

We too, have had our trials and difficulties. That we are to escape them in future is not to be hoped. It was to be expected when we entered upon this war that it would expose our people to sacrifices and cost them much both of money and blood. But we stood the nature of the war in which we were engaged. Nothing could be so bad as failure, and any sacrifice would be cheap as the price of success in such a contest.

But the picture has its lights as well as its shadows. This great strife has awakened in the people the highest emotions and qualities of the human soul. It is cultivating feelings of patriotism, virtue, and courage. Instances of self-sacrifice and of generous devotion to the noble cause for which we are contending are rife throughout the land. Never has a people evinced a more determined spirit than that now animating men, women, and children in every part of our country. Upon the first call, the men fly to arms; and wives and mothers send their husbands and sons to battle without a murmur of regret.

It was perhaps, in the ordination of Providence that we were taught the value of our liberties by the price which we pay for them.

The recollections of this great contest, with all its common traditions of glory, of sacrifice, and of blood, will be the bond of harmony and enduring affection amongst the people, producing unity in policy, fraternity in sentiment, and joint effort in war.

Nor have the material sacrifices of the past year been made without some corresponding benefits. If the acquiescence of foreign nations in a pretended blockade has deprived us of our commerce with them, it is fast making us a self-supporting and independent people. The blockade, if effectual and permanent, could only serve to divert our industry from the production of articles for export, and employ it in supplying commodities for domestic use.

It is a satisfaction that we have maintained the war by our unaided exertions. We have neither asked nor received assistance from any quarter. Yet interest involved is not wholly our own. The world at large is concerned in opening our markets to its commerce. When the independence of the Confederate States is recognized by the nations of the earth, and we are free to follow our interests and inclinations by cultivating foreign trade, the Southern States will offer to manufacturing nations the most favorable markets which over invited their commerce. Cotton, sugar, rice, tobacco, provisions, timber, and naval stores will furnish attractive exchanges. Nor would the constancy of these supplies be likely to be disturbed by war. Our confederate strength will be too great to tempt aggression; and never was there a people whose interests and principles committed them so fully to a peaceful policy as those of the Confederate States.

By the character of their productions they are too deeply interested in foreign commerce wantonly to disturb it. War of conquest they cannot wage because the constitution of their confederacy admits of no coerced association. Civil war there cannot be between states held together by their own volition only. The rule of voluntary association, which cannot fail to be conservative, by securing just and impartial government at home does not diminish the security of the obligations by which the Confederate States may be bound to foreign nations. In proof of this, it is to be remembered that at the first moment of asserting their right of secession, these states proposed a settlement on the basis of a common liability for the obligations of the general government.

Fellow-citizens, after the struggle of ages had consecrated the rights of Englishmen to constitutional representative government, our colonial ancestors were forced to vindicate that birthright by an appeal to arms. Success crowned their efforts, and they provided for their posterity a peaceful remedy against future aggression.

The tyranny of an unbridled majority, the most odious and least responsible form of despotism, had denied us both the right and the remedy. Therefore, we are in arms to renew such sacrifices as our fathers made to the holy cause of constitutional liberty. At the darkest hour of our struggle the provisional gives place to the permanent government. After a series of successes and victories, which covered our arms with glory, we have recently met with serious disasters. But in the heart of a people resolved to be free, these disasters tend but to stimulate to increase resistance.

To show ourselves worthy of the inheritance bequeathed to us by the patriots of the Revolution, we must emulate that heroic devotion which made reverse to them but the crucible in which their patriotism was refined.

With confidence in the wisdom and virtue of those who will share with me the responsibility, and aid me in the conduct of public affairs; securely relying on the patriotism and courage of the people, of which the present war has furnished so many examples, I deeply feel the weight of the responsibilities I now, with unaffected diffidence, am about to assume; and fully realizing the inequality of human power to guide and to sustain, my hope is reverently fixed on Him whose favor is ever vouchsafed to the cause which is just. With humble gratitude and adoration, acknow-

ledging the Providence which has so visibly protected the Confederacy during its brief but eventful career, to Thee, O God! I trustingly commit myself, and prayerfully invoke Thy blessing on my country and its cause.

This optimistic address, delivered in the early days of the Confederacy proved to be erroneous in the greatest part. However, it is believed by most historians that Davis was sincere at the time of this address, in his belief that the golden era pictured would come to pass.

INAUGURAL ADDRESS, LINCOLN'S FIRST —March 4, 1861. After an introduction by Senator Baker, a friend of Lincoln's from Springfield, Illinois, President-elect Abraham Lincoln read the following words:

Fellow Citizens of the United States: In compliance with a custom as old as the government itself, I appear before you to address you briefly, and to take, in your presence, the oath prescribed by the Constitution of the United States, to be taken by the President "before he enters on the execution of his office."

I do not consider it necessary, at present, for me to discuss those matters of administration about which there is no special anxiety, or excitement.

Apprehension seems to exist among the people of the Southern States, that by the accession of a Republican administration, their property, and their peace, and personal security, are to be endangered. There has never been any reasonable cause for such apprehension. Indeed, the most ample evidence to the contrary has all the while existed, and been open to their inspection. It is found in nearly all the published speeches of him who now addresses you. I do but quote from one of those speeches when I declare that "I have no purpose, directly or indirectly, to interfere with the institution of slavery in the states where it exists. I believe I have no lawful right to do so, and I have no inclination to do so."

Those who nominated and elected me did so with full knowledge that I had made this, and many similar declarations, and had never recanted them. And more than this, they placed in the platform, for my acceptance, and as a law to themselves, and to me, the clear and emphatic resolution which I now read:

"Resolved, That the maintenance inviolate of the rights of the states, and especially the right of each state to order and control its own domestic institutions according to its own judgement exclusively, is essential to that balance of power on which the perfection and endurance of our political fabric depend; and we denounce the lawless invasion by armed force of the soil of any state or territory, no matter under what pretext, as among the gravest of crimes."

I now reiterate these sentiments and, in doing so, I only press upon the public attention the most conclusive evidence of which the case is susceptible, that the property, peace, and security of no section are to be in any wise endangered by the now incoming administration. I add, too, that all the protection which, consistently with the Constitution and the laws, can be given, will be cheerfully given to all of the states when lawfully demanded, for whatever cause—as cheerfully to one section as to another.

There is much controversy about the delivering up of fugitives from service or labor. The clause I now read is as plainly written in the Constitution as any other of its provisions:

"No person held to service or labor in one state, under the laws thereof, escaping into another, shall in consequence of any law or regulation therein, be discharged from such service or labor, but shall be delivered up on claim of the party to whom such service or labor may be due."

It is scarcely questioned that this provision was intended by those who made it, for the reclaiming of what we call fugitive slaves; and the intention of the lawgiver is the law. All members of Congress swear their support to the whole Constitution—to this provision as much as to any other. To the proposition, then, that slaves whose cases come within the terms of this clause "shall be delivered up," their oaths are unanimous. Now, if they would make the effort in good temper, could they not, with nearly equal unanimity, frame and pass a law, by means of which to keep good that unanimous oath? There is some difference of opinion whether this clause should be enforced by national or by state authority; but surely that difference is not a very material one. If the slave is to be surrendered, it can be of but little consequence to him, or to others by which authority it is

119

done. And should anyone, in any case, be content that his oath shall go unkept, on a mere unsubstantial controversy as to how it shall be kept?

Again, in any law upon this subject, ought not all the safeguards of liberty known in civilized and humane jurisprudence to be introduced, so that a free man be not, in any case, surrendered as a slave? And might it not be well, at the same time, to provide by law for the enforcement of that clause in the Constitution which guarantees that "The citizens of each state shall be entitled to all privileges and immunities of citizens in the several states"?

I take the official oath today, with no mental reservations, and with no purpose to construe the Constitution or laws, by any hypercritical rules. And while I do not choose now to specify particular acts of Congress as proper to be enforced, I do suggest, that it will be much safer for all, both in official and private stations, to conform to, and abide by, all those acts which stand unrepealed, than to violate any of them, trusting to find impunity in having them held to be unconstitutional.

It is seventy-two years since the first inauguration of a President under our national Constitution. During that period fifteen different and greatly distinguished citizens have, in succession, administered the executive branch of the government. They have conducted it through many perils; and, generally, with great success. Yet, with all this scope for precedent, I now enter upon the same

task for the brief constitution term of four years, under great and peculiar difficulty. A disruption of the federal Union, heretofore only menaced, is now formidably attempted.

I hold, that in contemplation of universal law, and of the Constitution, the Union of these states is perpetual. Perpetuity is implied, if not expressed, in the fundamental law of all national governments. It is safe to assert that no government proper, ever had a provision in its organic law for its own termination. Continue to execute all the express provisions of our national Constitution, and the Union will endure forever,—it being impossible to destroy it, except by some action not provided for in the instrument itself.

Again, if the United States be not a government proper, but an association of states in the nature of contract merely, can it, as a contract be peaceably unmade, by less than all the parties who made it? One party to a contract may violate it—break it, so to speak; but does it not require all to lawfully rescind it?

Descending from these general principles, we find the proposition that, in legal contemplation, the Union is perpetual, confirmed by the history of the Union itself. The Union is much older than the Constitution. It was formed, in fact, by the Articles of Association in 1774. It was matured and continued by the Declaration of Independence in 1776. It was further matured and the faith of all the then thirteen states expressly plighted and engaged that it should be perpetual, by the Articles of Confederation in 1778.

And finally, in 1787, one of the declared objects for ordaining and establishing the Constitution was "to form a more perfect Union."

But if destruction of the Union, by one, or by a part only, of the states, be lawfully possible, the Union is less perfect than before the Constitution, having lost the vital element of perpetuity.

It follows from these views that no state, upon its own mere motion can lawfully get out of the Union, that resolves and ordinances to that effect are legally void; and that acts of violence, within any state or states, against the authority of the United States, are insurrectionary or revolutionary, according to circumstances.

I therefore consider that, in view of the Constitution and the laws, the Union is unbroken; and, to the extent of my ability, I shall take care as the Constitution itself expressly enjoins upon me, that the laws of the Union be faithfully executed in all the states. Doing this I deem to be a simple duty on my part; and I shall perform it, so far as practicable, unless my rightful masters, the American people, shall withhold the requisite means, or in some authoritative manner, direct the contrary. I trust this will not be regarded as a menace, but only as the declared purpose of the Union that it will constitutionally defend, and maintain itself.

In doing these there needs to be no bloodshed or violence; and there shall be none, unless it be forced upon the national authority. The power confided to me, will be used to hold, occupy, and possess the property, and places belonging to the government, and to collect the duties and imposts; but beyond what may be necessary for these objects, there will be no invasion—no use of force against, or among the people anywhere. Where hostility to the United States, in any interior locality, shall be so great and universal, as to prevent competent resident citizens from holding federal offices, there will be no attempt to force obnoxious strangers among the people for that object. While the strict legal right may exist in the government to enforce the exercise of these offices, the attempt to do so would be so irritating, and so nearly impracticable withal, that I deem it better to forego, for the time, the uses of such offices.

The mails, unless repelled, will continue to be furnished in all parts of the Union. So far as possible, the people everywhere shall have that sense of perfect security which is most favorable to calm thought and reflection. The course here indicated will be followed, unless current events, and experience, shall show a modification, or change, to be proper; and in every case and exigency, my best discretion will be exercised, according to circumstances actually existing, and with a view and a hope of a peaceful solution of the national troubles, and the restoration of fraternal sympathies and affections.

That there are persons in one section, or another who seek to destroy the Union at all events, and are glad of any pretext to do it, I will neither affirm nor deny; but if there be such, I need address no word to them. To those, however, who really love the Union, may I not speak?

121

Before entering upon so grave a matter as the destruction of our national fabric, with all its benefits, its memories, and its hopes, would it not be wise to ascertain precisely why we do it? Will you hazard so desperate a step, while there is any possibility that any portion of the ills you fly from, have no real existence? Will you, while the certain ills you fly to, are greater than the real ones you fly from? Will you risk the commission of so fearful a mistake?

All profess to be content in the Union, if all constitutional rights can be maintained. Is it true, then, that any right, plainly written in the Constitution, has been denied? I think not. Happily the human mind is so constituted, that no party can reach to the audacity of doing this. Think, if you can, of a single instance in which a plainly written provision of the Constitution has ever been denied. If, by the mere force of numbers, a majority should deprive a minority of any clearly written constitutional right, it might, in a moral point of view, justify revolution—certainly would, if such right were a vital one.

But such is not our case. All the vital rights of minorities and of individuals, are so plainly assured to them, by affirmations and negations, guarantees and prohibitions, in the Constitution that controversies never arise concerning them. But no organic law can ever be framed with a provision specifically applicable to every question which may occur in practical administration. No foresight can anticipate, nor any document of reasonable length contain express provisions for all possible questions. Shall fugitives from labor be surrendered by national or by state authority? The Constitution does not expressly say. May Congress prohibit slavery in the territories? The Constitution does not expressly say. Must Congress protect slavery in the territories? The Constitution does not expressly say.

From questions of this class spring all our constitutional controversies, and we divide upon them into majorities and minorities. If the minority will not acquiesce, the majority must, or the government must cease. There is no other alternative; for continuing the government is acquiescence on one side or the other.

If a minority, in such case, will secede rather than acquiesce, they make a precedent which, in turn, will divide and ruin them; for a minority of their own will whenever a majority refuses to be controlled by such minority. For instance, why may not any portion of a new confederacy, a year or two hence, arbitrarily secede again, precisely as portions of the present Union now claim to secede from it? All who cherish disunion sentiments are now being educated to the exact temper of doing this.

Is there such perfect identity of interests among the states to compose a new Union, as to produce harmony only, and prevent renewed secession?

Plainly, the central idea of secession is the essence of anarchy. A majority, held in restraint by constitutional checks and limitations, and always changing easily, with deliberate changes of popular opinions and sentiments, is the only true sovereign of a free people. Whoever rejects it does, of necessity, fly to anarchy or to despotism. Unanimity is impossible; the rule of the minority, as a permanent arrangement, is wholly inadmissible; so that, rejecting the majority principle, anarchy or despotism in some form, is all that is left.

I do not forget the position assumed by some, that constitutional questions are to be decided by the Supreme Court; nor do I deny that such decisions must be binding, in any case, upon the parties to a suit, as to the object of that suit, while they are also entitled to very high respect and consideration, in all parallel cases, by all other departments of the government. And, while it is obviously possible that such decision may be erroneous in any given case, still the evil effect following it, being limited to that particular case, with the chance that it may be overruled, and never become a precedent for other cases, can better be borne than could the evils of a different practice.

At the same time the candid citizen must confess that if the policy of the government, upon vital questions affecting the whole people, is to be irrevocably fixed by decisions of the Supreme Court, the instant they are made, in ordinary litigation between parties, in personal actions, the people will have ceased to be their own rulers, having to that extent practically resigned their government into the hands of that eminent tribunal. Nor is there, in this view, any assault upon the court or the judges. It is a duty from which they may not shrink, to decide cases properly brought before them; and it is no fault of

theirs, if others seek to turn their decisions to political purposes.

One section of our country believes slavery is right, and ought to be extended, while the other believes it is wrong, and ought not to be extended. This is the only substantial dispute. The fugitive-slave clause of the Constitution, and the law for the suppression of the foreign slave-trade, are each as well enforced, perhaps, as any law can ever be in a community where the moral sense of the people imperfectly supports the law itself. The great body of the people abide by the dry legal obligation in both cases, and a few break over in each. This, I think, cannot be perfectly cured; and it would be worse in both cases after the separation of the sections than before. The foreign slave-trade, now imperfectly suppressed, would be ultimately revived without restriction, in one section; while fugitive slaves, now only partially surrendered, would not be surrendered at all by the other.

Physically speaking, we cannot separate. We cannot remove our respective sections from each other, nor build an impassable wall between them. A husband and wife may be divorced, and go out of the presence, and beyond the reach of each other; but the different part of our country cannot do this. They cannot but remain face to face; and intercourse, either amicable or hostile, must continue between them. It is possible then to make that intercourse more advantageous, or more satisfactory, after separation than before? Can aliens make treaties easier than friends can make laws? Can treaties be more faithfully enforced between aliens, than laws can among friends? Suppose you go to war, you cannot fight always; and when, after much loss on both sides, and no gain on either, you cease fighting, the identical old questions, as to terms of intercourse, are again upon you.

This country, with its institutions, belongs to the people who inhabit it. Whenever they shall grow weary of the existing government, they can exercise their constitutional right of amending it, or their revolutionary right to dismember, or overthrow it. I cannot be ignorant of the fact that many worthy and patriotic citizens are desirious of having the national Constitution amended. While I make no recommendation of amendments, I fully recognize the rightful authority of the people over the whole subject, to be exercised in either of the modes prescribed in the instrument itself; and I should, under existing circumstances, favor rather than oppose a fair opportunity being afforded the people to act upon it.

I will venture to add that to me the convention mode seems preferable, in that it allows amendments to originate with the people themselves, instead of only permitting them to take, or reject, propositions originated by others, not especially chosen for the purpose, and which might not be precisely such, as they would wish to either accept or refuse. I understand a proposed amendment, however, I have not seen—has passed Congress, to the effect that the federal government shall never interfere with the domestic institutions of the states, including that of persons held to service. To

avoid misconstruction of what I have said I depart from my purpose not to speak of particular amendments so far as to say that, holding such a provision to now be implied constitutional law, I have no objection to its being made express and irrevocable.

The Chief Magistrate derives all his authority from the people, and they have conferred none upon him to fix terms for the separation of the states. The people themselves can do this also if they choose; but the Executive, as such, has nothing to do with it. His duty is to administer the present government, as it came to his hands, and to transmit it, unimpaired by him, to his successor.

Why should there not be a patient confidence in the ultimate justice of the people? Is there any better, or equal hope, in the world? In our present differences, is either party without faith of being in the right? If the Almighty Ruler of Nations with His eternal truth and justice, be on your side of the North or on yours of the South, that truth, and that justice, will surely prevail, by the judgment of this great tribunal, the American people.

By the frame of the government under which we live, this same people have wisely given their public servants but little power for mischief; and have, with equal wisdom, provided for the return of that little to their own hands at very short intervals. While the people retain their virtue and vigilance, no administration, by any extreme of wickedness or folly, can very seriously injure the government, in the short space of four years.

My countrymen, one and all, think calmly and well, upon this whole subject. Nothing valuable can be lost by taking time. If there be an object to hurry any of you, in hot haste, to a step which you would never take deliberately, that object will be frustrated by taking time; but no good object can be frustrated by it. Such of you as are now dissatisfied, still have the old Constitution unimpaired, and, on the sensitive point, the laws of your own framing under it; while the new administration will have no immediate power, if it would, to change either. If it were admitted that you who are dissatisfied, hold the right side in the dispute, there is still no single good reason for precipitate action. Intelligence, patriotism, Christianity, and a firm reliance on Him, who has never yet forsaken this favored land, are still competent to adjust in the best way, all our present difficulty.

In your hands, my dissatisfied fellow-countrymen, and not in mine, is the momentous issue of civil war. The government will not assail you. You can have no conflict, without being yourselves the aggressors. You have no oath registered in Heaven to destroy the government, while I shall have the most solemn one to "preserve, protect, and defend it."

I am loath to close. We are not enemies, but friends. We must not be enemies. Though passion may have strained, it must not break our bonds of affection. The mystic chords of memory stretching from every battlefield, and patriot's grave, to every living heart and hearthstone, all over this broad land, will yet swell the chorus of the Union, when again touched, as surely they will be, by the better angels of our nature.

When President - elect Lincoln finished, Chief Justice Taney, bitterly criticized by this same Lincoln for his opinion in the Dred Scott case of 1856, issued the oath of office to the sixteenth President of the United States.

INAUGURAL ADDRESS, LINCOLN'S SECOND—March 4, 1865. In contrast to his first inauguration, Lincoln was greeted by thousands of rain-drenched supporters when he appeared on the rostrum at the east side of the Capitol. As Lincoln began to speak, the rain stopped and the sun broke through :

Fellow Countrymen : At this second appearing to take the oath of the Presidential office, there is less occasion for an extended address than there was at the first. Then a statement, somewhat in detail, of course to be pursued, seemed fitting and proper. Now, at the expiration of four years, during which public declarations have been constantly called forth on every point and phase of the great contest which still absorbs the attention, and engrosses the energies of the nation, little that is new could be presented. The progress of our arms, upon which all else chiefly depends, is as well known to the public as to myself; and it is, I trust, reasonably satisfactory and encouraging to all. With high hope for the future, no prediction in regard to it is ventured.

On the occasion corresponding to this four years ago, all thoughts were anxiously directed to an impending civil war. All dreaded it —all sought to avert it. While the inaugural address was being delivered from this place, devoted altogether to saving the Union without war, insurgent agents were in the city seeking to destroy it without war—seeking to dissolve the Union, and divide effects, by negotiation. Both parties deprecated war; but one of them would make war rather than let the nation survive; and the other would accept war rather than let it perish. And the war came.

One-eighth of the whole population were colored slaves, not distributed generally over the Union, but localized in the southern part of it. These slaves constituted a peculiar and powerful interest. All knew that this interest was, somehow, the cause of the war. To strengthen, perpetuate, and extend this interest was the object for which the insurgents would rend the Union, even by war; while the government claimed no right to do more than to restrict the territorial enlargement of it. Neither party expected for the war, the magnitude or the duration, which it has already attained. Neither anticipated that the cause of the conflict might cease with, or even before, the conflict itself should cease. Each looked for an easier triumph, and a result less fundamental and astounding.

Both read the same Bible, and pray to the same God; and each invokes His aid against the other. It may seem strange that any men should dare to ask a just God's assistance in wringing their bread from the sweat of other men's faces; but let us judge not that we be not judged. The prayers of both could not be answered; that of neither has been answered fully.

The Almighty has His own purposes. "Woe unto the world because of offenses! for it must needs be that offenses come; but woe to that man by whom the offense cometh!" If we shall suppose that American slavery is one of those offenses which, in the providence of God must needs come, but which, having continued through His appointed time, he now wills to remove, and that He gives to both North and South, this terrible war, as the woe due to those by whom the offense came, shall we discern therein any departure from those divine attributes which the believers in a living God always ascribe to Him? Fondly do we hope—fervently do we pray—that this mighty scourge of war may speedily pass away. Yet, if God wills that it continue, until all the wealth piled by the bondman's two hundred and fifty years of unrequited toil shall be sunk, and until every drop of blood drawn with the lash, shall be paid by another drawn with the sword, as was said three thousand years ago, so still it must be said, "the judgements of the Lord, are true and righteous altogether."

With malice toward none; with charity for all; with firmness in the right, as God gives us to see the right, let us strive on to finish the work we are in; to bind up the nation's wounds; to care for him who shall have borne the battle, and for his widow, and his orphan —to do all which may achieve and cherish a just, and a lasting peace, among ourselves, and with all nations.

INDIANS, in the war—Both sides used Indians in the war, but the South used almost twice the number used by the North. It is almost impossible to give an accurate statement of the total number used by either side because of the continuous switching of sides by the Indians themselves. It has been said that most of the warriors, having no tribal tie with either side, would go with the winning side after each battle; however, no written proof exists to substantiate the totals involved in this maneuver.

Highest ranking Indian in the war on either side was General Stand Watie, a Confederate brigadier who holds the distinction of being the last Confederate general to surrender his troops (June 23, 1865). Highest ranking Indian officer in the Union army was Donehogawa, better known as General Ely S. Parker. Parker, a Seneca, is credited with having transcribed the penciled draft of the surrender papers into a "legible inked official document." He is also given credit with saving Grant's life at Spotsylvania.

General Albert Pike recruited Indians for the South, but disdained the use of modern weapons, and allowed them to use their tribal weapons of lances, spears, bows and tomahawks. Pike was not an Indian himself, but favored their recruitment.

Indian troops fought at many of the major battles, but seldom against each other. Perhaps the main distinction between the Indians on the two sides was their tribal backgrounds. The South had a large number of halfbreeds, and members of the Five Nations tribes (Cherokees, Choctaws, Creeks, Chickasaws and Seminoles); while the North used western Indians, some Creeks, and many northwestern Indians.

Although strongly opposed by a group of die-hards in the Lincoln cabinet, the policy of recruiting Indians gained momentum in the North, and the touted D'Epineuil's Zouaves (the Fifty-third New York Infantry) is said to have contained a large number of Tuscarora volunteers early in the war. At the battles of Pea Ridge and Locust Grove, Indian forces of both sides clashed in one of the few skirmishes where redmen met face to face. The Northern Indians carried both contests. Rumors flew concerning atrocities committed by "unmanageable" Indians.

When the highly respected General Albert Pike resigned his commission because of what he considered the "unfair . . . robbing of half-naked Indians of shoes . . . to clothe other troops," the Indians in the Confederate army split over whether to stay with the South, go home, or switch to the Northern army. As a result of his resignation, Pike was seized and imprisoned, but was later released. To add to this situation, Indian leader John Ross (Cherokee) "allowed" himself to be captured with some very important documents, by

127

Northern troops, and was rumored to have gone to Washington, handed over tribal treasures, and bartered for a position in the Union Army (using the promise of delivering his tribe to the Union as a lever).

The Cherokee nation split—one group ousting Ross as chief, and elevating fiery Stand Watie to the top post. Most of the half-breeds stood by Watie; the others either quit fighting altogether or went over to the union side. Bloody fighting broke out within the ranks of the Indians themselves, however, when the Confederacy lost in the West, and the Indians resorted to minor skirmishes and occasional raids.

The Union ledger lists 3,530 Indians officially employed by the Union, but the number far exceeds that when one considers the continuous switching of sides. A conservative estimate of the total number of Indians on both sides has been placed at close to 12,000. Many Indians supported the South because they themselves were slave holders. Outstanding Indian leaders were Stand Watie (Confederate), Ely Samuel Parker (Union), Colonel Peter B. Pitchlynn (Confederate), Colonel D. N. McIntosh (Confeder-(ate), and Lieutenant Colonel C. McIntosh (Confederate).

INTELLIGENCE OPERATIVES IN THE NORTH, Confederate—Colonel Jacob Thompson commanded most of the Confederate operatives in the North. He assembled them in Toronto, Canada, as early as August, 1864, to map out plans to slow down the Union effort and hinder homefront produc-tion. Thompson's official title was, "Special Commissioner of the Confederate States Government in Canada."

Among the more active of the operatives were Thomas H. Hines, the man who had engineered John Hunt Morgan's escape from an Ohio penitentiary in 1863, and the suspected Clement Laird Vallandigham. Vallandigham, leader of the Ohio "Copperheads," was also head of the "Sons of Liberty"—a peace organization which sympathized with the South. He had met with Thompson and Hines in June of 1864, in Windsor, Ontario, Canada, and offered the services of the Sons of Liberty.

Vallandigham offered the Confederate intelligence chief the services of 85,000 members in Illinois, 50,000 in Indiana, and 40,000 in Ohio. Whether he would have been able to produce or not is a question which remains unanswered.

Hines and sixty of his men were in Chicago rounding up sympathizers, arming them, and meeting with Copperhead leaders. Leaders of the Sons of Liberty movement assured Hines that they knew that a "general uprising . . . (would) result in glorious success."

Hines, and his men, were contemplating freeing and arming the more than 5,000 Confederate soldiers held at Camp Douglas, outside of Chicago. With these men, and others from nearby Rock Island Prison camp, Hines hoped to muster 13,000 men to rip apart Illinois around the Great Lakes region. However, the

Copperhead leaders were more talk than action, and the Sons of Liberty organization was unable to furnish even the 500 men that Hines needed to carry out his plan.

This is just an instance of situations all over the North where Thompson's men (who originally hoped to sit around stirring up riots and dissention) were unable to depend upon the dissenting factions in the North to aid them. The orders given to Hines and Thompson to "carry out any fair and appropriate enterprises of war against our enemies (the North)" that might occur to them, were applied only one time—at St. Albans, Vt., and that was more of a military operation than an intelligence maneuver.

The Confederate government made one mistake in its move to disrupt the Northern war effort—it relied too heavily on the word of the Copperhead leadership to lend support in their many efforts. The Copperheads never came through.

"INTELLIGENT CONTRABAND" — The term applied to Negro slaves who escaped to the Union side bringing vital information. Many were used as guides during the later years of the war, when the Union forces often found themselves in unfamiliar territory. The name "contraband" is misleading, however, for many of the Negroes supplying information and leading raiding parties were freed slaves before the war. Others acted as espionage agents while still in slavery.

Good examples of the former group were Harriet Tubman, who was working as a nurse in a military hospital when the government agreed to let her organize a band of guerrillas to raid the plantations of the South and free slaves, and Furnery Bryant, an ex-slave who had escaped from his master's plantation early in the war. Miss Tubman was given a blanket pass by General David Hunter which allowed her to go "wherever she wishes to go." This pass ordered all and sundry to give her free passage at all times on government transports. The old Boston *Commonwealth* newspaper describes one of her expeditions during which she served as a guide for a Union raiding party :

> Colonel Montgomery and his gallant band of 300 black soldiers under the guidance of a black woman, dashed into the enemy's country, struck a bold and effective blow, destroying millions of dollars worth of commissary stores, cotton, and brought off nearly 800 slaves and thousands of dollars worth of property without losing a man or receiving a scratch.

Bryant is credited with revealing to the Union the whereabouts of a Confederate cache of $800,000 in silver coin. He crossed the lines frequently during the war, serving as a spy until enlisting in a Negro regiment in late 1863.

William A. Jackson, Jefferson Davis' coachman was another who served as a spy for the Union. (See JACKSON, WILLIAM A.)

The exploits of slaves like Robert Small, William Morrison, A. Gradine, and John Small, who stole the Confederate steamer "Planter" right from under the guns of the Confederates, were given small notice during the war. (See SMALLS, ROBERT.) One Negro called "Prince" served as a pilot for boats winding their way through the difficult river channels of southern rivers. Many "intelligent contraband" performed in this manner.

Ex-slaves were most happy when acting as guides or scouts for expeditions into slave-holding territories with the intent to free slaves.

ISLAND NO. 10—Formerly an island in the Mississippi about forty miles below Columbus, Ky., near the Tennessee line. It has been washed away since the Civil War. There was formerly a line of islands lying below Cairo, Ill., which led directly into the heart of the Confederacy. The island received its name from its position as tenth in this chain from north to south.

It was fortified by the Confederates early in the war, under the direction of General Leonidas Polk. It was manned by about 7,000 Confederates under General W. W. Mackall (under Beauregard) when Commodore A. H. Foote of the Union navy bombarded this island for three weeks, using seven gunboats. This forced the surrender of the island on April 7, 1862. Polk evacuated as many of the Confederates as possible, under direct fire of two of Foote's gunboats, using a group of river transports to accomplish the task at night. Most of the Confederates were pursued into the swamps, and over 6,000 prisoners

were taken, in addition to large quantities of ammunition and supplies. Federal losses were extremely light.

J

JACKSON, Mississippi—Capital of the state of Mississippi. The city had a population of around 3,200 when war broke out, and it was there that the Mississippi legislature made that state the second to secede from the Union. Jackson was an important city strategically because of its dual role as state capital and as a railroad center.

The Battle of Jackson was fought when Grant assigned McPherson's and Sherman's Corps (and part of McClernand's) the task of capturing the city and destroying the railroads, bridges, factories, and arsenals there. Confederate General J. E. Johnston and his force attempted to delay the advance while removing records and other public property, but the Union forces battled their way into the city on the afternoon of May 14, 1863, and began to destroy the city's vital works.

Later, after the Union forces had evacuated the city, Johnston reoccupied Jackson and set up a defensive line flanked on the Pearl River. Vicksburg had been taken by the Union by then, and on July 11, 1863, Sherman began his siege of Jackson which lasted until the morning of July 17, when he found that the Confederates had withdrawn during the night. Sherman again entered the city, this time destroying all communications lines and gutting the city by fire. During the siege, the Union lost 129 killed, 762 wounded and 231 missing. Johnston lost 71 killed, 504 wounded, and 764 captured or missing.

JACKSON, THOMAS JONATHAN (1824–1863) — "Stonewall." Confederate Lieutenant General. Jackson graduated from West Point in 1846, and immediately entered the Mexican War. He resigned his commission in 1851 to teach at the Virginia Military Institute, and in this capacity, carried a group of cadets up to Harper's Ferry to see the hanging of abolitionist John Brown.

Jackson was not too successful in his prewar endeavors, and was opposed to secession and the war. At the start of the war, however, he was sent to Harper's Ferry for duty, and by June, 1861, was a brigadier general. At the first Bull Run, his troops stood firm against a continuously attacking Union force, prompting (according to legend) General Bee to comment, "There stands Jackson, standing like a stone wall." (See BEE.) The name took hold, and Jackson was known thereafter as "Stonewall" Jackson.

In October, 1861, Jackson became a major general, and carried his army into the Shenandoah. His campaign there in 1862 made him famous, and is termed one of the most brilliant campaigns of the war. During the Peninsular Campaign, he was called to Richmond, and fought (without much of his usual brilliance) at Dam Creek and White Oak Swamp. His troops fought exceedingly well at second Bull Run and Antietam. By October, 1862, he had risen to lieutenant general, and carried his force to Fredericksburg. He surprised Howard at Chancellorsville.

His death came as the result of a mistaken shot from a Confederate rifle in the dusk near the front at Chancellorsville. Jackson died on May 10, 1863, as a result of pneumonia brought about by the wound. He was most valuable as an independent commander, and exceedingly valuable to the Confederate cause. His force was often called the "Foot Cavalry" because of their rapid movement from one point to another.

Jackson was rather eccentric in manner (he loved to suck sour lemons) and often considered an "odd ball" by his troops; however, he was one of the fastest-moving, hardest-hitting Confederate generals in the war. Of him Lee said, "I know not how to replace him." (See HOTCHKISS, JEDEDIAH.)

JACKSON, WILLIAM A. — Coachman for Jefferson Davis. A Union spy, whose information gathered while serving as coachman for the President of the Confederacy, helped the Union cause considerably. Jackson was one of many Negroes spying for the Union. (See "INTELLIGENT CONTRABAND".) He is said to have learned many of the Confederate plans in his capacity as personal coachman for Davis. He would then steal through the Union lines and relay his information to Washington.

131

Historians describe him as "one of the most amazing of the 'Intelligent Contraband.'"

JAMES RIVER, THE ARMY OF THE—Created out of troops from the Department of Virginia and the Departments of Virginia and North Carolina. In April, 1864, the Army of the James came into being, and campaigned against Petersburg until early summer of that year under Union Major General Benjamin F. Butler. In the summer of that year, this army was trapped by the Confederates, bottled up, and rendered useless for all practical purposes.

JAMES RIVER, THE—The largest river in the state of Virginia, flowing from the Allegheny Mountains to the Chesapeake Bay—a distance of about 240 miles.

The James figured prominently in many of the campaigns during the war in the East, because of its winding nature and its transportation value. Its chief tributaries are the vital Chickahominy from the north and the Appomattox from the south. There are falls in the river below Richmond, Va.

JENKINS FERRY, Arkansas, the Battle of—April 30, 1864. Confederates under General Sterling Price and General E. K. Smith attacked Union General Frederick Steele at the Saline River and were repulsed.

JEWS — (See GENERAL ORDER NO. ELEVEN.)

JOHNNY REB—A nickname used by the Union forces applying to the Confederate soldier. The "Reb" is an abbreviation of their appellation, "Rebel." The Confederates in turn, called their opponents "Yanks," or "Bluebellies" (referring to the color of their uniforms).

JOHNSON, ANDREW (1808 – 1875)—Union Vice-President (1864–1865). A native of Tennessee and a Democrat. He was selected to run as Lincoln's co-candidate because the Republicans needed a stronger vote-getting combination in 1864. He assumed the Presidential seat upon the assassination of Lincoln (April 14, 1865).

In 1862, he had served as military governor of Tennessee. Johnson was considered a moderate.

JOHNSON, BUSHROD RUST (1817–1880)—Confederate Major General. Johnson was a native of Belmont, Ohio, and a graduate of West Point (1840). He served in the Mexican War, and was a member of the faculty of Western Military Institute at Georgetown, Ky., in 1847. He later served as superintendent of that institute from 1851 to 1855, when the institute merged with the University of Nashville.

Johnson took part in many major actions of the war, and was with Lee at the surrender at Appomattox. After the war, he served as Chancellor of the University of Nashville from 1870 to 1874.

JOHNSON'S ISLAND, Ohio — Union prison camp. An island at the mouth of Sandusky Bay near Lake Erie, used as a prison for Confederate soldiers during the war. The island, about one mile long and one and one half miles wide at the widest point, was used almost exclusively for officers, and was considered one of the "better" prisons.

JOHNSTON, ALBERT SIDNEY (1803–1812) — Confederate Full General. This native of Washington, Ky., was one of the valuable Southern leaders to fall at Shiloh. He graduated from West Point in 1826, and entered the Civil War as a full general in charge of western operations, following a brilliant prewar career. It is rumored that he traveled from the Pacific Coast overland to join the Confederate army.

It was this Johnston who set up the famous Kentucky line of defense, which would have changed the outcome of the Kentucky campaign had it been a shorter line and better manned. When troops under his command were defeated at Mills Springs, Fort Henry, and Fort Donelson, he withdrew to Corinth, Miss.

In the spring of 1862, Johnston struck Grant at Shiloh (Pittsburgh Landing, April 6, 1862), and had the Federal troops nearly routed when a leg wound knocked him out of the fight. The neglected wound bled profusely, and Johnston died from the loss of blood. His death, which could have been prevented with a simple tourniquet, disheartened his troops, and they retreated from Shiloh the next day when fresh Union troops arrived on the scene.

Johnston was overestimated as a strategist, but had a dogged type of determination which was very similar to the style of Grant. His type of leadership was very vital to the Confederate cause, and the loss of both him and Jackson in one year was a telling blow to the Confederate cause. His death did much to make Grant's way easier in the West.

JOHNSTON, JOSEPH EGGLESTON (1807–1891)—Confederate Full General. A native of Prince Edward County, Va., and an 1829 graduate of West Point, Johnston resigned his commission in 1837 to become a civil engineer. He returned to active duty to take part in the Mexican War, and was made Quartermaster General in 1860. In the same year, he became a brigadier general in the Union army, but resigned his commission to assume a similar rank in the Confederate army in May, 1861. He served with Beauregard at the first Bull Run, and was made a full general in August, 1861.

Johnston commanded the troops which eventually became famous as the Army of Northern Virginia, and was in charge of the retreat up the Virginia Peninsula by the Confederates until wounded at Seven Pines (Fair Oaks) in front of Richmond. Until November, 1862, when he was nominally placed in command of the West, Johnston was not heard from very much. His career (like so many) was hampered by disputes with Jefferson Davis. This brought about an ineffectiveness which seemed to become a part of his nature in the latter years of the war. He failed to relieve Pemberton at Vicksburg in the spring and summer of 1863, and failed to cut off Grant in mid-Mississippi.

However, Johnston conducted a masterful retreat to Atlanta after taking command of the Army of Tennessee in December, 1863, and attempted to draw Sherman into a trap deep in the heart of the Confederacy. To the surprise of both North and South, Johnston was relieved in front of Atlanta, and replaced for "failing to engage Sherman" (July 17, 1864). In February, 1865, he resumed command of the Army of Tennessee in time to surrender to Sherman on April 26, 1865.

Following the war, he served in Congress and entered business. He had great ability to keep a large, outnumbered force intact, and is best known for his strategic retreats. Naturally pessimistic, he was unable to be "directed" by Davis. It is possible that, had sufficient re-enforcements awaited him at Atlanta in 1864, the Southerners in Johnston's command might have wrecked Sherman's army as Johnston had planned.

JOMINI, ANTOINE HENRI, the Battle Theory of—Jomini was author of the strategy book, *Summary of the Art of War,* which greatly influenced most of the young West Point graduates in the early years of the Academy. Basically, his theory was one of the "holding offense," where the attacking general decided upon a place to which he would move, and then proceeded to take that position. The fallacy of the system was that it allowed no strategy for pursuit, retaliation, or retreat.

Jomini placed the emphasis on places instead of armies, and his pursuit phase was not vigorous at all. He relied upon his army to assume an offensive position so strong that the enemy would either be forced to withdraw or face annihilation. This was good in some respects. However, once the enemy withdrew, the strategy did not call for immediate or relentless pursuit. He is quoted as having said that he preferred the "chivalric war to organized assassination." Perhaps this is why he could not possibly have favored the relentless type of pursuit made famous by U. S. Grant.

Devoted followers of Jomini included McClellan, Lee, Sherman (until influenced by Grant), Beauregard, and Halleck, among others. Halleck, in fact, spent years translating Jomini's works, and Hardee's *Tactics* reflects a great many of Jomini's ideas. Dennis Hart Mahan began teaching this theory of war at West Point in 1824, thereby influencing most of the West Pointers in the Civil War period. The main factors of the theory were : (1) set an objective; (2) take the offensive; (3) use the mass of your troops against fractions of the enemy's force whenever possible; (4) use only the amount of troops necessary to dominate a theater of operation; (5) set up defensive interior lines behind offensive units; and (6) maintain a unity of command, with as little dispersion of authority as possible. Lee was considered the greatest follower of Jomini within the Confederate ranks.

JONES, CATESBY (1821–1877)—Confederate naval officer. Jones was serving in the army as a lieutenant when war broke out. Prior to the war, he assisted Lieutenant J. A. B. Dahlgren in the development of the famous Dahlgren gun while working at the Washington Navy Yard. Jones joined the Confederacy with the rank of lieutenant, and was made executive officer aboard the rebuilt "Merrimac" (renamed the "Virginia"). He replaced the injured Captain Franklin Buchanan in command of the vessel on March 9, 1862, after a naval battle with the Union ships "Cumberland" and "Congress," and was, therefore, in command of the vessel when the famous battle with the Union ironclad "Monitor" was fought. In 1863, he was promoted to commander, and was placed in charge of ordnance production for both the army and the navy, at Selma, Ala., not far from his home of Fairfield, Ala. Jones died as the result of a wound received in a quarrel with his neighbor at Selma in 1877.

JONES, DAVID R. (1825–1863)—Confederate officer. This West Point graduate (of 1846) served as Beauregard's chief of staff in the early phases of the war, and was the officer who carried the terms of surrender to Anderson at Fort Sumter in April, 1861.

JONESBORO, Georgia, the Battle of—August 30, 1864. A Confederate loss which eventually resulted in the fall of Atlanta. During an extensive maneuver around the city of Atlanta,

Sherman moved his force to East Point, Ga., about six miles southwest of Atlanta, in an attempt to cut off the communications of that sector. A similar move had been made at Ezra Church in July.

Sherman's troops, under General Thomas, were busy destroying about thirteen miles of railroad line and building a battle line in conjunction with forces under Couch and Schofield when Hardee's troops, in conjunction with the corps under one of the Lees, hit O. O. Howard, on Thomas' right. Because Hardee's attack was (in the words of his supporter S. D. Lee) "a feeble one and a failure, with the loss to my corps of about 1,300 men killed and wounded," the attack failed. The entire loss by Hardee was 1,700, while the Union force lost only 179 killed or wounded in the combined attack.

The fighting had, however, left Hardee entrenched and covering Jonesboro. After a hard-fought battle between his forces and those under Union General Jeff Davis, Hardee retreated under cover of darkness to Lovejoy, Ga., leaving Jonesboro and the surrounding terrain to the Union.

JORDAN, THOMAS (1819–1895)—Confederate army officer. Jordan was a veteran of the Seminole and Mexican Wars when he resigned his Union commission in 1861 to serve as chief of staff under General P. G. T. Beauregard. Prior to the war, after graduating from West Point in 1840, he had introduced steam navigation on the Columbia River (1856–1860). After the war, he took part in the Cuban Revolution as commander of the Cuban insurgents, defeating the Spanish at Guaimaro, January, 1870.

K

KANAWHA, the Army of—Confederate. This army was under Brigadier General John B. Floyd, and fought in the section of Virginia that later became West Virginia (fall, 1861).

KAUTZ, AUGUST V. (1828–1895)— Union Major General. Kautz, a native of Ispringen, Germany, graduated from West Point in 1852. The son of German immigrants who settled in Ohio, he proved to be one of the best officers in the Union army. His greatest battle was at Petersburg, June 9, 1864. The career officer remained in the army until 1892.

KEARNY, PHILIP (1814–1862)—Union Major General. Kearny was called "the most perfect soldier" by General Winfield Scott. Born in New York, and a graduate of Columbia University (1833), he entered the U.S. Army in 1837 as a lieutenant of the First Dragoons.

The young officer studied cavalry tactics in France, and fought with the French Army in Algeria prior to entering the Civil War. Resigning his position on the staff of General Scott in 1846, Kearny returned to enlist for service in the Mexican War. Here, he gained notice by chasing the fleeing Mexicans into Mexico City after the Battle of Churubusco. He

again resigned his commission in 1859, and returned to Europe where he joined the French Army again and fought in Italy.

On May 17, 1861, Kearny was appointed a brigadier general in the Union army, commanding the cavalry of the Army of the Potomac (and serving with particular merit in the Peninsular Campaign). On July 7, 1862, he was made major general of volunteers, but was shot while reconnoitering near Chantilly, Va., after the Battle of Bull Run. He died just three months after receiving his promotion.

Considered an exceptionally able soldier and cavalry leader, Kearny operated in the style of Stuart and Ashby, but possessed the polish and tactical know-how of the European horseman.

KELLY'S FORD, Virginia, Engagements at—Numerous engagements took place at this strategic point on the Rappahannock River just above the point where it meets the Rapidan. The first of these was fought between cavalry forces in August, 1862. In March of the following year, Union General W. W. Averell and 2,100 cavalrymen crossed the ford after a heated exchange with forces under Confederate General Fitzhugh Lee, but were driven back. Still later, on November 7, 1863, Union forces under General W. H. French forced their way across the river, enabling the Army of the Potomac to cross without too much opposition on the 8th. Most of the engagements fought at Kelly's Ford were between cavalry units.

KEMPER, JAMES LAWSON (1823–1895) —Confederate Major General. Kemper graduated from Washington College (now Washington and Lee) in 1842. He served in the Mexican War, and was a representative in the Virginia legislature for ten years. During the Civil War, Kemper rose from colonel to major general, and led the charge of the right wing of Pickett's force during the famous "Pickett's charge" at Gettysburg, Pa. (July, 1863). After the war, he served as governor of Virginia as a Democrat from 1874 to 1878.

KENNESAW MOUNTAIN, Georgia — Above Atlanta, Confederate troops set up a pocket of resistance during the retreat in 1864, and forced Sherman's troops to bypass this point. Sherman, like Grant, preferred to bypass unimportant defenses which might prove costly to take. Eventually, the Confederates evacuated the mountain, but Federal forces, storming in force, were never able to assume complete command of the ranges of the mountain during this march. The area is now a national park.

KENTUCKY, the Army of—Confederate. This army fought under a number of generals during the brief period from late 1861 to early 1862 when it operated as a separate entity. On November 20, 1862, it was merged into the Army of Tennessee under General Braxton Bragg.

KERNSTOWN, Virginia, the Battle of —March 22, 1862. When Jackson began his retreat up the Shenandoah Valley, closely followed by Union General James Shield and his division, the tide turned for the Confederates on March 20, when Shields was recalled to Winchester. Jackson, finding that his pursuer had begun to return over the pursuit route, turned his forces and began to chase the Federal force. Turner Ashby engaged Shields on the afternoon of the 22nd at Kernstown, Va. During the fighting, Shield received a shell wound which put him out of action. Erroneous information caused Jackson to believe that the Federal forces had only four weak regiments, while, in reality, Shields had over 8,000 men with cavalry and artillery support. Jackson, although possessing twenty-seven guns to Shields' twenty-three, had only 3,000 men.

Colonel N. Kimball, under attack by Jackson's forces, staged a counterattack, broke Jackson's line, and forced the Confederates into a full retreat, leaving their dead and wounded behind. Jackson referred to this fight as fiercer than "any portion of the battle of Manassas." Union losses totaled 118 killed, 450 wounded, and 22 missing. Jackson lost 80 killed, 375 wounded, and 263 missing.

KILPATRICK, HUGH JUDSON (1836–1881)—Union Major General. Kilpatrick graduated from West Point one month early (1861) because of the Confederate attack on Fort Sumter. He was made a captain of volunteers in the Union army, and was severely wounded in June, 1861, at the Battle of Big Bethel, Va., the first engagement of the war between aligned troops of the two armies.

Soon after, he was made lieutenant colonel of the cavalry, and remained in this rank until made a major in the regular army in 1863, just before Gettysburg. He led the abortive "Kilpatrick Raid" on Richmond, Va., in an attempt to release the prisoners of Libby Prison. Kilpatrick was again severely wounded at Resaca, Ga., in 1864, and was still unable to ride when he joined Sherman on the "March to the Sea."

After the war, he became minister to Chile from 1865 to 1868, and was reappointed to the post in 1881. He died in Chile on December 2nd of that year.

KILPATRICK RAID, THE—(See KILPATRICK, HUGH JUDSON).

KING COTTON DIPLOMACY—The misconception within the Confederacy that the power of its cotton would lure the European powers to the Southern side, resulted in what has been termed "King Cotton Diplomacy." The economic pressure brought about by the Northern blockade of Southern ports paid little dividends, although there was some unemployment in the factories of England. Just as the pinch was being felt in Europe, Lincoln (in one of the smartest political maneuvers of the war) threw the slavery issue into the picture by announcing the Emancipation Proclamation. This offset any feelings of alignment that might have arisen within the foreign countries. Whereas many nations might have been willing to side with a group of rebels, or revolutionaries, not one was willing to go before the world as a nation supporting slavery and opposing the Union which advocated the freedom of the Negro.

With the opening of the cotton markets of India and the Near East, the power of the Confederacy's cotton waned, and consequently bales of cotton rotted in warehouses. Worse still, speculators were reduced to selling cotton to the North in order to obtain necessary items which could not be brought in through the ever tightening blockade. Cotton failed as a diplomatic weapon because of the industrial power of the North. Most foreign markets felt that it was not worth the loss of Northern trade to cultivate Southern cotton merchants. In many instances, the withholding of raw cotton from the mills of England actually enraged the lower and middle class Englishmen, turning them against the South.

The original move in the "King Cotton" farce was designed to force England to break down the Northern blockade in order to get cotton to operate her mills. It failed completely.

KING, RUFUS (1814–1876) — Union Brigadier General. The New York born journalist graduated from West Point in 1833, and became adjutant general of the state of New York shortly after (1839–1843). He served as associate editor of the Albany (N.Y.) *Advertiser* and the *Journal*. King was commissioned brigadier general of the Wisconsin volunteers in May, 1861, and commanded a division in the Department of the Rappahannock in mid-1862. He served as a member of the military tribunal at the trial of General Fitz-John Porter (1862–1863), but resigned his commission in 1863 to serve as minister to Rome for the next four years.

L

LEE, FITZHUGH (1835–1905)—Confederate Major General. The nephew of Robert E. Lee, and a graduate of West Point, 1856. Lee entered the Confederate army in May, 1861, and served as a staff officer and lieutenant colonel of the cavalry until July, 1862, when he was promoted to brigadier general. He conducted several cavalry raids. He commanded at Kelly's Ford and at Chancellorsville, and was again promoted, in August, 1863, to major general. In 1864, Lee fought in the Virginia campaign, and spent a brief time with Early in Shenandoah. Near the end of the war, he commanded the cavalry of the Army of Northern Virginia.

Following the war, he became governor of Virginia, and returned to the Union army to command a corps in the Spanish-American War. He was considered a hard-hitting cavalry officer, but is best known nationally for his postwar political activities.

LEE, ROBERT EDWARD (1807–1870)— Confederate Commander - in - chief. This Lee was born in Stratford, Westmoreland County, Va., and reared in Alexandria, Va. The son of the famous "Light Horse Harry" Lee, he graduated from West Point in 1829, ranked number two in his class scholastically (with no demerits). Lee served in the army for seventeen years in various commands, while living the life of a Virginia gentleman in his native area. He married Mary Ann Randolph Custis, the great - granddaughter of Martha Washington, in 1831, and they had seven children.

During the Mexican War, he served as a captain in various engineering capacities, following which he worked on the construction of forts around the United States and served as superintendent of West Point. In 1855, he joined the Second Cavalry as a colonel, but was with his troops in Texas only occasionally. He was the Lee who commanded the marine troops in 1859 during the storming of "Brown's Fort" at Harper's Ferry (SEE HARPER'S FERRY).

Although a Southerner, Lee professed little sympathy with secession. In fact, he had freed his own slaves before the Civil War broke out, and was so well thought of by Union officials that he was offered the command of the Union army when war finally came. In early 1861, Lee was made a full colonel, and was offered top rank with the position of commander of the Union armies in April, 1861. He refused the latter rank, and resigned his commission on April 20, 1861, to "fight for Virginia."

Lee served as commander of the

Virginia forces and as military adviser to Jefferson Davis with the rank of general. At this time, he was not the highest ranking officer in the Confederate army, as many think. In July, 1861, he failed to hold the Union invasion of West Virginia, and was reassigned to organize defenses on the Atlantic Coast from November, 1861, until March of the following year. He later returned to assist Davis.

When Joe Johnston was wounded on May 31, 1862, Lee took command of what was to become the Army of Northern Virginia. He kept this command until Appomattox, successfully forestalling and defeating every Union attempt to entrap him until Grant took over the eastern forces. He defeated Hooker, McClellan, Burnsides, Meade, and even Grant, on some occasions. Most believe that, with the resources of men and materials at the disposal of the Northern generals, Lee would have taken Washington in late 1863. At Fredericksburg, he defeated Burnside, and almost destroyed Hooker at Chancellorsville in May, 1863.

Beginning a second Northern invasion—his first had been halted at Antietam in Maryland in 1863—Lee moved this time into Pennsylvania. He was halted again—this time by Meade, at Gettysburg—and forced to again retreat into Virginia where he ran out the year in engagements around Bristoe Station and Mine Run. In the Wilderness campaign of Grant, Lee's forces soundly defeated the Union army as in the past, but were surprised to find that Grant did not quit, but simply moved around the blockading Confederate army to continue to move southward. Following this, Spotsylvania, Cold Harbor, and North Anna were all victories for Lee on the field, but his losses of men and equipment began to tell. Grant was relentlessly moving towards Petersburg. Too late, the Confederate administration made Lee commander-in-chief of all Confederate armies in February, 1865—a move opposed by Davis.

Forced to evacuate Petersburg, April 2–3, 1865, Lee retreated towards Appomattox, and a possible junction with Johnston, who was opposing Sherman along the lower coast. This move was cut off by Grant, and Lee, possibly the greatest stategist in U.S. military history, was forced to surrender at Appomattox Courthouse because of lack of supplies and manpower—and a general disenchantment with the war as expressed by the homefront. The surrender on April 9, 1865, ended Lee's part in the war. After the war, he became president of Washington College, now named Washington and Lee University in his honor.

His name became legend around the nation and the world. Considered a splendid gentleman and an able judge of men, Lee was a profound strategist of the Jomini (q.v.) school, who adapted the West Point-taught strategy to the needs of a mobile army like his own, and made the move pay off. He generally won his battle with inferior numbers and superior maneuvering. His strongest point, perhaps, was his ability to inspire his men to greater effort. His farewell address to his men at Appomattox brought tears to their eyes.

LEE, ROBERT EDWARD, THE FAREWELL ADDRESS OF—April 10, 1865. When Lee appeared at the door of the McLean farmhouse after signing the articles of surrender, a profound silence settled over the normally noisy troops of both sides, and tears stained many hardened cheeks as the leader said, "Men, we have fought through the war together; I have done my best for you; my heart is too full to say more." This was April 9, 1865, and was actually his final word to his troops in person.

The following day, Lee issued his last order :

After four years of arduous service, marked by unsurpassed courage and fortitude, the Army of Northern Virginia has been compelled to yield to overwhelming numbers and resources. I need not tell the survivors of so many hard-fought battles, who have remained steadfast to the last, that I have consented to this result from no distrust of them but, feeling that valor and devotion could accomplish nothing that could compensate for the loss that would have attended the continuation of the contest, I have determined to avoid the useless sacrifice of those whose past services have endeared them to their countrymen. By the terms of the agreement, officers and men can return to their homes and remain there until exchanged. You will take with you the satisfaction that pro-

ceeds from the consciousness of duty faithfully performed; and I earnestly pray that a merciful God will extend to you His blessing and protection. With an increasing admiration of your constancy and devotion to your country, and a grateful remembrance of your kind and generous consideration of myself, I bid you an affectionate farewell.

LEE, STEPHEN DILL (1833–1908)— Confederate Lieutenant General, and a member of the West Point class of 1854. Lee served in Florida and the West before resigning to join the Confederate ranks at Fort Sumter. After fighting in the Peninsular campaign, second Bull Run, and Antietam, he was promoted to the rank of brigadier general. At the end of the Vicksburg campaign, he was again elevated, and held the rank of major general until June, 1864, when he became the youngest lieutenant general in the Confederate army. His participation in the Atlanta and the Nashville campaign earned Lee the command of a corps.

His postwar activities as planter, public figure, and writer earned more plaudits for him. He was considered capable and often *too* daring by his subordinates during the war.

LEXINGTON, Missouri—Here, 12,000 Confederates overran the famous Chicago Irish Brigade of 1,000 members, after an eight-day battle. The Union force, under Colonel James A. Mulligan, surrendered on September 20, 1861, after defense of the town became impossible.

LIBBY PRISON — The Confederate prison at Richmond, Va.

LIGHT BROOKE RIFLE—This weapon was characterized by a three-inch bore which could hurl a ten pound projectile a distance of 3,500 yards. In some instances, a heavy shot took almost fifteen seconds to reach the target, and could actually be seen in flight.

LINCOLN, ABRAHAM (1809–1865)— Union President. Born near Hodgenville, in Hardin County, Ky. His family moved to Spencer County, Ind., in 1816 and to a farm near Decatur, Ill., in 1830. Lincoln served in the Black Hawk War and returned to the Decatur-New Salem area to study surveying and law at the end of the war. In 1842, he married Mary Todd, daughter of a prominent Kentuckian. In 1834, he was elected to the Illinois State Legislature, and served there for four terms. Lincoln left politics in 1848 to resume his law practice. He became a member of the new Republican party in 1856, and received one-hundred and ten votes for the vice-presidential nomination in that party's convention, but this was not enough to give him the second spot on the 1856 ticket. Lincoln became famous through his debates with Stephen A. Douglas in the senatorial race in 1858. Lincoln, who had been a member of the House of Representatives from 1846–1848, met Douglas in a series of debates on the expansion of slavery and the popular sovereignty issue. In the fall election, Douglas defeated Lincoln,

but both profited nationally by the debates. Although the underdog in the 1860 Republican convention, Lincoln was able to win the nomination because of his moderate stand, his many friends, and the skillful maneuvers of his managers, who promised each contesting group a political favor should Lincoln win. Lincoln did not campaign generally, and barely won over his other three opponents in the fall elections, receiving less than half of the total votes cast. He was inaugurated March 4, 1861 (see INAUGURAL ADDRESS, LINCOLN'S FIRST), and was forced to battle a split cabinet throughout his first term because of campaign promises made to various Republican factions during the convention, which made it almost mandatory for certain individuals like Seward, Chase, and Cameron to be appointed to cabinet posts. Yet, Lincoln is said to have ruled his cabinet with an iron hand. He often acted without cabinet or congressional consent or advice, and was called "dictatorial" and "unconstitutional" by some of his opponents. Lincoln's main objective during the war was *not* the ending of slavery as many believe. His consummate goal was the preservation of the union. The Emancipation Proclamation *(q.v.)* did not free a single slave actually, but was a shrewd move to halt recognition of the Confederacy by England and other European nations. This document and the Gettysburg address are considered his greatest works, either written or oral. He defeated General George B. Mc-

Clellan in the 1864 election—an election which Lincoln did not believe he would win because he had both the Abolitionists and the Peace Democrats against him. However, a strong soldier vote carried the election and Lincoln began a second term. Abraham Lincoln was assassinated just five days after Robert E. Lee surrendered at Appomattox. He was shot while sitting in a box at the Ford Theatre in Washington, by actor John Wilkes Booth. He died the next day.

Noted for his ability to take dissident groups and mold them into a working unit, Lincoln skillfully used a "homespun" guise to get his points across. Although of humble, rural origin, Lincoln was far from "homespun" in his later years. He was, instead, a shrewd, ambitious, dynamic politician, who had a complete grasp of a situation and the ability to adapt himself to that situation and use it to his own benefit. He was a keen judge of human nature, a bit too generous and lenient (if his cabinet members are to be believed), and dedicated to the cause of the union. His good acts have been magnified and his faults overlooked in the passage of time, but this is perhaps good, for Lincoln, even with his faults, must loom as one of the greatest of Presidents. Had he lived through the Reconstruction years, perhaps his image would have been a bit tarnished, for his Reconstruction plans were bitterly opposed by his own party. But it is strongly believed by many that he would have succeeded in having at least a part of his program passed had he lived.

His arbitrary acts aroused much opposition, and his orders suspending the privilege of habeas corpus have been questioned down through the years . Yet, there are few who discount his impact upon the American scene.

LOCOMOTIVE CHASE, the Great—(see ANDREWS RAID, the)

LOGAN, JOHN ALEXANDER (1826–1886) — Union Major General. Logan, a veteran of the Mexican War, was a lawyer in civilian life, holding local and state offices prior to 1858, when he entered Congress as a Democrat. He possessed a talent for old-fashioned oratory and was considered very persuasive. Many felt that he was a Southern sympathizer because of some of his congressional stands, but he was actually a strong Union man. He became a colonel of a regiment which he raised and outfitted in Illinois, and fought at Belmont, Fort Donelson, and Vicksburg. After Donelson, he was made a brigadier general, and was promoted to major general after Vicksburg. In the Atlanta fighting, Logan commanded a corps. He later commanded the Army of the Tennessee, but was relieved by Grant, because Sherman still mistrusted Logan's political persuasions (while praising his military ability).

Logan helped organize the Grand Army of the Republic after the war, and served in both the House and the Senate as a Republican. He was considered a "political general," but rated highly for his military ability (a quality very rarely found in "political generals").

LOGAN'S CROSSROADS—(see FISHING CREEK).

LONGSTREET, JAMES (1821–1904)—Confederate Lieutenant General. Longstreet was a graduate of West Point and a veteran of the Mexican War when the Civil War broke out. His 1842 West Point class furnished many of the leading officers in both armies. His rank in the Union army at the start of 1861 was major (in the paymaster's office). He resigned this commission and was made a brigadier general in the Confederate army in June, 1861. After fighting at Bull Run, he was promoted to major general in October, 1861. Longstreet served in the Peninsular campaign, at second Bull Run, and at Antietam. He commanded half of the Army of Northern Virginia as one of Lee's two favorite lieutenants (Jackson was the other). His corps participated in the main part of the defense of Fredericksburg. He was given semi-independent command against Suffolk, Va., and on numerous occasions thereafter.

Following the death of Jackson, he became Lee's principal lieutenant. He was, however, the center of a controversy over the movements during the attack at Gettysburg. He was accused of delaying in his execution of Lee's plans because he disagreed with the strategy. Following this battle, he was sent to Georgia to command. Longstreet served with Bragg at Chickamauga, 1863, but failed in an effort to capture Knoxville as an independent commander. He was severely wounded at the Wilderness, May 6, 1864, but returned to duty in November of that year. After the war, he became an active Republican, and was made commander of the militia in Louisiana. Longstreet was slow to move, but an excellent officer. He was disliked by many Southerners because of his postwar activities.

LOST MOUNTAIN, Georgia—Above Marietta, near Cartersville, Ga. A defensive position during the battle for Atlanta. Here, Johnston held until Sherman's forces threatened to flank the position and move toward Atlanta.

LOVEJOY STATION, Georgia—Below Atlanta, south of Jonesboro, Ga. Here, Hood set up a defense line after moving out of Atlanta.

LOWE, THADDEUS SOBIESKI COULINCOURT (1832–1913)—Union balloonist, Chief of Aeronautics. Lowe is called the "Father of the U.S. Air Force," because of his activities as a military balloonist. He served as chief of aeronautics for the Union, and made his first military observation flight for General McDowell following the first Bull Run. He crashed in enemy territory, but escaped without being injured or captured.

Prior to making this flight, Lowe built the largest balloon in history—the "Great Western"—in preparation for a flight across the Atlantic. He landed in South Carolina in the midst of the uproar which followed the beginning of the war, but escaped capture through assistance received from admirers, and proceded north to join the Union forces. Following his Bull Run flight, Lowe was ordered by President Lincoln to organize a corps of five observation balloons, with the title "Chief of Aeronautics, U.S. Army." This newly created office eventually led to today's U.S. Air Force.

LYNCHBURG, Virginia—Unofficially, the last capital of the Confederacy. The Confederate president, his cabinet members, and other high-ranking officials fled there when Richmond fell to Grant.

LYON, NATHANIEL (1818–1861) — Union captain. Born in Ashford, Conn., Lyon graduated from West Point in 1841, and served in Florida and Mexico prior to the outbreak of the Civil War. He was very active in early western operations. As a captain, he was at the St. Louis arsenal in 1861, and was largely responsible (along with Francis P. Blair) for seizing Camp Jackson from the pro-Southern forces under Frost.

Lyon organized Federal troops in Missouri, and pushed state troops out of Jefferson City and Booneville, Mo., in June, 1861. He fought the Confederates at Wilson's Creek, August 10, 1861, near Springfield, Mo., but was killed in action. His death came as a great blow to the Union cause, for Lyon was considered one of the most brilliant leaders in the West at the time.

M

MCCLELLAN, GEORGE BRINTON (1826–1885) — Union General-in-Chief. Born in Philadelphia, Pa., and finished second in his graduating class at West Point (1846). McClellan studied military affairs in the Crimea during the Crimean War, and is famous for developing the "Mc-Clellan Saddle," a cavalry saddle. He resigned from the army in 1857 to become chief engineer for the Illinois Central Railroad. Later, he became the Illinois Central Railroad vice-president, moving to president of the Ohio and Mississippi Railroad in 1860.

At the outbreak of war, McClellan was given command of all Ohio forces, and promoted to the rank of major general in the regular army (May, 1861) commanding the Department of the Ohio. He was very successful in the Virginia campaign, and was given the command of the Division of the Potomac, and reorganized it into the Army of the Potomac. In November, 1861, McClellan succeeded Winfield Scott as general-in-chief of the Army, and fell under pressure to move on Richmond. His procrastination resulted in his being relieved from command as general-in-chief, March, 1862. He remained, however, in command of the Army of the Potomac until relieved from command and replaced on November 7, 1862. From that time on, he served in minor command capacities until the end of the war.

McClellan relied heavily upon reports brought to him by Allan Pinkerton, whom he had designated as his intelligence chief. Most of this information was faulty, and often led McClellan to believe that he was hopelessly outnumbered.

The Army of the Potomac while under his command was characterized by its spit and polish nature—but also by its failure to win the major battles. It was constantly setting out toward Richmond, only to retreat towards Washington after coming face to face with Lee's force. McClellan was a great organizer, but he lacked the combat knowledge and inclination. His proper place was at a desk. He was intensely egotistical, but greatly loved by his men and the general public.

Before the end of the war, he was the Democratic nominee for President in 1864, but lost the election. He served as governor of New Jersey after the war.

MCCLERNAND, JOHN ALEXANDER (1812–1900)—Union Major General. Born near Hardinsburg, Ky. Admitted to the bar, 1832, and entered Illinois politics as a Jacksonian Democrat. He served in the U.S. House of Representatives from 1843 to 1851, and again from 1859 to 1861. He left Congress to become a brigadier general, and fought at Belmont, Fort Henry, and Fort Donelson before being promoted to major general in March, 1862. A political general, he was strongly criticized by Grant following the battle of Shiloh for his laxness and slowness in following orders.

In October, 1862, he was authorized by Lincoln to gather a force to attack Vicksburg, and did so under the assumption that he would lead the expedition. McClernand was greatly disappointed when Grant assumed personal command. Intensely ambitious, he attempted to set aside Grant, but failed. McClernand commanded a corps in the Vicksburg campaign, and is partly responsible for allowing Pemberton to escape from a trap before the Vicksburg siege began.

Removed from command by Grant in June, 1863, for issuing an unauthorized order criticizing the campaign, he used his influence to regain his command of another corps in the West in February, 1864, but resigned in November of that year. McClernand was more interested in his personal success than in the successful pursuit of the war. His fellow generals criticized him a great deal.

MCDOWELL, IRVIN (1818–1885) — Union Major General. Born in Columbus, Ohio, and graduated from West Point in 1838. Having served in the Mexican War as a staff officer, he continued in this post after that war. By 1856, he had risen to major, but became a brigadier general when the Civil War broke out. He organized the army in front of Washington, D.C., and carried an unprepared army (following orders) toward Manassas Junction after political pressure from civilian politicians forced the move. McDowell was soundly defeated, July 21, 1861, and forced to retreat to Washington.

He was replaced by McClellan, but continued as a major general leading a division in Washington. He commanded a corps in the second Battle of Manassas, August 29–30, 1862, and was again severely criticized—this time for his battle action. Relieved of command, McDowell did no more major fighting after that battle.

He was an able staff officer and a brilliant desk general. However, like most of the early Union command choices, he was not suited for the battlefield because of his limited experience. McDowell was a serious, devoted officer, but not very brilliant in actual battle, and prone to make mistakes under pressure.

MCPHERSON, JAMES BIRDSEYE (1828–1864)—Union Major General. Born in Sandusky, County, Ohio; died northeast of Atlanta, Ga. A graduate of West Point, 1853 (at the head of his class), he went from first lieutenant to major general from 1861 to 1863. He became an aide to Halleck as a captain in August, 1861, and a brigadier of volunteers by 1862. His troops re-enforced Rosecrans at Corinth. He became a major general (January, 1863) and commanded a corps. Serving in the Vicksburg campaign, he was given command of the Army of Tennessee in March, 1864, under Sherman. He fought at Kennesaw Mountain in the march on Atlanta. McPherson was killed July 22, 1864, near Atlanta while heading toward the sound of battle from a point near Marietta, Ga. He had

been conferring with Sherman during the night. Hardee's troops were responsible for his death after he had left the Howard House to the northeast of Atlanta. He was replaced by O. O. Howard. He had failed to follow through on his victory at Resaca that might have crushed the Confederate cavalry. One of the ablest generals in the Union army, McPherson was known as the "Whiplash of the Army," and was greatly respected by soldiers of both sides.

MCWITTIER, M. H.—(see ARIZONA, the Confederate Territory of)

MAGRUDER, JOHN BANKHEAD (1810–1871)—Confederate Major General. A West Point graduate, 1830, Magruder served in Texas, Florida, and Mexico before being made a regular army captain and brevet colonel just before the start of the Civil War. He became a full colonel in the Confederate army, May, 1861. Magruder held commands on the Peninsula in Virginia, and was promoted to brigadier general in June, 1861, after the fight at Big Bethel. He became a major general in the fall of 1861.

At the defense of Yorktown, Magruder bluffed McClellan into believing that the Confederates (numbering only 12,000 men) actually outnumbered a far superior Union force. He had trouble with Lee as the result of mistakes made during the Seven Days campaign, and was subsequently sent to Texas to command that district. He captured Galveston in January, 1863. (see GALVESTON BAY)

Magruder was more concerned with the social benefits of being an officer than in the actual fighting of a war. He was called "Prince John" because of his dress and manner. A rather quick-tempered individual, he was willing to fight, but reluctant to take orders which were not to his liking. Magruder displayed spots of brilliance, but can not be considered a really great commander.

MAHONE, WILLIAM (1826–1895)— Confederate Major General. Mahone was a graduate of Virginia Military Institute, 1847, and worked as a railroad engineer before taking over the Norfolk District as a colonel in the army. He joined the Army of Northern Virginia (or what was to become that army) at the outbreak of the war, and was promoted to brigadier general by November 16, 1861. Mahone served with that army throughout the war, and successfully defended the Crater at Petersburg— one of his feats of military brilliance. He was made a major general following the Petersburg engagement, and ended the war with that rank. He was well-liked by his men and fellow officers. Mahone became a railroad executive after the war, and later a U.S. senator.

MANASSAS, the Battle of—(see BULL RUN, the Battle of)

MALLORY, STEPHEN RUSSELL (1813–1873)—Confederate Secretary of the Navy. Born in Trinidad while his father was working there for the government, Mallory was reared in Key West, Fla. His early education was limited, but he studied law on his own, and rose to great heights in Southern political circles prior to the war. He was elected to the U.S. Senate in 1851 and 1857, and served as chairman of the naval affairs committee. He left the Senate when Florida seceded, and was appointed secretary of the non-existent Confederate navy in February, 1861. He held that office until the end of the war.

Mallory was one of the few cabinet members who was able to avoid trouble with Jefferson Davis. He is referred to as "ingenious," and his administrative ability was unquestionable.

MANNING, PEYTON T.—Confederate officer. Chief of Ordnance for Longstreet.

MEADE, GEORGE GORDON (1815–1872) — Union Major General. Meade was born in Cadiz, Spain, during the time when his father was U.S. naval agent to Spain for the United States. He graduated from West Point in 1835, and served in Florida and in Mexico as an engineer. At the outbreak of the war, he was a captain in the topographical engineers, and was appointed brigadier general of volunteers in August, 1861. Meade commanded a brigade in the Seven Days campaign, and was badly wounded there. He fought at second Bull Run, South Mountain, and Antietam. By November, 1862, Meade had risen to the rank of major general and had command of a corps. He served in this capacity at both Fredericksburg and Chancellorsville.

On June 28, 1863, he replaced Hooker as commander of the Army of the Potomac, although he did not want the appointment. He promptly settled down to stop the invasion of Pennsylvania, and was victorious at Gettysburg. However, he was criticized for allowing the defeated Confederates to get safely back into Virginia without launching a counterattack against them. Meade nominally commanded the Army of the Potomac until the end of the war, but Grant actually directed the field operations for the latter portion of the Appomattox campaign. Meade fought at Rapidan and Mine Run, and was made a regular army major general in 1864. He commanded several departments after the war.

Stubborn and not overly brilliant, Meade made an outstanding commander under Grant's style of fighting. He worked well with Grant, but was not extremely popular with other officers or the enlisted men.

MECHANICSVILLE, the Battle of— June 26, 1862. Part of the Seven Days campaign. A Confederate force under General Robert E. Lee's command and led by General Thomas "Stonewall" Jackson struck Union forces commanded by General Fitz-John Porter at Mechanicsville. The Confederates had turned McClellan's flank and were able to strike Porter with a superior force. The Union

army outnumbered the Confederates 100,000 to 85,000 but the Southerners were still jubilant over an earlier victory in the Shenandoah Valley, and had confidence in their leader, General Jackson.

Accurate figures are not available for the campaign, but estimates give the Union 1,735 killed, 6,055 missing and 8,065 wounded. About 90,000 union soldiers took part in the battle. Lee engaged all of his 85,000 men, and lost 3,480 killed, 16,265 wounded and 875 missing during the total campaign. There are no accurate individual statistics available for the individual battles of the Seven Days campaign. This battle is also known as the battle of Beaver Dam Creek.

MERRIMAC, The—A Union frigate which was sunk by the naval force at the Norfolk Navy Yard in 1861, but was raised by the Confederates and renamed the "Virginia." The Confederates converted the vessel into an ironclad, mounting fifty guns, and started her northward hoping to smash the North's wooden ships. However, the North countered with the ironclad "Monitor," and the two engaged in a classic struggle off Hampton Roads, Va., in March, 1862. Neither ship was able to claim a clean victory. The newly christened "Virginia" continued to be known by its former name "The Merrimac" throughout its short naval career. Her crew scuttled her to keep the North from recapturing her.

MERRETT, WESLEY (1834 – 1910) — Union Major General. Merritt was a member of the surrender team which Grant assigned to meet Lee's Commissioners at Appomattox. He graduated from West Point in 1860, and rose to the post of commander of the cavalry of the Army of Shenandoah before joining Grant in the final stages of the war.

MINIE BALL, the—Throughout the war, the greatest number of wounds were inflicted by the well-known minie ("Minnie") ball fired from either a Springfield musket or a .577 Enfield. Minie balls were wrapped in a paper catridge containing powder, which had to be bitten off before being stuffed into the weapon. The ball was a conical bullet with a hollow base, made of soft lead which expanded on impact (similar to the "dum-dum" bullet of today), causing a large, ragged wound. In principle, it was very similar to the dum-dum in that it entered heavily and emerged leaving a larger, more ragged wound which bled profusely. The minie was approximately one inch long and differed in caliber. The North used a .58 caliber minie, while the South used the .577. Later in the war, the minie was replaced by more solid bullets which did not splatter upon contact.

MISSIONARY RIDGE, the Battle of— November 25, 1863. After Hooker had forced the Confederates to evacuate Lookout Mountain, Grant moved on Bragg with a force of 56,000 men. Bragg, recuperating from two major defeats, still had 46,000 men at his disposal. The Con-

federate force had moved to the second of the key heights in this area approximately twenty-four miles east of Chattanooga, Tenn., and actually held a position as favorable for defense as any held during the entire war. They had entrenched along the crest of a five-mile long, 500-foot high ridge and were dug in deeply.

Sherman assaulted the position first, but the north end of the ridge proved too tough for his forces to take. Had he succeeded there, Grant would have been able to cut off Bragg's supply line and could have settled down to regular siege procedures. When Grant saw that Sherman's forces were in danger, he sent Thomas to stage a demonstration against the first line of Southern trenches. Thomas sent 20,000 men with instructions to create a diversion which would relieve some of the pressure from Sherman. The troops, after clearing the first trenches, continued up the hill in a spontaneous movement (without orders) and carried the top of the ridge. The Eleventh Ohio was conspicuous in this action. When questioned about this movement without orders, Thomas is quoted as having said, "When those fellows get started, all hell can't stop them."

The Union lost 5,800 men in the encounter, and the Confederates lost 6,600. Bragg was forced to retreat to Georgia, with three consecutive major defeats to his credit. It was at this point that Grant left the area to assume command of all of the Union armies, turning the western sector over to Sherman.

MISSISSIPPI, the Army of—Confederate. Formed in March, 1862, under General Pierre G. T. Beauregard. This was a major army of the Confederacy until the death of A. S. Johnston after Shiloh (Pittsburgh Landing). Beauregard was succeeded by Johnston, but resumed command of the army after Johnston's death from a wound received in the Shiloh fighting. The army later merged with that of Kentucky to form the Army of Tennessee in November, 1862.

MISSISSIPPI, the Army of—Union. Organized in February, 1862, and commanded by Major General John Pope. This army fought at Island No. 10 under Pope, and followed his directions until June 26, 1862, when Pope was called east.

Major General W. S. Rosecrans assumed command from that time until October 26, 1862, when that army was discontinued. The army took part in the battles of Iuka and Corinth before being disbanded.

MISSOURI, the Army of Southwest—Union. Created in December, 1861, and active in most of the battles in Missouri and Arkansas, including Pea Ridge. This army was in existence only one year, and was then merged into the Department of Missouri in late 1862.

MORGAN, JOHN HUNT (1825–1864)—Confederate Brigadier General. Known as "Morgan the Raider," this successful rebel scout received his early education at Lexington, Ky., and served in the Mexican War before joining the Confederate army when Civil War broke out. He rapidly rose to the rank of captain. In April, 1862, he began his career as a raider, and was appointed to the rank of colonel. By December, 1862, he had risen to brigadier general. His most famous raid was one which began on July 2, 1863, when he and his Second Kentucky Cavalry rode out of Burkesville, Ky., with orders to raid behind the Union lines in order to set up a diversion which would allow Bragg to withdraw his troops from Tullahoma to Chattanooga. The raiders left Kentucky (contrary to orders received by Morgan) and crossed the Ohio River into Ohio. Running into thousands of militia and regular Union cavalry, Morgan continued his trek north into Indiana and northern Ohio, hitting East Liverpool, Ohio, in an attempt to gain the Pennsylvania border.

An aroused Union cavalry was pushing the raider unit hard, and Morgan was forced to surrender his remaining 300 men to Captain Edwin Burbick—who was, at the time, already a prisoner of Morgan's —under the condition that parole would be given to each of his men. The Ninth Kentucky cavalry (Union) refused to honor Burbick's terms, and carried Morgan and his men to Cincinnati for trial. The Chicago *Tribune* conceded, "The capture of the raiders releases five times their numbers of Federal troops who were engaged in the business of catching them."

Instead of being put into a regular prison camp, Morgan and his men were put into the Ohio State Penitentiary at Columbus, Ohio, and treated as common criminals. On November 27, 1863, Morgan and six of his captains escaped via a rope fashioned of bedclothes. They found their way back to the Confederate lines, and Morgan assumed command of the Department of Southwest Va. On September 3, 1864, Morgan attacked Union forces near Knoxville, Tenn. While resting for the night, he was surrounded at Greeneville, Tenn. and was killed while trying to escape.

Morgan's raids covered five states and hit as far north as the Ohio-Pennsylvania border.

MOSBY, JOHN SINGLETON (1833–1916)—Confederate Colonel. Known as "The Gray Ghost," Mosby and his men were among the most famous of Confederate raiders. He enlisted in the cavalry at the start of the war, after having practiced law in Virginia. Mosby began his independent operations following successful service on Stuart's staff during the Peninsular campaign, at second Bull Run, and at Antietam. He started operating in Laudain County, Va., with only a few men in early 1863. It was here that he earned the sobriquet, "Gray Ghost." With a very elusive force of rangers, he was very successful in harassing Union lines, and his operation grew. On numerous occasions, Mosby refused command over regular troops in order to continue to lead his rangers. The troops were officially called the Forty-third Virginia Cavalry.

Mosby's major coup came when he led 29 men through six Union regiments and a brigade (the Second Vermont) to Fairfax, Va., in a move to capture a colonel who had called Mosby a horse thief. Instead, he captured Union General Edwin H. Stoughton (a former classmate of Fitzhugh Lee's), 30 other prisoners, and 58 horses. The raiders stayed in the town for an hour without firing a shot. When the raid ended, it was found that the "Gray Ghost" had taken 29 men twenty-five miles behind and through the Union lines, captured a total of 100 prisoners (with pickets captured on the way back to Confederate lines), and returned to the Southern lines with one general and two captains among his prisoners. About 50 prisoners escaped enroute, but the column reached the Confederate lines without interference. Lee called it "a feat unparalleled in the war." Mosby rose from lieutenant to major in two weeks because of this feat.

Mosby's rangers operated under the partisan ranger law which allowed the raiders to split captured public property among themselves. Mosby carried four guns most of the time. His area of operation came to be known as "Mosby's Confederacy," and extended from northern Virginia south of the Potomac, and east of the Blue Ridge Mountains.

After Union General Custer executed six of Mosby's rangers for their part in the raids, Mosby executed seven Union prisoners in reprisal. This ended the execution of Mosby's rangers.

Mosby disbanded his eight companies of men when Lee surrendered, but was not personally pardoned until February, 1866. After the war, he resumed his law practice, and was appointed consul to Hong Kong in 1878. He remained there until 1885 when he returned to serve as land agent in Colorado, and as assistant attorney for the Department of Justice. He died in Washington, D.C., at the age of 83.

"MOSBY'S CONFEDERACY" — (see MOSBY, JOHN)

MOSES, RAPHAEL J.—Confederate Commissary Officer. Moses is called by many Southerners a traitor to the Confederacy because of his part in the handling of the Confederate treasury in the last days of the war. A native of Charleston, Moses served as chief commissary officer for Longstreet, and was given a large sum (alternately described as $35,000 and $40,000) by Jefferson Davis during the administrator's flight through Washington, Ga., in May, 1865. This sum was supposed to have been used to purchase food for the injured Confederate veterans who would be ill and needy since the breakdown of communications lines. Moses claimed that he turned the money, which was in silver bullion, over to the Federal provost general in Augusta for that purpose, but the money still remains unaccounted for, with both sides blaming the other for stealing the funds.

There is an official Confederate order showing that Moses was given the money by Davis, but there is neither a Federal record of the disposition or receipt of the funds, nor was Moses able to produce a receipt from the Augusta provost which would show that he had turned the money over as he claimed.

MOUNTAIN DEPARTMENT, the Army of the—Union. Organized under Major General John C. Fremont to operate against the Confederate General Thomas "Stonewall" Jackson. Jackson was victorious at both McDowell and Cross Keys against this army. In June, 1862, the army was discontinued.

"MUD MARCH," the—This term refers to the march made by the Army of the Potomac along the banks of the James River in a futile attempt to cross north of Lee's army during the rainy season. The move resulted in the loss of wagons, equipment, and soldiers because of the freezing rain and deep mire along the bank. The Confederates relaxed in the relative comfort of their defenses and watched the bedraggled Union forces return to the Washington area cold, disgusted, and defeated.

N

NAPOLEON, the—A cannon. The weapon was capable of firing more than one kind of shot, and could be used according to the tactical situation. It was a smoothbore piece, twelve-pounder, with a fairly accurate scope. The Southerners liked this weapon because it fitted into their ammunition-shy program. It was used by both sides of the war.

NASHVILLE, Tennessee—Capital of Tennessee. This city was fought for throughout the war, but the major attack came in December, 1864. On December 15, Thomas came out of his entrenchments and pushed the Confederate force back along the Franklin and Granny White pikes towards Overton Hill. Hood's force numbered about 23,000 men able to answer muster, while George Thomas and Schofield combined a force of over 55,000 men. Thomas had fortified the city during the two weeks before the fighting actually began (Hood had arrived outside of the city the first week of December).

On December 16, Thomas attempted to hit Overton Hill again, but the Union forces were thrown back. At this point, forces under Darius Couch and John McArthur stormed the hill. The collapse of Hood's left and center exposed the right, commanded by Stephen Lee, to the danger of being overrun. Only the coming of a heavy rain allowed Hood to retreat toward Franklin without being completely crushed. He resigned his commission within a month's time. (see HOOD)

"NASHVILLE," the — Confederate raider. This raider was engaged in raiding the commerce lines of the Union merchant fleet during the war. The vessel was considered one of the best of its kind. A now-famous water color sketch of the "Nashville" run-

ning the blockade in April, 1862, was painted by the Earl of Dunmore.

NAST, THOMAS (1840–1902) — Reporter-Artist. Nast, working for *Harpers*, viewed the parade of the Seventh New York Regiment down Broadway on April 19, 1861, and captured the pomp and gala atmosphere on canvas. The picture lives as one of the masterpieces of the time. The work was enlarged in oil by Nast eight years later, and is now in the Seventh Regiment Armory in New York City.

NEGRO INSURRECTION PLOT IN ARKANSAS, the—June, 1861. In Monroe County, Arkansas, a plot was uncovered among the slaves to murder all the white men in the county and try for freedom. A number of Negroes were arrested, and three were hanged (among them a girl). It is generally conceded that the size of the plot was "ballooned" to add to the propaganda that the "Negroes will take over the county." The plot was similar to that of Denmark Vesy, but was not as well planned.

NEGRO TROOPS, the use of—The Negro was originally used by Federal commanders to construct roads, build bridges, cook, and serve officers. When the numbers of refugees magnified to such an extent that even this use of the former slave had to be discounted, the government (realizing the potential of this vast reserve of manpower) authorized the arming of former slaves or freed Negroes into military units. The regiments were to be composed of Negroes, officered by whites, and to be re-garded as troops of the line, ready for field duty if needed.

The white troops objected. They did not mind fighting the war, but they were not about to fight it side-by-side with a lowly former slave. Race prejudice was more common in the North at that time than it is today, and very few of the Union soldiers looked upon the Negroes as equals. However, the fact that the use of the Negroes opened up the ranks for promotions a bit more, soothed the fears of many of the non-commissioned officers and young second lieutenants. Even privates were commissioned to take command of these regiments as lieutenants and captains, since the white officers declined the positions.

By 1863, the North was anxiously recruiting Negroes to serve on front line duty. The use of these troops became so popular that abolitionists, always looking for instances of abuse of former slaves, raised the cry that these people were being used as "cannon-fodder." The number of Negroes in Union uniforms reached as high as 150,000 during the war. Most were on garrison duty only, but many saw front line action in 1863, 1864, and 1865.

Major Martin R. Delany, a gradu-ate of Harvard Medical School, broke the officer barrier and became the first Negro officer to hold a field command (see DELANY, MARTIN R.).

Of these combat troops, General Benjamin Butler said, "I knew that they would fight more desperately than any white troops in order to prevent capture, because they knew . . . if captured, they would be returned to slavery." This was the lesser of two horrible fates. After the Fort Pillow Massacre, Southerners took the "no quarter" attitude to-wards Negro troops, and slaughtered them rather than take them pris-oners. Negro troops were used extensively by Butler, a rabid abol-itionist.

Negro troops were not paid on the same scale as their white counter-parts, and this raised an issue for the abolitionists to grasp in the late-1864 period.

NEW ORLEANS, the capture of—April 24, 1862. Under Rear Admiral David G. Farragut, a fleet of war-ships, complimented by eighteen or nineteen mortar schooners, hit the forts defending New Orleans. Al-though the Confederates used mor-tars, fire rafts, and rams, the Union force bypassed the forts, wrecked the defending crafts, and forced New Orleans, Baton Rouge, and even Natchez to surrender. The Union had control of all of the Mississippi except the Vicksburg area. Forts Jackson and St. Philip fell with New Orleans.

NORTH CAROLINA, the secession of— May 20, 1861. When Lincoln issued a call for 75,000 men to "put down the insurrection," this hastened the secession of Virginia and North Carolina. Lincoln's blockading order would have affected North Carolina anyway, and the state decided to cast its lot with that of South Carolina, Alabama, Mississippi, Florida, Virginia, Arkansas, and Tennessee (states which had already seceded).

NOVELTY IRON WORKS, the—New York. This iron works specialized in the manufacturing of boilers and engines for river steamers, but was responsible for turning out the revolving turret of the famous ironclad, "Monitor." Known as the "Novelty Iron Works," it also was listed as the "Stillman Allen & Company Works." The shop had been in operation for a number of years prior to the war.

O

OAK HILL, the Battle of (see WILSON'S CREEK, the Battle of).

OFFICERS OF THE UNION, Top Military:

President and Commander-in-Chief: Abraham Lincoln, Mar. 4, 1861 to Apr. 15, 1865. Andrew Johnson, Apr. 15, 1865 to Mar. 4, 1869.

Secretary of War: Simon Cameron, Mar. 4, 1861 to Jan. 14, 1862. Edwin M. Stanton, Jan. 15, 1862 to May 28, 1868.

General-in-Chief of the Armies: Winfield Scott, Brevet-Lt. Gen. June, 1841 to Nov. 5, 1861. George B. McClellan, Maj. Gen. Nov. 6, 1861 to Mar. 11, 1862. No commander between Mar. 11, 1862 and July 11, 1862. Henry W. Halleck, Maj. Gen. July 11, 1862 to Mar. 12, 1864. Ulysses Grant, Lt. Gen. Mar. 12, 1864 to Mar. 4, 1869 (promoted to full general, July 25, 1866).

Note: Halleck became chief of staff on March 12, 1864, and held that post until April 19, 1865.

O'LAUGHLIN, MICHAEL (1838–1867)—Conspirator. O'Laughlin was a Baltimore, Md., clerk who got involved in the Surratt plot to kidnap a number of high government officials (including the President) during the latter part of the war. He refused to take part in the plan when he found out that the schemers planned to murder the officials instead of simply kidnapping them. He received a prison sentence for his part in the plot which resulted in the death of Lincoln and the assault upon Seward.

"OLD OSAWATOMIE"—(See BROWN JOHN.)

"OLD STRAIGHT" — (See STEWART, ALEXANDER P.)

OLUSTEE, Florida, the Attack on— A Union expedition of white and Negro troops attempted to take a section of Florida early in 1864, and met defeat at the hands of the Confederates in February of that year. The victory would have been of no importance to the Union, and the fight was simply a waste of manpower, in a sector of the country which had no valid strategic importance.

ONE-TENTH PLAN, LINCOLN'S — This Reconstruction measure proposed by Lincoln in 1864 would have allowed any seceded state to return to the

Union fold by simply having at least one tenth of its eligible voters set up a loyal government and declare that government loyal to the Union. The Congress would then recognize that government as the legal government of the state. The proposal was turned down by the U.S. legislators.

ORCHARD KNOB, Tennessee—Situated to the front of Missionary Ridge, outside of Chattanooga, Tenn.

ORDER 191 — Confederate battle order. The famous "lost order" from Lee to his commanders describing in detail the battle plan for the invasion of Maryland. A copy of this order fell into the hands of Union General McClellan, but he procrastinated for an entire day before taking action on this information.

The order, allegedly found in a meadow by a Union soldier, was wrapped around three cigars, and was obtained only because the soldier noticed the cigars. The loss of this order by the unknown courier resulted directly in the defeat of Antietam for the Confederate forces and the end of their invasion of Maryland.

By the order, McClellan was informed that Lee had split his force into three parts, but the Union leader failed to direct his army against either of the three sections before Lee found that the order was missing and began to pull his forces together.

OX HILL, the Battle of—(See CHAN-TILLY, VA.)

P

PAINE, LEWIS (1846–1865)—One of the eight accused assassins involved in the plot to kill the top Union government officials. Lincoln was killed by John Wilkes Booth, and Paine was assigned to kill Secretary of State Seward, but bungled the job, only wounding the Union official. He was tried, found guilty, and hanged.

PARKER, ELY—(See DONEHOGAWA).

PARROTT, the—A cannon. One of the larger siege guns, used by the Confederate forces mainly. Frequently this gun blew up when fired at long range for too long a period of time. It was capable of hurling a 100-pound projectile four miles. It was a tremendously heavy weapon.

PELHAM, JOHN (1838–1863)—Confederate Major. Called the "Boy Major" because of his youth, Pelham was attending West Point when war broke out, and resigned to join the Confederate army. He formed a battery of horse artillery as a captain under Stuart, and won fame at the Seven Days campaign. As a result, Pelham was promoted to major. He held vital points at both Antietam and second Bull Run, and was with Stuart on his raids in Loudoun County, Va. He was also with Stuart at Fredericksburg, where his unit again held a crucial point against overwhelming odds. Pelham was killed at Kelly's Ford, March 17,

1863. He was a bit rash, but a daring leader. He was also called the "Gallant Pelham."

His action at Fredericksburg was his most notable. There, with a Blakely Rifle and a twelve-pound smoothbore, Pelham held an entire Union force in check on December 13, 1862. Until his death, he served as Stuart's chief of horse artillery.

Some list his birthplace as Cane Creek, Ala. He actually died at Culpeper, Va., where he was carried after being wounded at Kelly's Ford. He carried a Bible given him by Confederate spy Belle Boyd, which bore the inscription :

"I know thou are loved by another now,
I know thou wilt never be mine . . ."

Of him, Jackson once said, "With Pelham on each flank, I believe I could whip the world." Pelham boasted that he had never lost a gun, and was always allowed to select his own spots on any battlefield under Jackson's command.

PEACE AND CONSTITUTIONAL SOCIETY, the—This anti-Confederate society came into being in Van Buren County, Ark., in late 1861, and was formed by men who were against Arkansas' move to leave the Union. In late 1861, a number of members of this secret society were arrested and the information was released that there were several hundred members of this society in Van Buren County alone.

According to Dr. Georgia Tatum in her work *Disloyalty in the Con-federacy*, p. 25, there were about "seventeen hundred in the whole state." Each member was sworn to aid the other members in distress, to encourage desertion, and to attempt to build a Federal army in Arkansas. Death was decreed as the penalty for divulging secrets of the organization. This society flourished in the northwestern part of the state where the residents were almost solidly against secession. (See PEACE SOCIETIES.)

PEACE SOCIETIES—From the organization of the first peace society within the Confederacy—the Peace and Constitutional Society of Arkansas—to the well organized and extremely active organizations which existed in Alabama, Tennessee, Georgia, Mississippi, and Florida, peace societies played an annoyingly vital part in the move to get the South back into the Union and out of the war.

In the fall of 1861, it was revealed that a peace society existed in Van Buren County, Ark. This was the first inkling that such subversive organizations were in operation. The Arkansas group is believed to have been the first. Actually, there were only three major peace societies : the two mentioned above, and one known as the Order of Heroes of America *(q.v.)*, which was founded in North Carolina and eastern Tennessee, extending even into western South Carolina and parts of southwest Virginia.

Very little was known about these societies until around 1863 when the effects of their anti-war sentiment began to be felt in the deep South. They performed (under cover) the same functions basically that the Copperheads performed in the North, with the added inducement of a "secret" order. The societies encouraged desertion from the armies, asked home front family members to refuse to serve, and even called upon mothers to write to their boys to "come home." The secret societies had handshakes, passwords, and signs. In some of the more widely distributed orders, members did not know each other, and signs varied.

According to Dr. Tatum's book, the societies even permeated the ranks of active duty soldiers, and Federal pickets were said to have honored Confederate secret signs and passwords when the person was able to prove himself a member of the society. Dr. Tatum writes that,, "If in prison, the word 'Washington' repeated four times would secure release within twenty-four hours, if guarded by the faithful."

New members were initiated into the peace societies just as into fraternal orders of less secret societies. (See SPECIFIC SOCIETIES.)

PEACE SOCIETY, THE—This was perhaps the widest in coverage of any peace society of its kind, extending through Alabama, east Tennessee, Georgia, Mississippi, and parts of Florida. It had passwords, grips and signs which differed a bit from state to state and sector to sector, but was loosely united by common interest. Because of its wide distribution, the effects of this society were felt more among the various military units than any other society of its kind. Men who had been part of other lesser secret peace societies joined this group once they were inducted into the military service, where they came in contact with peace society members from other parts of the Confederacy. Its main function was similar to that of other peace societies (q.v.).

PEMBERTON, JOHN CLIFFORD (1814–1881)—Confederate Lieutenant General. Born in Philadelphia, Pa., and a graduate of West Point in 1837, Pemberton fought in Florida, in Mexico, and in the West before the outbreak of the Civil War. He married a Virginia woman, and (despite his Northern birth) joined the Confederacy when war broke out. The Southerners were suspicious of him because of his Northern background, and the army officials confined his activities to organizational work in Virginia in the early stages of the war. However, by February, 1862, he was promoted to major general in command of South Carolina, Georgia and Florida. In October of that year, he was again promoted, to lieutenant general, and given command of the depot along the Mississippi.

Pemberton defended Vicksburg during the siege, and attempted to surrender his fortress on July 3rd instead of July 4th, when he learned it was rumored that Grant was simply waiting until that holiday to march into the city. Prior to the siege, Grant had defeated Pemberton near Jackson, but Pemberton outfoxed McClernand at Big Black River and retreated to the safety of the city of Vicksburg. Following the fall of Vicksburg, Pemberton resigned his rank to become a lieutenant colonel of the artillery for the duration of the war. Southerners blamed him for the fall of Vicksburg.

PENINSULAR CAMPAIGN, the—A series of skirmishes and battles involving 105,000 Union and 90,000 Confederate troops and extending from just southeast of Richmond over the entire area covered between the James and York Rivers. General McClellan engaged Confederate Generals J. E. Johnston and Robert E. Lee throughout the campaign.

McClellan, never enthusiastic about the campaign, moved his troops in his characteristically cautious manner up the peninsula, giving the Confederates adequate time to prepare defenses and plan their operation at a site of their own choosing. Throughout the campaign, Lee was able to dictate when and where the battles would be fought. Yorktown, Va., fell before McClellan's troops without a fight on May 3, 1862, and the campaign (which actually started April 4) was underway full scale. Williamsburg fell on May 5th.

The tide turned in favor of the Confederacy on May 31, when Lee caught Sheridan with his force split on both sides of the flooded river at Seven Pines (Seven Oaks). Johnston was wounded, and Lee took command of the Army of Northern Virginia. He immediately sent J. E. B. Stuart on a raid of Union supplies which is known as "Stuart's Ride." Stuart completely circled the McClellan forces, raising havoc as he went.

Lee recalled Jackson from the Shenandoah Valley and engaged McClellan at Mechanicsville on June 26, Gaines Mill on June 27, Savage's Station on June 29, Frayser's Farm (Glendale) on June 30, and Malvern Hill on July 1st. His assaults forced McClellan back across the peninsula to the upper James River. Union casualties totaled 16,000; Confederate losses soared to 20,000. McClellan failed miserably, but he did inflict losses upon Lee which could not be afforded by the Confederacy at that time. Lee emerged as the outstanding military leader on the eastern front, and permanent commander of the Army of Northern Virginia.

PICKETT, GEORGE EDWARD (1825–1875)—Confederate Major General. An 1846 graduate of the Military Academy, Pickett finished last in his class. He served in Mexico and in the Northwest territory before accepting a commission as colonel in the Confederate army when war broke out. By January, 1862, he had risen to brigadier general.

Pickett gained fame at Seven Days, during which campaign he was wounded. He was promoted to major general in October, 1862, and commanded at Fredericksburg and in the Suffolk campaign. His most famous day was when his force led other divisions in a wild, reckless "charge" (really a half-trot, and often a walk) against the strong right center of the Union line at Gettysburg, July 3, 1863. Pickett later commanded the Department of Virginia and North Carolina. He fought at Five Forks near Richmond, April 1, 1865, but, after this battle, was relieved of command for "dereliction of duty" during the attack.

PICKETT'S CHARGE — July 3, 1863. Pickett commanded three brigades which he sent forward in two main lines along the right flank of forces under General James Pettigrew. The force advanced about 500 yards from a swale in which they had assembled, did a left oblique (which brought them closer to Pettigrew) and dipped into a hollow about midway between the two armies where they formed while Confederate artillery shelled the Union artillery positions.

Coming out of the hollow, Pickett learned that the Union guns had only stopped firing in order to conserve ammunition, and the Confederates faced a withering fire at almost point-blank range. The charge, actually made at a half-trot (and made walking at many points) caused such extensive damage to the Confederate force that Pickett (safely back at Gordi's farmhouse well to the rear while the action was taking place) was forced to send his reserves into action. The Confederates breached the Union line at three points, and (had the reserves not already been committed) re-enforcements might have carried the battle for the Southerners. Hand-to-hand fighting ensued, and the tired Southerners were soon pushed back by rallying Federal forces. This ended, for all practical purposes, the Battle of Gettysburg. Lee withdrew southward.

In the charge, over three-fourths of the 4,800 men under Pickett fell. All of the field officers except one were downed, and the Southern invasion of Pennsylvania was ended.

PIGEON'S RANCH—(See GLORIETTA, the Battle of.)

PILLOW, the massacre at Fort—(See FORT PILLOW, the massacre at.)

PINKERTON, ALLAN (1819–1884)— Head of the Union Secret Service under McClellan. A native of Glasgow, Scotland, Pinkerton had gained a reputation as a detective as a result of a spectacular capture of a gang of counterfeiters. He operated one of Chicago's underground railway stations as an abolitionist, and became the city's first private detective, operating his own agency. This agency was the first of its kind in the world.

Under McClellan, he organized a secret service branch for the Union, but gave such erroneous information and overestimates of the Confederates' strength that he seriously hampered the Peninsular campaign. A reluctant McClellan used these figures to excuse his failures to attack the enemy, claiming that he was "outnumbered."

When McClellan was removed

from command, Pinkerton resigned and returned to work as a private detective. His private practice was highly successful, but his Civil War work was sketchy and not to be depended upon. He did little or no good for the Union cause in his role as a spy.

PITTSBURG LANDING, Tennessee—(See SHILOH, the Battle of.)

POLK, LEONIDAS (1806–1864)—Confederate Major General. Because of the influence of a friendly chaplain, Polk resigned his commission from West Point (Class of 1837) to study theology, and became an Episcopal priest in 1831. He rose to the status of bishop of the Southwest in 1838, following a tour of the sector as missionary bishop. He became the bishop of Louisiana in 1841, and founded Sewanee (the University of the South) in 1860 at Sewanee, Tennessee.

Polk accepted the rank of major general when Jefferson Davis called upon him to join the Confederacy in June, 1861. He fortified Columbus, Ky., and defended the Mississippi while serving under Johnston. Polk fought at Belmont, Shiloh, Perrysville and Murfreesboro as a corps commander. He had difficulties with Bragg, and was accused of being slow to attack at Chickamauga.

In June, 1864, Polk was killed in the fight at Pine Mountain near Marietta, Ga., while taking part in the defense of Atlanta. He was described as a competent yet not a great leader, whose religious convictions had a great influence upon men serving under him. His near fanatical zeal could have done much for the Confederacy had he directed it into a military vein.

POPE, JOHN (1822–1892) — Union Major General. Pope, a topographical engineer prior to the Mexican War, was an 1841 graduate of West Point. Although only a captain when the Civil War broke out, he was promptly promoted to brigadier general of volunteers after the fighting began.

His forces captured Madrid, Mo., while he was commander of the Army of the Mississippi. Island No. 10, a fortified island on the Mississippi near New Madrid, fell to his force in April, 1862. By this time, Pope was a major general (March, 1862). He was called east to command the forces scattered around Washington. These forces later became the Army of Virginia, and still later, the Army of the Potomac.

Because of a very poor showing at second Bull Run (which saw Union forces in rout to Washington) Pope was relieved of command in September, 1862, and his army dissolved. He spent the remainder of the war handling Indian trouble in the Northwest. He showed great ability in his western duties, and it is thought that his poor showing at Bull Run was to be attributed to overconfidence.

PORTER, DAVID DIXON (1813–1891)— Union rear admiral. The son of a naval officer, Porter followed his father to sea without the benefit of too much formal education, and became a midshipman at the age of sixteen. He served in the Mexican War doing coastal surveys, and was a lieutenant at the outbreak of the Civil War.

Porter commanded a flotilla in the attack on New Orleans (see "PORTER'S POTS"), and captured the forts below the city. He commanded the Mississippi river squadron as an acting rear admiral during the Vicksburg campaign, and is credited with organizing the unsuccessful Red River campaign. He worked very effectively with Grant. Leaving the West, his North Atlantic blockade was very highly effective. The squadron captured Fort Fisher (aided by land troops) on the North Carolina coast.

After the war, he served as a vital member in the organization of the Naval Academy, serving as superintendent of the institution. Porter succeeded Farragut as admiral in 1870. He had excellent administrative ability and was a capable battle commander. His most effective operations were in co-ordination with land movements.

PORTER, FITZ-JOHN (1822–1901) — Union Brigadier General. After graduating from West Point in 1845, Porter served in the Mexican War and was a colonel when war broke out. By May of 1861, he had risen to brigadier general of the Shenandoah Volunteers, and rose from there to the command of a division on the Peninsula. Later, he assumed command of a corps.

Porter defended Mechanicsville and Gaines Mill ably, and was sent North to aid Pope in defending Washington. Longstreet's corps kept him from attacking Jackson at second Bull Run by their maneuvering. Porter also led a corps at Antietam, but did not engage in combat, because his troops were held in reserve. He was relieved of command in November, 1862, and faced charges of disobedience, disloyalty and misconduct filed by Pope. Found guilty, he was turned out of the army, and did not return to military service until 1882 after a long and continuous effort to regain his commission. He was, however, put on the retirement list immediately, and did not see active service after his trial.

Generally, it is felt that Porter was treated unnecessarily harshly by the military tribunal, and that his outspoken manner in support of his friend McClellan did much to add to his army troubles. All in all, he was an able leader of men, and "should have been dealt a better hand."

"PORTER'S POTS"—Admiral David D. Porter added tremendous firepower to his flotilla by mounting twenty-one huge mortars aboard barges, and using these batteries to shell coastal forts. He was most effective in the bombardment of the forts below New Orleans. The "Pots" hurled a 285-pound shell, and featured a thirteen-inch bore. In appearance, they were squat, kettle-shaped weapons mounted on heavy stationary bases. These mortars fired a missile every ninety seconds at the besieged forts. Their size gained them the name, "Porter's Big Pots."

POSTON, CHARLES D. (1825–1902)— (See ARIZONA, the Union Territory of.)

POTOMAC, the Army of the—Established August 20, 1861, out of the Military District of the Potomac and scattered troops in and around Washington. It was the major army for the Union in the East. Units from this command fought (not too admirably) at first Bull Run on July 21, 1861, under McDowell. Mainly organized by McClellan, this army was considered a "spit and polish" army by other Union forces. Under every commander prior to Meade, the army's maneuvers were characteristically defeatist in attitude. At Richmond, during the Peninsular campaign, at Fredericksburg, and at Chancellorsville, the army was handed defeats by Lee's Army of Northern Virginia. At Antietam, the army emerged victorious, but failed to follow up its victory by smashing Lee's force. Victorious again at Gettysburg, the army followed the pattern of its leaders and failed to wreck the enemy.

Commanded by McClellan, Burnside, Hooker, and Meade, the army changed its complete character once Grant began to supervise Meade's maneuvers. Before Meade assumed command, the general policy of the army had been to attack, get soundly defeated by an inferior force, and then retreat to the Washington area to lick its wounds. This army proved,

after being commanded by Grant, that it could fight (given the proper leadership). One writer summed up the attitude of the Army of the Potomac in this manner :

> Loved with deep affection, George B. McClellan; disliked Burnside; lacked confidence in Hooker; respectful of Meade; and intensely proud of Grant. As an army, it had taken it on the chin time and time again but had never disintegrated. It could suffer defeat and tremendous physical losses but remained a fighting force that grew in experience and strength until it became by the war's end, the mightiest army on earth at the time.

This army suffered the greatest losses of the war. In the latter stages of the war, the losses were so heavy that the civilian populace labeled Grant "the Butcher" and many other uncomplimentary names in the same vein.

POWELL, DR. J. W. (1834–1902)— Confederate surgeon. Powell served with Gregg and A. P. Hill, and was responsible for a number of field innovations in medical care with these forces.

PRESTON, SALLY BUCHANAN CAMPBELL—Confederate belle. This lady's "fatal" charms gained fame around the Confederacy after she was announced as the woman who had lost more lovers in battle than any woman in U. S. history. According to the *Diary of Mrs. Chestnut*, "Buck (Sally) had a knack for being fallen in love with at sight, and of never being fallen out of love with." Mrs. Chestnut stated also that ". . . there seemed a spell upon her lovers; so many were killed or died of the effect of wounds." Among the warriors who fell in love with Sally and later fell in battle were: Ransom Calhoun, Braddy Warwick, Claude Gibson, and two relatives referred to as "The Notts." This totals five sweethearts for one woman killed in battle within a four-year period.

PRICE, STERLING (1809–1867)—Confederate Major General. A lawyer before the war, and a Missouri legislator. He was elected to the U.S. Senate in 1844, and resigned to serve as a colonel in the Mexican War, and later as a brigadier general. He was governor of Missouri from 1852 to 1856.

At the outset of war, Sterling Price favored the Union, but switched his allegiance to the Confederacy when local Unionists angered him. He served with the Missouri state militia under McCullough, and was instrumental in the Wilson Creek victory. His troops captured Lexington, Mo., and then retreated into Arkansas. They also fought at Pea Ridge as an independent unit, after which fight, Price was made a major general in the Confederate army. He later fought at Iuka and Corinth, Mississippi, and was greatly responsible for the Union setback at Red River in 1864. His last Missouri raid was in 1864, after which he retreated to Texas.

Greatly influential, Price was one of the leading Southern commanders in the West, but received little mention from historians for his part in the war because of the erroneous conception that the Civil War was fought entirely east of the Mississippi.

"PRINCE JOHN" — (See MAGRUDER, JOHN BANKHEAD.)

Q

QUAKER GUNS—Logs painted to look like cannons. The South used these in the early stages of the war to deceive Union scouts. McClellan fell victim to this type of ruse, and withheld his attack upon Confederate forces at Yorktown as a result. The guns were first found at deserted rebel posts in the eastern sectors.

QUANTRILL, WILLIAM CLARKE (1837–1865)—Guerrilla. Born in Canal Dover, Ohio. Quantrill, a former school teacher, assumed the name of Charley Hart, and settled in Lawrence, Kan., after traveling westward from his home in Ohio, via wagon train. In Lawrence, he became known as a gambler, horse thief and suspected murderer. His connection with the Confederacy was as an irregular, and he was more a "freelance" guerrilla than a military leader.

Quantrill organized what has been called the "most virulent brand of partisan warfare" during the war, in Kansas, Missouri, Arkansas, and surrounding territories. He was declared an outlaw by Northern military leaders in 1862, and joined the regular Confederate service in August of that year, becoming a captain. On August 21, 1863, Quantrill and 450 men raided Lawrence, Kansas, butchering 150 men and burning part of the town. The raid served no useful purpose to the Confederacy, and it is doubtful that he was acting under direct orders from the military when he staged the raid. He committed a similar massacre at Baxter Springs, Kan., in October of 1863.

Quantrill's band broke up in 1864, as a result of dissension among the deserters and outlaws fighting under its banner. Quantrill escaped capture for more than another year, but was killed near Taylorsville, Ky., in 1865, by Union troops, while on a robbing and foraging raid with another group of raiders which he had organized.

Such unsavory characters as "Wild Bill" Anderson, Jesse James, and Cole Younger rode with Quantrill. He is generally considered to have contributed more outlaws to the cause of western crime than any other leader in the history of the country. His efforts towards aiding the Southern cause were minimal, and most Confederate leaders felt that his band only offered a haven for deserters. It is felt that bands like Quantrill's had no qualms about attacking Southern sympathizers as well as Union supporters.

QUANTRILL'S RAIDERS—(see QUANTRILL, WILLIAM CLARKE.)

RANDOLPH, GEORGE W. (1818–1867)— Confederate Cabinet member

R

RAWLINS, JOHN AARON (1831–1869)— Union Major General. Born in Galena, Illinois. Rawlins practiced law in Galena as a pro-Union Democrat before the war. In August, 1861, Grant asked him to be his aide, and the two became the closest of friends. Many refer to Rawlins as "Grant's watchdog," inferring that Rawlins was placed under Grant's command continually in order to keep Grant from slipping back into his old drinking habits. This has never been verified, and has no concrete foundation. From 1861 to 1865, Rawlins rise was rather slow, but in March, 1865, he became a brigadier general and chief of staff of the army. By April, he had risen to major general of the regular army.

After the war, Rawlins served as secretary of war under Grant (1869) but died just five months after his appointment. He was also called "Grant's Conscience," and served mainly as a staff officer under Grant during the war. He was a man of "exceptional talents" in the field of military administration.

REID, WHITLAW (1837–1912) — A journalist born in Xenia, Ohio, who served as a war correspondent for the Cincinnati *Gazette*. He was considered one of the top reporters of his day, and was selected to the Ohio Newspaper Hall of Fame. In 1872, Reid bought control of the New York *Tribune*. In 1892, he was the unsuccessful Republican candidate for the vice-presidency. His pseudonym during the Civil War was "Agate." In 1905, he was appointed ambassador to Great Britain, and held that post until his death.

RESACA, Georgia — Johnston entrenched at Resaca during the Union march to Atlanta, but was skillfully flanked out of the entrenchments by moves by Sherman. The Southerners fell back to Adairsville, then Cassville.

RICH MOUNTAIN, West Virginia—July 11, 1861. Union General McClellan staged a flanking march over the back roads of the mountain country in western Virginia, and hit the Rebel forces at Rich Mountain and Laurel Mountain. He dislodged them, and forced them back into the Shenandoah Valley. The site of the battle of Rich Mountain was near the small community of Beverly. McClellan's force routed the 4,500 Confederates, clearing western Virginia of the Southern threat for a temporary period. The Union officer commanded over 20,000 troops. Confederate commanding general Robert S. Garnett was killed in a rear-guard skirmish during this engagement. The South lost 700 men killed or captured. This victory set McClellan in his pattern of "maneuvering rather than fighting."

RIPLEY, JAMES W. (1794 1870) Union Chief of Ordnance. Ripley was replaced by Lincoln after the President found that the former had refused to purchase the Spencer repeating rifle because he thought it

a "gadget." Lincoln personally tested the weapon and ordered it supplied to the troops on the line.

ROANOKE ISLAND, the Fall of—In 1862, a combined amphibious force under Flag Officer Louis M. Goldsborough and Brigadier General Ambrose Burnside hit the North Carolina Sounds area from Hatteras Inlet. Among the positions to fall before this force was Roanoke Island. With the fall of New Bern, Fort Macon and Elizabeth City, the Union gained control of almost all of the North Carolina coast, and tightened the blockade.

ROSECRANS, WILLIAM STARKE (1819–1898)—Union Major General. Born in Delaware County, Ohio, and a graduate of West Point, 1842. Rosecrans resigned his commission in 1854 to practice engineering and enter business. Shortly after the outbreak of the Civil War, he became a regular army brigadier general and served with McClellan in western Virginia, winning the Battle of Rich Mountain.

Under Grant, in Mississippi, Rosecrans was successfully able to command troops in 1862, with victories at Iuka and in the subsequent defense of Corinth. He was promoted to major general in 1862. He succeeded Buell in Kentucky, and fought at Stone's River, one of the bloodiest battles of the war. He conducted a skillful campaign in the summer of 1863, near Tullahoma, Tenn., and forced Bragg back into Chattanooga. He then proceeded to

167

maneuver Bragg back out of the city, and took over the area.

The Confederates overcame his thinly manned defense line at Chickamauga in September, 1863, and his army was bitterly crushed. Because of this defeat, he was relieved of duty and saw very little active duty thereafter. He remained in the service until the end of the war, but resigned his commission in 1867.

ROUND TOPS, the—(See GETTYSBURG.)

RUFFIN, EDMUND (1794–1865)—Honorary Confederate Private. Born in Prince George County, Va. This avid secessionist claimed to be the man who fired the first shot at Fort Sumter in April, 1861. He was known as a pure "state's righter" who voiced his sentiments loudly and continuously before the first shot was fired. A member of the Virginia plantation aristocracy, he wrote much on the merits of a separate South and authored the work, *Slavery and Free Labor Described and Compared.*

Ruffin went to Morris Island, S.C., on April 9, 1861, because he had heard that a battery on that island would soon fire on Fort Sumter. Because of his status as a leader in the secessionist movement, he was made an honorary private in the Palmetto Guard, and given the opportunity to fire the first shot of the war. According to his diary, he fired the first shot at approximately 4:30 A.M., on April 12, 1861, hitting the fort at the northeast angle of the parapet.

Ruffin also claimed to be the person who started the helter-skelter rout at the first Bull Run. This claim is supported by some eyewitnesses (all members of the Palmetto Guard). One description of the rout is as follows:

The Yankees had come to the Club Run bridge, crowding and shoving to get away from the deadly Confederate fire. The road was jammed with artillery, trains, baggage wagons, and ambulances. As the first wagon in the retreat drove onto the bridge, Ruffin fired a load of buckshot into the lead horses. They reared, upsetting the wagon, and thereby blocking the bridge and the road.

Ruffin himself recalls that, "The whole mess of fugitives escaped on foot as quickly as possible. Thus all the wagons and artillery were abandoned and everything else by the terrified fugitives." The fighting portion of the war ended for Ruffin on that day, for he was deafened by the volume of the gunfire, and never shouldered a musket again. In his final entry in his diary, he declared his undying hatred for the Yankees, placed a pistol to his temple and pulled the trigger.

Prior to the war, Ruffin had contributed much to the betterment of the Southern farm system. His experiments in crop rotation, drainage, plowing and fertilizing had done much to improve the crop output in his native Virginia. His claims concerning his part in the war (most of which are unverified) have been disputed by many, but no one has been able to positively disprove them. He committed suicide June 18, 1865, in Amelia County, Va.

S

SAILOR'S CREEK, Virginia, the Battle at—April 6, 1865. During the retreat towards Appomattox, the Confederates were constantly harassed by Sheridan's cavalry. At Sailor's Creek, the blow which smashed all Southern hopes fell, when the Federal forces wrecked a Southern supply train, and hit Lee's rear guard at a crucial time. General Dick Ewell was captured, the Sixth Corps (the old nemesis of the Shenandoah Valley) overwhelmed the staggering Army of Northern Virginia's rear support, and, on April 8th, Custer seized four supply wagons. The morale and fighting fibre of the mightiest army of the Confederacy was shattered.

ST. ALBANS, the Raid on—Vermont. Confederate raiders struck St. Albans, Vt., from Canada, in an attempt to strike fear into the hearts of the Union civilian population while taking funds from the three banks there. During the raid, one of the raiders is alleged to have said, "This is the way Sherman hits our homes." Lieutenant Bennett H. Young, a graduate of Center College in Danville, Ky., led the raiders on an October 19, 1864, attack on the three banks of the town, escaping into Canada with over $201,522 in currency and negotiable bonds.

The raiders arrived in the town in twos and threes, and registered at the American House Hotel on the main street of St. Albans, beginning Saturday, October 15. By Wednesday morning, October 19, all twenty-one raiders (mostly Confederate ex-cavalry men who were living in Canada) were in the town. At 3:30 P.M., on that day, the raiders hit the three town banks simultaneously, taking $58,000 from the First National Bank, $73,522 from the St. Albans Bank further down the street, and $70,000 from the Franklin County Bank (also on the main street). No more than four of the raiders entered any one bank at a time, and the remainder of the crew was busy rounding up those citizens of the town who had happened to be walking or riding down the main street at the time.

The raid, beautifully executed, would have gone off without a hitch had it not been for Union Captain George P. Conger, home on leave from the First Vermont Cavalry. Conger was captured while walking down the street in his Union uniform, but escaped and alerted the townspeople amidst a hail of Confederate bullets. At the same time, fiery old E. D. Fuller, one of the proprietors of the local livery stable, was fighting off a band of the raiders who were attempting to take over his horses. The only drawback in his magnificent stand was that the pistol he had picked up was empty.

With Conger's alarm, and the successful robbery of the bank, the raiders fled the town closely pursued by the aroused townspeople. They crashed across the Canadian border without stopping at the border check, and assumed that they were safe from the Americans. However, Captain Conger took command of the townspeople and also tore into Canada without stopping at the customs and immigration station. They pursued the raiders into the area around Montreal and captured ten of them. While attempting to take them back across the border, Conger's force was stopped by Canadian authorities and the raiders were placed in protective custody by the Canadians. It almost stirred up an international incident of major proportions, for only $86,000 of the original booty was turned over to the St. Albans people at that time by the Canadian government. The remained of the money from the robberies has not been recovered to this date.

The Canadian Parliament appropriated $70,000 in gold to turn over to the St. Albans Banks, but this did not still the uproar, especially when the courts released the raiders deeming them belligerents of a foreign nation at war. A total of fourteen of the twenty-one raiders were captured; one was killed during the raid, and four were wounded. Ironically, the raiding group was exactly the same size as that of Union Captain Andrews whose force stole a Confederate locomotive. (See AR-DREWS RAID, the.) The town of St. Albans suffered extensive damage from delayed incendiary bombs left by the raiders upon their escape. Lieutenant Young returned to his native Kentucky at the end of the war, but was refused President Johnson's amnesty. He died in 1919 at the age of seventy-six. (See YOUNG, BENNETT H.) The raid was authorized by a special order dated June 16, 1864, and signed by Secretary of War James A. Seddon of the Confederacy. It authorized Young to "organize for special service a company not to exceed twenty in number from those who belong to the service and are at this time beyond the Confederate states."

Killed in the battle during the raid were one St. Albans citizen, E. J. Morrison, and one of the four wounded raiders. While in jail, the raiders sent humorous little cards and letters to the St. Albans citizens taunting them about the raid. Young even sent for a subscription to the St. Albans *Messenger*. Another raider paid his hotel bill through the mail, regretfully stating that he had been forced to leave the town rather suddenly, and asking that the proprietor of the American House extend best wishes to the fine "young lady who occupied the room adjacent to mine." This raid hit farther north than any other action of the war.

SANTA FE, New Mexico, the Evacuation of—March 4, 1862; April 5-6, 1862. The capital of New Mexico, defended by a small garrison of Union troops under quartermaster Major J. L. Donalson, was forced to evacuate in early 1862, when Confederate troops under Charles J. Pyron threatened the supplies stored there. The Union force returned in April, after the Confederates evacuated on April 5th and 6th.

SAVAGE STATION, the Battle of—June 29, 1862. Confederate forces under Magruder struck the retreating Union army of McClellan above Richmond, while the Federals were pulling back from the siege of that city. The action was fought mainly between the strong rear guard of McClellan and Magruder's smaller force. The Southerners had to break off the action when ·expected support from "Stonewall" Jackson failed to materialize. This battle immediately preceded the Battle of Frayser's Farm.

SCHOFIELD, JOHN MCALLISTER (1831–1906)—Union Major General. Born in Chautauqua County, N.Y. An 1853 graduate of West Point. Schofield entered the army and taught physics at Washington University in St. Louis in addition to his regular army duties. At the outbreak of war, he was serving as chief of staff to Captain Nathaniel Lyons. In November, 1861, he was made a brigadier general of volunteers and from October, 1862, to April, 1863, headed the Army of the Frontier in Missouri, becoming a major general while holding that position. By May, 1863, he had assumed command of the whole Department of the Missouri. Eight months later (February, 1864), he took over the Army of the Ohio and served under Sherman as its commander in the Atlanta campaign. Schofield held off Hood's advance on Nashville at the Battle of Franklin, and later fought under Thomas at Nashville. He ended the war under Sherman in North Carolina.

His war record was not considered outstanding, but he was personally considered to be an able commander when serving directly under a good tactician. Following the war, he became secretary of war (1868–1869), and later became a regular major general. In 1888, he became the commanding general of the army, gaining the rank of lieutenant general in 1895.

SCOTT, WINFIELD (1786–1866) — Union General-in-Chief. Born near Petersburg, Va., Scott studied law before joining the army in 1808 at the age of twenty-two. He served during the War of 1812, where he won the brevet rank of major general because of his outstanding combat record. His subsequent military career was a distinguished one, including command in the Black Hawk War, in 1835 in Florida, and in the Mexican War. He was mentioned for the Presidency in 1840, but was made general-in-chief of the army in 1841 instead. He held that post for twenty years before resigning under pressure when the Civil War broke out.

He was known as "Old Fuss and Feathers" because of his mannerisms. He played no outstanding part in the prosecution of the war except to advise Lincoln against attempting to reprovision Fort Sumter prior to the shelling of that fort. His advice was not heeded

SEBASTIAN PLAN, the—This was a plan proposed by anti-Confederate Arkansas Unionists to get their state back into the Union. Simply, the

171

plan called for W. K. Sebastian, whose term as a U.S. senator had not expired, to return to his seat in the United States Senate as though nothing had happened. It was felt that this would signify to the Union that the state of Arkansas was back in the Union.

Chief exponents of this plan were Confederate officers William Fishback and E. W. Gantt. Fishback had deserted to the Union in June, 1862. Gantt, once a brigadier general in the Confederate army, became convinced of the futility of the Southern cause while a prisoner in a Union war camp. Both were members of the Peace Society of Arkansas. Both felt that, should the people instruct Sebastian to resume his seat in the Senate, the Union would accept the move as representatives of the State's wishes, and return Arkansas without any other retaliatory action.

SECOND BULL RUN—August 29–30, 1862. Manassas. Lee sent Jackson behind Pope's army to burn the Union supply depot at Manassas Junction, Va., about twenty-five miles west of Washington. Pope, following Jackson's strategically retreating force, was drawn back to the scene of the first major Union defeat, Bull Run. Here, at Groveton, on August 28, Pope and Jackson engaged in a hot skirmish which lasted over to the 29th. (See DOGAN'S HOUSE.) Pope, unable to dislodge Jackson, was surprised by a flank attack from Longstreet on the 30th, resulting in a rout of the Federal forces, forcing them to retreat to Washington in almost an exact enactment of the first Bull Run rout. Union casualties totaled 14,500. The Confederates lost 9,500. As in most of the contests of the war, the Union force of 75,000 greatly outnumbered the 55,000 Confederates. As a result of this defeat, Washington was again seriously threatened by the South's army.

SEDDON, JAMES ALEXANDER (1815–1880) — Confederate Secretary of War. Born in Fredericksburg, Va. A University of Virginia graduate, Seddon practiced law in Richmond prior to the outbreak of the war. He served as a member of the House of Representatives (1845–1847, 1849–1851), and was socially prominent in Virginia. Seddon served as a member of the Confederate Congress until he resigned in November, 1862, to replace George Randolph as secretary of war. He resigned that post in 1865, following heated disputes with the Confederate Congress regarding his prosecution of the war. He retired to his Virginia estate, where he remained until he died in 1880.

SEDGWICK, JOHN (1813–1864)— Union Major General. Born in Cornwall Hollow, Conn. A member of the West Point class of 1837, Sedgwick served in Florida, in Mexico and along the Canadian border prior to the Civil War. He was a lieutenant colonel serving on the frontier when the war broke out, but was promptly promoted to brigadier general.

Sedgwick served during the Peninsular campaign, in command of a division, and was wounded there. He was again wounded (after becoming a major general of volunteers) at Antietam. Following service against Fredericksburg, Chancellorsville, Gettysburg, and Mine Run, Sedgwick was killed while leading his Sixth Corps in the Spotsylvania fighting, May 9, 1864. Known affectionately as "Uncle John" to his men, Sedgwick rated highly in the ranks of hard-fighting generals of the Union.

SEMMES, RAPHAEL (1809–1877)— Confederate Rear Admiral. Born in Charles County, Md. Died in Point Clear, Ala. Naval raider captain. Appointed a midshipman in the U.S. Navy in 1826, Semmes studied and practiced law during his leaves, in Maryland and Ohio. He served in the Mexican War, and was naval aide to the Army during the campaign to Mexico City. Semmes resigned from the navy with the rank of commander, in order to accept the same rank in the Confederate navy at the outbreak of the Civil War.

He commanded the C.S.S. "Sumter" (the first Confederate Cruiser), taking fifteen prizes in six months, while raiding Northern commercial shipping lanes. Blockaded in Gibraltar by Union ships in April, 1862, Semmes escaped and went to England to take command of the "290" built at Laird's shipyard in Birkenhead, England. Actually, he took command of the ship at Terceira, an island in the Azores. The "290" was renamed the "Alabama," and Semmes nearly swept the ocean clean of Union merchantmen as her captain. In six months, he captured or destroyed ten ships, sinking the Union warship "Hatteras" on January 11, 1863, in Galveston Bay.

Labeled a pirate by the North, Semmes raided as far away as the Indian Ocean and the China Sea. His ship was destroyed by the "Kearsarge" on June 19, 1864 (see "ALABAMA"). He was rescued by an English yacht, and returned to the South to receive a promotion to rear admiral. During the war, ships commanded by Semmes captured eighty-two Union merchant vessels valued at six million dollars. He boarded 386 ships and took over 2,000 prisoners during his time as captain of the "Alabama" (twenty-two months). He is rated one of the greatest naval figures in the war.

SEVEN DAYS BATTLES (June 26–July 2, 1862)—Near Beaver Creek Dam. These engagements took place between June 26 and July 2, 1862, and were part of the Peninsular campaign (q.v.). During these seven days of battles and skirmishes, twenty-one Confederate regiments attacked Union positions near Beaver Creek Dam. Strongly entrenched, and backed by artillery and cavalry, the Federal forces inflicted severe damage on the forces led by the famous Confederate General Stonewall Jackson, during the first day of the fighting. However, at the end of the Seven Days, Union commander McClellan was frantically wiring

Washington for re-enforcements. One of his wires to Lincoln read : ". . . if you do not know now, the game is lost. If I can save this army, I tell you that I owe no thanks to you or any persons in Washington. You have done your best to sacrifice this army." This wire was addressed to President Lincoln, and was thought so outrageous by the men in the telegraph office that parts were deleted. Notwithstanding, McClellan was relieved from command following the Peninsular campaign, and replaced by Halleck.

Battles included in the Seven Days campaign were :

June 26 : Mechanicsville, or Beaver Dam Creek

June 27 : Gaines Mill, or First Cold Harbor

June 28 : Running skirmishes.
June 29 : Savage Station.
June 30 : White Oak swamp,

Frayser's Farm, or Glendale
July 1 : Malvern Hill
July 2 : McClellan retreats.

SEWARD, WILLIAM HENRY (1801–1872)—Union Secretary of State. Born in Florida, N.Y. A graduate of Union College, 1820, Seward settled in Auburn, N.Y., to practice law, and became associated with prominent political leader Thurlow Weed. As a result, he entered the state legislature and was subsequently elected to the governorship as a Whig, 1838–1840, after an earlier defeat. Politically, Seward was an outspoken anti-slavery proponent. He served in the Senate from 1848 until he resigned to take the post of secretary of state in Lincoln's cabinet. His senate record shows complete opposition to any and all slavery compromises. He was viewed as an extremist on the subject.

Seward had sought the Republican Presidential nomination in 1860, but was bypassed for Lincoln after some strong political maneuvering by Lincoln's managers prior to the voting. Together with Chase, Seward was one of the two selections for cabinet posts made personally by Lincoln. All others came as a result of pre-voting promises and compromises made by his managers. Earlier, Seward had attempted to get the Whig party and the New Republican Party to merge, but without success.

He went into the cabinet with the thought of becoming the power behind the Presidential chair, but (by his own admission) began to respect Lincoln more when the latter refused to allow him to take over control of things. Nevertheless, Seward wielded tremendous power in the cabinet. He tried to "bully" England (and even urged a foreign war) over the "Trent Affair."

Seward was injured in a carriage accident in early 1865, and was stabbed on the night of the assassination of Lincoln by Lewis Paine (one of the Booth conspirators). He recovered to serve the Johnston administration successfully. It was during the Johnston administration that he negotiated for the purchase of Alaska—termed at that time, "Seward's Folly."

SHARPESBURG, the Battle of—(see ANTIETAM).

SHENANDOAH VALLEY, the—In 1864, Grant planned to lay waste to this area which had been pro-Southern in its sympathies from the outbreak of the war. He ordered Sigel and Hunter to "make all of the valley south of the Baltimore and Ohio Railroad a desert . . . all provisions and stock should be removed and the people notified to get out." This is some indication of the value and strategic importance of the Shenandoah Valley during the war.

It was in this valley that Thomas "Stonewall" Jackson gained his reputation as a great strategic wizard. It was here also that the cadets of the Virginia Military Institute routed Sigel and saved the wheat crop for the Confederacy (see VIRGINIA MILITARY INSTITUTE) and it was here that General Hunter gutted Virginia Military Institute because he claimed to have found a proclamation issued by the governor of Virginia "inciting . . . guerrilla warfare on my troops."

Earlier in the war, Jackson roamed the valley at will, and inflicted defeats upon most of the Union armies sent there to confront him. Throughout the war, the valley (called the "breadbasket of the South") was the scene of major battles and skirmishes. The South kept a force there from the beginning of the war until just before Lee's surrender in April, 1865.

SHENANDOAH, the Army of—

CONFEDERATE. The name given to the troops in the Shenandoah Valley under General Joseph E. Johnston early in the war. The name was dropped after this army moved to the first Battle of Bull Run to aid in the fighting there.

UNION. Created expressly to fight Jubal Early in his invasion of the Shenandoah Valley in August, 1864. This army drained the valley of its produce and left a trail of "burnt earth" behind it, under orders from Grant to "make all the valley south of the Baltimore and Ohio Railroad a desert."

SHEPHERD, HAYWOOD (?–1859) — Civilian. If the action at Harper's Ferry is to be construed as the first "battle" of the war, Shepherd then becomes the first casualty of the war. However, it would be hard to tell which side he would have been listed as fighting for. Shepherd was a free Negro, serving as station master at Harper's Ferry when he was felled by a bullet from the gun of one of Brown's men. (See HARPER'S FERRY, the raid on.)

SHERIDAN, PHILIP HENRY (1831–1888)—Union Major General. Born in Albany, N.Y. (according to his own statement), but it is strongly suspected that his actual birthplace was aboard a ship enroute to the United States from Ireland. An 1853 graduate of West Point, Sheridan graduated only after a rather stormy career at the Academy, which found him being threatened with expulsion on two occasions.

He served in the West, and was a captain when war broke out. By May, 1862, he had risen to a captaincy in the cavalry. By June of that year, he had been promoted to brigadier general following action at Booneville, Mo. Sheridan was one of the few victorious Union commanders at Stone's River, and won laurels at Perrysville also.

In December, 1862, he again won promotion, and commanded a corps as a major general of volunteers. He fought at Chickamauga, Missionary Ridge, and in numerous other engagements. Sheridan commanded the Army of the Potomac's cavalry under Grant and Meade. In August, 1864, Sheridan took command of the Army of the Shenandoah, and pushed the Confederates out of the valley, following Grant's "scorched earth" policy as he went. This type of warfare made the name of "Little Phil" hated in that area.

Because of his famous "twenty-mile ride" which brought him to the scene of battle just as his troops were beginning to waver at Cedar Creek, Sheridan is credited with inflicting one of the few clear-cut defeats on Jubal Early (October 19, 1864). This battle closed major engagements in the Shenandoah Valley.

Sheridan (promoted to a regular army major general in November, 1864) turned the Confederate flank at Petersburg, winning Five Forks, and participating in the final campaign in Virginia to Appomattox. He was accused of retaliating against the South after the war. He succeeded Sherman as commander-in-chief of the Army in 1883, and became a full general in 1888.

Aggressive, relentless, and uncompromising as a leader, Sheridan formed the final rung in the three-step ladder of spoilers for the Union. Together with Grant and Sherman, his style of fighting was a compliment to the triumvirate of "unconditional surrender" generals of the Union's latter years. He was extremely capable, and loved a fight.

SHERMAN, WILLIAM TECUMSEH (1820–1891)—Union Major General. Born in Lancaster, Ohio. Known as "Cump." Sherman graduated from West Point in 1840, and served in the Mexican War before resigning in 1853 to take up banking. Failing at this, he became superintendent of a military college (now Louisiana State University), and refused high rank in the Confederacy when war broke out. He refused, in fact, to enter the war at all at the outset, preferring to remain as president of a St. Louis street railway for a short time before entering the Union service as a regular colonel in May, 1861.

After the fighting at first Bull Run, Sherman was promoted to brigadier general, and given command in Kentucky. Because of his peculiar nervous habits, he was (unjustly) labeled "odd," and was relieved of his command. He was, however, restored in time to fight at Shiloh. Sherman commanded at Memphis in July, 1862, as a major general, but failed in the attack on Chickasaw Bluffs at Vicksburg. Although opposing the Vicksburg campaign, he led a corps throughout the fighting. Late in

1863, Sherman was sent to relieve Chattanooga, and later fought at Missionary Ridge.

When Grant moved east, Sherman took over command of the West, advancing to Atlanta with three armies and capturing the city in a campaign which featured few major conflicts, many small scale battles, and much maneuvering. Hood was relieved of duty in front of Atlanta for "failing to stop Sherman." In 1864, Sherman was made a regular army major general. He left Atlanta on November 15, 1864, and advanced through Georgia. The world lost contact with this army until it reappeared at Savannah after "cleaning up" the countryside in this famous "March to the Sea."

Like Grant and Sheridan, Sherman believed in destroying and commandeering property that might be used profitably by the enemy. The excessive practice of this policy during the Georgia march (whether with or without Sherman's consent) did much to earn the Union lasting condemnation in parts of that state. His troops fought one of the last battles of the war at Bentonville, N.C., after which he accepted Joseph E. Johnston's surrender, April 18, 1865. (See SURRENDER TERMS, the Durham Station.)

SHILOH, the Battle of—April 6–7, 1862. The Confederates, in an effort to halt the movements of Union forces along the Tennessee, moved to attack Grant east of Memphis. The combined forces of Beauregard and Albert Sidney Johnston totaled 40,000, but were outnumbered by forces under Grant and Buell which numbered 61,000.

Grant, expecting Buell to re-enforce him from Nashville, allowed Johnston to surprise his force while still in camp. The Union army was camped in the river at Pittsburg Landing (lending still another name to the battle) in a wooded area surrounding the Shiloh Meeting House. Johnston's force, coming up from Corinth, Mississippi, forced the Federals back with heavy losses, only to be stopped by desperate fighting and heavy cannon fire as they approached the river.

Buell's force arrived on the 7th with supplies and fresh troops to fill the gaps created in the Union line. They beat back the exhausted Confederates, forcing them to retreat towards Corinth, with Grant and Buell continuing their campaign on the river. General Johnston was killed in the contest, but might have been saved had proper care been given his not-too-serious wound. (See JOHNSTON, ALBERT SIDNEY.)

SICKLES, DANIEL EDGAR (1825–1914) —Union Major General. Born in New York, N.Y. Sickles attended the University of the City of New York, and became a printer and lawyer after graduation. He entered state politics, and later became a member of the U.S. House of Representatives from 1857–1861, gaining the infamous distinction of having shot Phillip Barton Key because of Key's attention to Mrs. Sickles while the congressman was away attending his congressional duties. Key was the son of Francis Scott Key, the author of the national anthem. Sickles was acquitted, and raised a troop of volunteers at the start of the war. He was made a brigadier general at the start of the Peninsular campaign, and was promoted to major general and given command of a corps in early 1863. He commanded the Second Corps at Gettysburg.

At Gettysburg, Sickles advanced his command to the Peach Orchard, without orders, on July 2nd, and was badly beaten. As a result of a wound received in this encounter, he lost a leg, and was severely criticized for his actions. Throughout the war, he served in a rather irresponsible manner, gaining his promotions through influence and politics. Definitely a "political general" in the phrase's worst connotation, Sickles served as governor of South Carolina until dismissed under fire because of mismanagement. In 1869, he was appointed U.S. minister to Spain; later he returned to serve in Congress again. He is best described as ill-tempered, stubborn, cantankerous, and irresponsible. He leaned heavily on his political contacts during the war.

SLIDELL, JOHN (1793–1871) — Confederate. Unofficial minister to France. Born in New York, N.Y. Slidell, a Columbia University graduate, failed in business in New York, and moved to New Orleans to practice law. He was an active Democrat, and served as U.S. commissioner to Mexico in 1845. He was U.S. senator from 1853 to 1861, when he resigned after Lincoln's election. He was named minister to France by the Confederate government, although the French government had not officially recognized the Confederacy.

He and James Mason, commissioner to England, were taken off the British steamer "Trent," and detained by Captain Charles Wilkes, in Boston. This touched off the famous "Trent Affair" which developed into one of the most tense international situations of the period, between the United States and Great Britain. The two were later released. Slidell arranged for ship construction and loans to France, and attempted to get Napoleon III to recognize the Confederacy. He never returned to the United States after the war.

Slidell, a moderate Union man before Lincoln's election, was politically powerful during the Buchanan administration. He was not greatly trusted in Europe, "because of his shrewdness."

SMALLS, ROBERT (1839–1915) — Union steamer captain. Born in Beaufort, S.C. A slave who became the first Negro captain of a vessel in the Union merchant fleet, after stealing a Confederate steamer from under the guns of the Charleston Harbor defenses. Smalls was owned by one Henry McKee, and was hired out by his master as a slave seaman at the rate of $16 per month, with $15 going to McKee.

At the age of twenty-three, Smalls (and a group of Negro seamen) stole a paddle-wheel steamer, the

"Planter," from Charleston Harbor and boldly sailed by the Charleston defenses. The move took place on May 12, 1862, and the slaves were bold enough to drop anchor beside the Confederate merchant-man, "Etowan" and dispatch a rowboat to pick up their waiting families before departing. Smalls, wearing the cap and coat of the steamer's captain, saluted the harbor defenses in the customary fashion, and sailed past the guns. Reaching the Union fleet three miles outside of the harbor, he raised a white flag and surrendered the ship to the Union. Because of this feat, he was made captain of the "Planter" and served in that capacity for the duration of the war.

After the war, Smalls served as representative in the South Carolina legislature, and later the U.S. Congress.

SMITH, CHARLES F. (1807–1862)— Union. Formerly commandant of cadets at West Point, but assigned to handle volunteer troops in the early stages of the war. With Grant (whom he taught at West Point), Smith led the assault which cracked the outer defenses of Fort Donelson. He commanded a division in that battle. Smith was considered too stiff and formal to win the affection of the less formal western troops under Grant. He was, however, considered a good soldier.

SMITH, EDMUND KIRBY (1824–1893)

Confederate General. Smith graduated from West Point in 1845. He was born in St. Augustine, Fla., and signed his name "E. Kirby Smith."

He served in the Mexican War and on the frontier prior to the war. He resigned the rank of major to enter the Confederate army, becoming a brigadier general in June, 1860, and was wounded at the first Bull Run. In October, 1861, Smith was promoted to major general, and was high in command circles of Bragg's invasion army of Kentucky, becoming a lieutenant general in October, 1862. He assumed command of the Trans - Mississippi Department in February, 1863, and set up an army so far from the Confederate action that it became known as "Kirby's Kingdom." In February, 1864, Smith was promoted full general, and his troops repulsed the abortive Red River invasion in April of that same year. He surrendered the last main force of the Confederacy on June 2, 1865. He is known to historians as just plain "Kirby Smith."

Following the war, he became chancellor of the University of Nashville, and later held a teaching post at the University of the South. He was a very able field general, but not suited to high level administrative work. He was very daring, and loved a good fight.

SMITH, GUSTAVUS W. (1822–1896)— Confederate Cabinet member. (See CONFEDERATE CABINET, THE.)

SMITH, THE WILLIAM R.—Confederate troop train. (See ANDREWS RAID, THE.)

SOUTH CAROLINA, the Secession of—The South Carolina Secession Convention originally met at Columbia, S.C., on December 17, 1860, but was forced to move to Charleston because of an epidemic of smallpox in Columbia. The convention met on December 18, in Institute Hall in Charleston, but did not officially vote for secession until December 20, making their intention known by the issuance and signing of an ordinance of secession. Wild celebrating followed the move, as people paraded through the streets wearing a multitude of different flags (but none wearing the colors of the United States). South Carolina had officially declared herself no longer a part of the Union of States.

SPENCER, CHRISTOPHER MINER (1833–1922)—Union inventor. Born in Manchester, Conn. Spencer invented the Spencer repeating rifle used by the Union during the latter part of the war. He also invented a steam-driven automobile. He worked for the Colt Firearms Company. In March, 1860, Spencer was issued patent no. 27,393 for a repeater, a self-loading rifle. He had trouble selling the rifle to the army because Brigadier General James W. Ripley, chief of the Bureau of Ordnance, had no faith in the "gadget." Spencer sold his first large order to the Navy after a demonstration.

Army General Thomas Wilder used some of the rifles which he had purchased at his own expense, and found them very effective.

Through a friend, Charles Cheney, Spencer got an interview with President Lincoln on August 17, 1863, and convinced the President to personally test the weapon on an improvised firing range near the Washington monument. Lincoln did so on August 18, and as a result the rifles were ordered. Ripley was replaced, and the Union gained a very valuable and much-needed weapon.

The Confederates described the weapons in a very prophetic manner : "Them Yankees can load in the morning and fire all day." The rifle was a seven-shot, lever action repeater. The metal cartridge was the main reason that the Confederates were unable to use captured Spencers effectively. The South could not manufacture the ammunition for the Spencer.

SPENCER RIFLE, the—Patent issued, March, 1860, No. 27,393. Invented by Christopher Miner Spencer for use by the Union. A seven-shot, lever action repeater, it was shorter than the old musket, and much lighter. The Spencer could be fired five to seven times as fast as the .58 caliber muzzle-loading rifle. It used a metal, self-containing cartridge, and became standard cavalry equipment for the Union as early as 1864.

SPOTSYLVANIA, the Battle of—May 9–19, 1864. After Grant pulled his troops out of the Wilderness, the next point south was Spotsylvania. A race between Federal and Southern forces began, with each trying to reach the point forty miles north of Richmond first. Grant was forcing Lee to push tired troops into a forced march in order to protect the Confederate capital.

Lee won the race, and entrenched his army deeply after defeating a small cavalry force that had reached the Courthouse far ahead of the main Union army. On the 9th, both sides dug in, and there was mild skirmishing. Sedgwick was killed on this day in a minor engagement, and Anderson took over the Union's Sixth Corps. (See SEDGWICK, JOHN.) The Union began a swinging movement in an attempt to either bypass the Confederates or cut them off. The Confederates followed each move with a countermove from the 12th to the 18th, causing the battle line to take on the appearance of a huge pendulum.

However, on the 19th, the Confederate line moved a bit too much, allowing Grant to bypass Spotsylvania and move toward Richmond. A running battle followed, with losses continuing to pile up. The South lost roughly 9,000, and the Union almost 17,000. This battle caused the Northern populace to raise the cry of "Butcher Grant," but Grant was steadily moving southward, refusing to fight Lee on the latter's chosen ground as the previous Northern commanders had done.

SPRINGFIELD, the Battle of—(see WILSON'S CREEK, the Battle of).

SPRING HILL AFFAIR, the—(November 29, 1864). Hood had a chance to cut off Federal forces under Schofield above Nashville, Tenn., but did nothing. This failure to act by Hood has been labeled the "Spring Hill Affair," and ranks as one of the great lost opportunities of the war. Hood *did* attack on November 30, but Schofield was able to make a stand at the town of Franklin (see FRANKLIN, the Battle of). Hood's failure to hit Schofield before the Union commander could entrench changed an almost sure victory into a resounding Confederate defeat.

STANTON, EDWIN MCMASTERS (1814–1869)—Union Secretary of War. Born in Steubenville, Ohio, and attended Kenyon College. Stanton never finished college, but he was admitted to the bar in 1836, and became a successful lawyer. Leaving Steubenville in 1847, he moved to Pittsburgh, but did not stay there long. In 1856, he served as special counsel to the government in a fight over land claims resulting from the Mexican War.

From the start, Stanton strongly supported the Union. On December 20, 1860, President Buchanan appointed him to the post of attorney general. Stanton, a Democrat, lost this post very shortly after when the new Lincoln cabinet was appointed, but became secretary of war after Simon Cameron was removed. Prior to this appointment, Stanton had strongly criticized Lincoln, and mistrusted his motives. The breach was widened when Lincoln removed McClellan—one of Stanton's good friends.

When Stanton took over the War Department, he completely revised the system, setting up an efficient and well oiled machine which did much to aid the Union prosecute the war. His appointment to the post came January 15, 1862, and he served in the cabinet until May, 1868, when he resigned. Stanton made many mistakes in the operation of his post, but these are far outnumbered by his organizational ability and production. He broke with his friend McClellan when the general's obvious reluctance to move his troops into battle became apparent to War Department officials. At the same time, Stanton directed much of the criticism of the Lincoln administration's prosecution of the war towards himself, thus taking the pressure from Lincoln at a crucial time. He had a tremendous ability to arm and supply troops, and he was blasted by the press because of his tendency to "muzzle" reporters, not allowing them the free run of the War Department that his predecessor had.

When Lincoln was assassinated, Stanton is quoted as having said, "Now he belongs to the ages." This phrase turned up on a sheet of paper found in the belongings of Lafayette C. Baker, indirectly accusing Stanton of masterminding the plot. No proof was found to substantiate the charge, although many historians today lend credence to the charge. Many, however, feel that Clement L. Vallandigham was a more likely suspect (q.v.).

Stanton was prominent in the impeachment proceedings involving President Andrew Johnson. His association with the radical Republicans placed him in a peculiar situation when the proceedings failed to find Johnson guilty. It was over the attempted removal of Stanton that most of the trouble arose. Consequently, Stanton resigned when Johnson won his impeachment trial.

Grant named Stanton to the Supreme Court in December, 1869, but Stanton died before taking the bench. He was a highly controversial person (devious on occasions) but, nevertheless, one of the best suited men for the post of secretary of war during this period. It is felt that his censorship of the press had much to do with the rumors of his anti-Lincoln activities.

"STAR OF THE WEST," the—Union supply ship. This ship sailed from New York on January 5, 1861, with men and supplies for Fort Sumter. Nearing Charleston Harbor's entrance, the troops and arms were secreted below decks, but the batteries at Morris Island, S.C., manned by cadets of the South Carolina Military Academy, fired upon the ship before it could reach the fort. Major Robert Anderson refused to fire upon the batteries in support of the ship because he did not feel that he had the authority. Consequently the unarmed merchant ship was forced to turn about and return to New York.

182

STEAM GUN, the—Built in Baltimore, Md., but described as "not likely to be of much service," this gun was a forerunner of today's tank or armored weapons carrier. The gun was a steam-powered machine gun which could have made land warfare entirely different during the crucial period of 1861-1863. It was set on four wheels with a boiler similar to that of the steam engine of the time. The cylinder was upright. There was but one barrel, made of steel, and set upon a pivot. It was fed through a hopper set directly over the pivot. The barrel, which had the appearance of the ordinary musket barrel of the time, had a rotary motion, and moved the circumference of the pivot at least 1,500 times per minute. It would discharge a two-ounce ball (about 300 per minute) but was not as accurate as it could have been, with the misses coming either to the left or the right of the target. The gun could be worked so that it would fire in any direction, but it had a range of not over 100 yards. The whole machine weighed 6,700 pounds, and was about the size of a steam engine of that day.

Had the officials of that day had the foresight, the invention could have improved upon and used as a very effective weapon. Later, a Southerner named Dickenson built a similar machine, but it too failed to impress the authorities involved.

STEELE'S BAYOU, Mississippi—Above Vicksburg. The scene of the entrapment of the ironclad fleet of Rear Admiral David Dixon Porter during the attempts to get to the rear of Vicksburg. The Confederates felled trees across the narrow passage, and fired down upon the ships from the trees. Sherman's force came to the rescue of the fleet, and also ended the attempts to get to Vicksburg via a rear route.

STEPHENS, ALEXANDER HAMILTON (1812-1883) — Confederate Vice-President. Born in Wilkes County, Ga. A graduate of the University of Georgia, 1832, Stephens taught school, practiced law, and served as a member of both the Georgia legislature and the U.S. House of Representatives prior to the war. He was a Whig, and strongly favored slavery, after taking an earlier stand against the institution. He was never a rabid secessionist, but was elected to the post of vice-president of the provisional Confederate government on February 9, 1861. He did not enjoy the post, because his beliefs were not as strongly against the Union as was necessary to carry out the duties of the position. He began to oppose Davis and Davis' appointees; he gathered a corps of generals who disagreed with Davis's tactics and did much to bypass some of Davis' more impractical orders. Stephens' most noted move came in February, 1865, when he led a delegation northward to meet Lincoln at Fortress Monroe, in an effort to obtain an armistice.

At the end of the war, he was arrested and held prisoner at Boston until October, 1865. Following his release, he re-entered politics, and was elected to the Senate in January,

1866. He was not, however, allowed to take his seat. Returning home, he began to campaign for a seat in the House which he won and was allowed to take in 1872.

Stephens possessed a brilliant mind and persistent nature. He was an uncompromising idealist, and was respected much more than Jefferson Davis in both Northern and Southern quarters.

STEWART, ALEXANDER PETER (1821–1908)—Confederate Lieutenant General. Born in Rogersville, Tenn., and a graduate of West Point, 1842. Stewart resigned three years after graduation to teach mathematics and philosophy at Cumberland University (later Nashville University) in Tennessee. Prior to the war, he opposed secession, and was a Whig politically. Nevertheless, he joined the Confederate army and became a major. He fought at Belmont, and served as brigadier general at Shiloh. He was promoted to major general by June, 1863, and commanded a division of Hardee's troops.

He campaigned at Chattanooga, Chickamauga and Atlanta, earning still another promotion (to lieutenant general) in June, 1864, and assumed command of a corps. His forces opposed Sherman in the last days in North Carolina, under J. E. Johnston. He was called "Old Straight" by his troops, and was of very high moral character. An able military leader, and a competent worker in every field into which he entered. After the war, he became chancellor of the University of Mississippi.

STONE FLEETS, the Great—Fearing that the Union military heads would send men-of-war into Charleston's harbor, Governor Francis W. Pickens ordered four huge hulks loaded with stones and sunk across the main channel entrance. The first of these "fleets" was sunk on December 12, 1861. The second fleet was sent to the bottom on January 20, 1862.

STONE'S RIVER, the Battle of—December 31, 1862–January 2, 1863. At the fork of the Stone River, Rosecrans's forces cornered Bragg and fought a close and hotly contested battle. The point, about thirty miles southeast of Nashville, Tenn., proved another disaster for the Federal forces, as Bragg (outnumbered 47,000 to 38,000) forced the Union troops to retreat. Both sides lost roughly 12,000 men, and the Confederates leisurely retired southward after the Federals rallied to hold their positions. The river has been alternately called "Stone" River and "Stone's" River.

STONEMAN, GEORGE (1822–1894)—Leader of a luckless expedition of cavalry during the Chancellorsville raid which failed to accomplish its mission against Southern strongpoints and resulted in the loss of almost 7,000 Union horses. Stoneman was severely criticized by both administrators and military leaders for his leadership during the abortive raid toward Richmond.

"STONEWALL" — The nickname applied to Thomas Jackson. The origin of this nickname has been debated for a number of years, with the general consensus leaning towards the legend that Confederate General Bernard Bee, retreating under fire at the first Bull Run, ordered his troops to rally around Jackson's troops with the words, "There stands Jackson like a stone wall."

Other chroniclers, however, applied the name to Jackson's brigade, and state that Jackson received his nickname only because he was the commander of the "Stonewall Brigade." It evolves into the age-old question of which came first, the chicken or the egg. The name was applied to both Jackson and the brigade throughout the remainder of the war. The "Bee version" first appeared in the Charleston *Mercury* four days after the battle. The "Brigade version" is supported in *Mrs. Chestnut's Diary* and the Richmond *Whig and Advertiser* (August 9, 1861).

STUART, JAMES EWELL BROWN (1833–1864)—Confederate general. Known affectionately as "Jeb." Born in Patrick County, Va. Stuart, a graduate of West Point, served in the West prior to the outbreak of the war. In May, 1861, he resigned his commission in the Union army and became a colonel in the First Virginia Cavalry. Following service at Bull Run, he was made a brigadier general (September, 1861).

Stuart executed a wild, but brilliant ride around McClellan's entire army on the Peninsula, and became a hero as a result. McClellan, on the other hand, was one of the most embarassed generals in the Union army when the news became public information. Stuart fought at the Seven Days battles, and made more steps towards promotion to major general (which came in July, 1862).

His Chambersburg, Pa., raid stirred fear in the hearts of Northerners, and he later attempted to duplicate his earlier feat of riding around the Union army, but the results were disasterous for the Southerners. At the time that Stuart proposed his second "ride," he was serving as Lee's main probing force, and was responsible for keeping the Confederate leader informed of Federal strengths and weaknesses. Without Stuart to give this information, Lee went into the battle of Gettysburg almost completely uninformed as to the number of Federal troops in the vicinity of the town. This ignorance may have cost the Southerners a victory. Stuart accomplished nothing on his second ride, but did leave Lee without his "eyes" (a term applied to Stuart's cavalry).

Stuart supported Lee in the Wilderness, and his forces outraced Phil Sheridan for the Yellow Tavern crossroads north of Richmond, Va. His delaying action there allowed Lee to recoup his losses and to dig in for the defense of the Confederate capital. On May 11, 1864, just two days after the start of the race for Yellow Tavern, Stuart was wounded in a skirmish, and died the following day in Richmond.

To the Southerners, "Old Jeb" epitomized the cavalier spirit about which they had read in Scott's novels. To the Northerners, the work of fighting the war was a serious business to be treated with precise and well-planned efficiency—Stuart's carefree brand of warfare was a slap in the face to these soldiers. Although carefree, Stuart was deadly serious when planning for a raid or a battle. He executed each maneuver in a relaxed (yet precise) manner, and was seldom beaten in an even battle. He was one of the South's most idolized leaders.

STUART'S RIDE—(see STUART, JAMES EWELL BROWN)

SULLIVAN ISLAND—Called also Sullivan's Island. This island lies just to the north of the entrance to Charleston Harbor. It was heavily manned with artillery batteries designed to protect the harbor from Northern invasion during the war.

"SUMTER," the C. S. S.—The first Confederate cruiser. Its first captain was the famous raider Raphael Semmes (1861–1862).

SURRATT, JOHN (1844–?)—Conspirator. Son of Mary Surratt, who, it is believed, was supposed to kill Grant at the same time that John Wilkes Booth assassinated Lincoln. Surratt claimed to have been in Canada on April 14, and thus could not have taken part in the plot to kill all top top Union officials. He escaped sentence.

SURRATT, MRS. MARY (1820–1865)—It was in her boardinghouse that the plot to assassinate Lincoln and all of the top officials of the government was first hatched by John Wilkes Booth and seven other conspirators. Mrs. Surratt's son was allegedly involved in the plot, but escaped punishment. She was hanged, along with Lewis Paine, George Atzerodt, and David Herold. Mrs. Surratt is accused of having thought of the original scheme to abduct Lincoln and his top cabinet members. However, the plot thickened, and progressed from kidnapping to murder.

SURRENDER TERMS, THE DURHAM STATION—April 18, 1865. Sherman offered the following terms to Confederate J. E. Johnston and Confederate Secretary of War John C. Breckinridge :

Confederate regiments were to be allowed to march to their state capitals, disbanding there after depositing their weapons at storage places to be provided.

Each man was to sign a pledge never to take up arms again.

Each state was to recognize its duty, and to be recognized by the Union once its administrators pledged to support the Constitution of the United States of America.

No person was to be punished for taking part in the rebellion or for supporting secession.

All political rights were to be guaranteed.

The rights of person and property were to be respected as defined in the Constitution.

Congress refused to ratify these terms.

Earlier, Lincoln had instructed his field commanders to offer liberal terms, but not to step into the political realms such as readmission to the Union, the restoration of political rights, or the question of slavery. Lincoln might have been able to retain much of the liberal aspects of the treaty—but he had been assassinated four days earlier. (See DURHAM STATION.)

The surrender terms were completely out of character for Sherman, who had been depicted as a "spoiler" and "unrelentless in pursuit of the total destruction of the Confederacy." Like Grant (and even more so) Sherman offered the beaten foe liberal terms. Now it was the turn of the politicians to be "uncompromising."

T

TAYLOR, RICHARD (1826–1879)—Confederate Lieutenant General. Born in Louisville, Ky. A graduate of Yale, 1845. Taylor was the only son of Zachary Taylor, and became a planter in Saint Charles Parish, La., after graduation from college. He was known as one of the most learned men in Louisiana. Taylor joined the Confederacy, and became a colonel of the infantry. In October, 1861, he was made a brigadier general, and served with Jackson in the Shenandoah Valley. In July, 1862, he became a major general, and later commanded the District of Western Louisiana. As commander there, he directed the moves which halted the Red River campaign of Union General Nathaniel Banks in April, 1864. For this piece of work, he was moved up the ladder to lieutenant general, and given command of the Department of East Louisiana, Mississippi, and Alabama.

Taylor had the unwanted honor of surrendering the last major Confederate force east of the Mississippi on May 4, 1865. Although not to be considered a brilliant general, Taylor was certainly one of the more capable of the South's leaders, despite his limited military experience prior to the war.

TENNESSEE, the Army of—Confederate. One of the principal armies of the Confederacy, but assigned to cover too much territory to be effective. It came into being on November 20, 1862, when the Army of Kentucky and the Army of Mississippi were united to form the Army of Tennessee under the command of Braxton Bragg. It remained in existence until April 26, 1865, when Johnston surrendered to Sherman at Durham Station, North Carolina.

The failure of the Confederate patriots across the Mississippi to affect the Union military might in that area did much to lessen the striking power of the Army of Tennessee. Like the Army of Northern Virginia, it finally resorted to a defensive and strategic retreat as a weapon, in order to consolidate the dwindling forces at its command into a fighting force strong enough to hold its territory. It did not succeed. The army had three major commanders—

187

Bragg, J. E. Johnston, Hood, and Johnston again. It was, however, blessed with a talent-laden roster of lesser commanders such as Forrest, Hardee, A. P. Hill, Joe Wheeler, Cleburne, Cheatham, and Stewart (to name just a few).

The strategic retreat of this army in the fight for Atlanta is considered one of the military masterpieces of the war. Johnston was in command at the time. Forces of this army did much to hamper the shipments of supplies to the West by Union quartermaster units. Johnston was replaced by Hood in front of Atlanta, but later took command again for the final campaign in North and South Carolina. This was a hard-fighting army of Georgians, Kentucky mountaineers, Texans, and Tennessee woodsmen.

TENNESSEE, the Army of the—Union. This force, composed mainly of troops up from the river campaigns under Grant and of the Shiloh men, was known as the Army of West Tennessee before October 16, 1862, when it assumed the title of "The Army of the Tennessee." It took part in the siege of Vicksburg, the battles around Chattanooga, and the campaign for Atlanta. Parts of this army were with Sherman on his "March to the Sea," in 1864–1865.

When Grant moved east, Sherman was named commander of this army, and later was replaced by Major General James B. McPherson when he (Sherman) took over command of the whole western sector. McPherson took over on March 26, 1864, and served as commander of the army until his death on July 22, 1864. He was succeeded by O. O. Howard, after Major General John A. Logan had held temporary command for five days. Sherman is given credit for molding this group of unruly westerners into an effective fighting machine. He used it as his main weapon for the systematic pushback of the Confederate army, just as Grant used the Army of the Potomac.

This army was reportedly the roughest, most dogged of all Union armies. Confederate soldiers generally preferred fighting the easterners to doing battle with the westerners. The Army of the Tennessee worked more on respect than on discipline, until Sherman took over. A fair comparison would be that the easterners were closer to the European idea of an army, while the Army of the Tennessee was reminiscent of the American army of the Revolution because of its homespun make-up. These men referred to the men of the spit-and-polish Army of the Potomac as "clerks."

TENNESSEE, the Secession of—May 7, 1861. Tennessee seceded immediately after Arkansas (May 6), and in the aftermath of the Lincoln proclamation calling for 75,000 men to put down the rebellion. Immediately following the issuance of the call to arms, Virginia seceded (April 17), and was then followed by Arkansas. The move "forced" four states out of the Union, of which Tennessee was the third.

TEXAS, the Secession of—February 1, 1861. Texas became the seventh state to secede from the Union on February 1st, following South Carolina (December 20, 1860); Mississippi, (January 9, 1861); Florida (January 10); Alabama, (January 11); Georgia, (January 19); and Louisiana (January 26). Delegates from the state attended the Alabama Secession Convention at Montgomery, February 4, 1861.

THIRTEENTH AMENDMENT, the — December 15, 1865. This amendment was based upon the Emancipation Proclamation and actually freed the slaves, whereas the Proclamation had little actual power to do so. It was ratified by the states on December 15, 1865.

THOMAS, GEORGE HENRY (1816–1870)—Union Major General. Born in Southampton County, Va., and a graduate of West Point, 1840. A Southerner by birth but not by sentiment, Thomas chose to remain with the Union when war broke out, even though his family boycotted him as a result, and never forgave him. When war broke out, Thomas was a major general with experience garnered from combat duty in the Mexican War, and in the West. He rose to the rank of colonel before the spring of 1861 ended, and became a brigadier general in August of that same year.

After having led a brigade at Shiloh, Thomas led victorious forces at Mill Springs (Logan's Cross Roads), January 19, 1862. He was made a major general while serving under Buell, in April, 1862, and took part in the Corinth campaign as a commander of volunteers. He remained with Buell until the end of the Kentucky campaign. When offered the post held by Buell, Thomas refused it, and chose to serve under Buell's successor, Rosecrans. He served at Stone's River, and won lasting fame at Chickamauga. There his forces held Snodgrass Hill against a tidal wave of victory-incensed Confederates, earning the name "the Rock of Chickamauga" for Thomas. He replaced Rosecrans as commander of Cumland and took Missionary Ridge. His army joined Sherman in the Atlanta campaign, but was sent back to defend Nashville after Sherman began his "March to the Sea."

Criticized by some for delaying in his attack on Hood's forces at Atlanta, Thomas, instead of being relieved of duty, was promoted for his handling of the battle at Nashville. He was called "Pap" by his men. He was regarded as one of the best tacticians of the war, although considered a bit too slow and deliberate at times. He was, in fact, described by one of his fellow officers as being "large, deliberate and slow-moving."

TOMPKINS, SALLY LOUISA (1833–1916)—Confederate captain. Born in Poplar Grove, Va. Unassigned captain of the cavalry. This nurse was the only woman officer of the Confederacy, and was commissioned by Jefferson Davis to skirt the Confederate congressional order that no civilian could supervise a hospital caring for military personnel. Miss Tompkins had opened the Robertson Hospital to the first soldier patients on July 31, 1861, ten days after the first Bull Run. The Richmond home of Judge John Robertson was used to house the wounded. The hospital received wounded until April 2, 1865, and the last soldier was discharged June 13, 1865. During the war, Miss Tompkins catered to 1,333 wounded men, and only 73 men died while under her care. This was an exceptionally low rate as far as hospital mortality rates of that day were concerned.

She never married, retiring to the Home for Confederate Women in Richmond in later years. Two chapters of the United Daughters of the Confederacy were formed in her name, and she was made an honorary member of the Robert E. Lee Camp of Confederate Veterans.

TOOMBS, ROBERT AUGUSTUS (1810–1885) — Confederate Secretary of State. Born in Wilkes County, Ga. Toombs attended both the University of Georgia and Union College of New York. He engaged in politics prior to the war, and served as a member of the state legislature of Georgia, the U.S. House, and the U.S. Senate. He left the Senate in 1861, expecting to be named president of the Confederacy. Instead, he was named secretary of state.

Dissatisfied, Toombs broke with Davis in July, 1861, and took over command of a brigade in Virginia.

Although he favored compromise measures, Toombs thought that secession was imperative. This attitude of compromise may be the reason he was not elected president of the Confederacy. His antagonistic nature built up much enmity between him and his superior officers. He was forced to resign because the high command continuously bypassed him for promotions. Strictly a "political general," Toombs exerted strong influence on the Reconstruction of the South after the war.

TOTOPOTOMOY CREEK, Va. — This area was the scene of a four-day series of battles between the forces of Lee and Grant in the move against Richmond in 1864. The fighting began on May 28 along the banks of the creek, and ended with Lee entrenching at Cold Harbor, Va., on June 1.

TRIMBLE, ISAAC R. (1802–1888)— Confederate Major General. Born in Kentucky. Trimble was a West Point graduate, and a citizen of Maryland by adoption. He finished the Academy in 1822, and became a professional engineer. Trimble was accused of burning a number of railroad bridges in the Baltimore-Washington area when war broke out, and joined the Confederate army. He promptly rose to the rank of major general (the highest rank achieved by any Maryland officer). He lost a leg at Gettysburg, and was captured. Stanton refused to grant permission for his exchange, and refused him permission to communicate with anyone because (as Stanton described him) he was a "dangerous man." Trimble was not exchanged until just a few weeks before the end of the war. Not much is known about his postwar activities.

TWO-NINETY, the—(see "ALABAMA" and SEMMES, RAPHAEL)

TURNER, WILLIAM F.—(see ARIZONA, the Union Territory of)

U

"UNCLE JOHN" — (See SEDGWICK, JOHN).

"UNCONDITIONAL SURRENDER"—(See GRANT, U. S.).

UNDERWOOD'S FARM, Missouri—The scene of a minor skirmish between pro- and anti-Union forces in the summer of 1861.

UPSON, CHRISTOPHER COLUMBUS— Associate Justice of the Arizona Territory for the Confederate Government. Upson was a native New Yorker who was practicing law in Texas when the war broke out. He served in the war during the first year, as a member of Whiting's staff at the Seven Days campaign. Later in that year, he assumed his post as associate justice.

V

VAN DORN, EARL (1820–1863)—Confederate Major General. Born in Port Gibson, Miss., and a graduate of West Point, 1842. Van Dorn served in Mexico, Florida, and the West prior to the outbreak of war. Shortly after being appointed colonel in the Confederate army, Van Dorn was promoted to major general (September, 1861). He served in Texas until this time. In January, 1862, Van Dorn was given command of the Trans-Mississippi area. His forces were defeated at Pea Ridge (Elkhorn Tavern) in March of that year, and were beaten at Corinth, on the other side of the river, in October. He conducted a well-planned raid on the Federal supply depot at Holly Springs, Miss., in December.

Van Dorn's record does not give a clear indication of his natural ability as a cavalry leader. He ranks with a few others as one of the outstanding cavalry officers of the Civil War. Van Dorn met his death at the hands of a jealous husband in May, 1863. The shooting took place at his headquarters at Spring Hill, Tenn.

VICKSBURG, the Battle of—April 16–July 4, 1863. Vicksburg, on the Mississippi at the Arkansas-Mississippi border, was the scene of one of the longest, most devastating sieges of the war. The fall of Vicksburg gave the Union complete control of the Mississippi, and split the Confederacy in half.

Grant attacked the city from both above and below the port of entry, with most of the frontal assaults failing completely, and none succeeding sufficiently to carry the fortress. Even the famous "Grierson's

Raid" by Colonel Benjamin Grierson and 1,000 men in an effort to pull defending Confederates away from Vicksburg failed to accomplish its objective. After all efforts to storm the elevated city failed, the Union forces settled down to a long and effective siege of the city. Just seventy days after Grant's forces had boarded transports to ferry across the Mississippi, Vicksburg fell. Joseph E. Johnston, Confederate commander in the West at the time, had attempted to relieve the Vicksburg garrison during the siege, but General W. T. Sherman intercepted him and held him off. After forty-two days of siege, the starving garrison surrendered. Pemberton, commander of the garrison, and classmate of Grant, was disturbed over the fact that Grant would accept no terms other than unconditional surrender. In a single stroke, Grant had eliminated the danger of an entire army of the Confederacy, scored the most telling victory of the war up to this point, and cleared the Mississippi from Canada to the Gulf of Mexico for Union use. Lincoln called him east to take on Robert E. Lee.

Grant had the Twelfth Corps under McClernand, two brigades of Logan's Seventeenth Corps under McPherson, and two of Sherman's divisions under his command. Grant's force totaled about 33,000 men. Grant had ordered an assault on Vicksburg on May 19 but it failed. He ordered another on the 22nd which fell short also. The stage was set for the siege. The navy commanded the waters, Grant's forces controlled all land accesses, roving cavalry units stood between the city and re-enforcements. Pemberton was trapped.

Grant had no siege guns other than Porter's mortars. He foraged in the country between the Yazoo River and the Big Black River for provisions for his army. It was during this period that McClernand wrote his letter of dissatisfaction over "treatment received." The siege developed into one in which pickets of each side would exchange foodstuffs on a small scale. On July 3rd, a white flag appeared above the city. Pemberton sent forth terms by General Bowen and Colonel Montgomery which read:

I have the honor to propose an armistice for —— hours, with the view to arranging terms for the capitulation of Vicksburg. To this end, if agreeable to you, I will appoint three commissioners to save further effusion of blood, which must otherwise be shed to a frightful event.

Grant received Bowen (who had been one of his neighbors when he lived in Missouri) and sent him back to the fort with a note which read:

The useless effusion of blood you propose stopping by this course can be ended at any time you may choose, by the unconditional surrender of the city and garrison.

Pemberton raged at the terms, but appeared at the suggested point at three P.M., accompanied by Bowen and Montgomery. Grant was accompanied by Ord, McPherson, Logan,

A. J. Smith, and others. Although Grant and Pemberton had served together in the Mexican War, Grant refused to consider a compromise of his terms. Pemberton conceded. That night at ten P.M., Grant submitted his terms. They read :

In conformity with agreement of this afternoon, I will submit the following proposition for the surrender of the city of Vicksburg, public stores, etc. On your accepting the terms proposed, I will march in one division as a guard, and take possession at 8 A.M. tomorrow. As soon as rolls can be made out and paroles be signed by officers taking with them their side-arms and clothing; and the field, staff, and cavalry officers one horse each. The rank and file will be allowed clothing but no other property. If these conditions are accepted, any amount of rations you deem necessary can be taken from the stores you now have, and also the necessary cooking-utensils for preparing them. Thirty wagons also, counting two-horse or mule teams as one, will be allowed to transport such articles as cannot be carried along. The same conditions will be allowed all sick and wounded officers and soldiers as fast as they become able to travel. The paroles for these latter must be signed, however, whilst officers present are authorized to sign the roll of prisoners . . .

On July 4th, 1863 (the date on which the foot soldiers of Grant's army vowed would be their date of occupation), Union troops entered the city. Over 31,000 prisoners surrendered with 172 cannons, 60,000 muskets, and a large quantity of ammunition and small arms. Upon hearing that Vicksburg had fallen, Gardner at Port Hudson surrendered to Banks with nearly 6,000 more prisoners, 51 cannons, and 5,000 small arms. Casualties totaled 10,000 for the Confederacy, plus 37,000 prisoners, and for the Union, 9,300 casualties.

VIRGINIA, the Army of Northern— Confederate. Commanded principally by Robert E. Lee. Prior to his assumption of command, the forces in Virginia were known as the Army of the Potomac. Lee gave the army its name, and commanded it until the surrender at Appomattox Courthouse. The army received its name on June 1, 1862, when Lee took over in front of Richmond. It participated in most of the major eastern battles of the war : Seven Days, second Bull Run, Antietam, Fredericksburg, Chancellorsville, Gettysburg, the Wilderness, Spotsylvania, Cold Harbor, Five Forks, Petersburg, and the Appomattox campaign. Only one corps of this army ever fought anywhere other than in the east—Longstreet's corps at Chickamauga in the fall of 1863. This army had some of the greatest leaders of the war : Jackson, Longstreet, A. P. Hill, Early, Ewell, and countless others.

In the main, the Army of Northern Virginia fought defensive battles, but campaigns such as the Maryland invasion and Early's strike at Washington, coupled with the Shenandoah Valley campaign and the Pennsylvania campaign, were decidedly offensive maneuvers. It was a highly mobile force, the most mobile in the world at that time. It gained world acclaim for deftly outmaneuvering a larger, more cumbersome opponent throughout the first three years of the war.

The final surrender of the army came as a result of shortages of equipment, men, food, and, above all, a reluctance to continue an obviously losing fight. This last feeling permeated the ranks as a result

of letters from home telling of privations and general disgust with Davis and "his confederacy." All in all, the Army of Northern Virginia was perhaps the most spirited and most loved and respected army in U.S. History —giving a possible close second to the minutemen of 1776.

VIRGINIA, the Union Army of—Organized from various units in and around Washington, under Major General John Pope. Its primary purpose was the defense of Washington. Set up on June 26, 1862, the army saw combat in August of that year against the Confederates in the second Battle of Bull Run. It was soundly defeated, and retreated to the Capitol in humiliation.

This army never was a cohesive unit, for it was made up of too many diverse factors. Pope was not capable of handling an assignment of this size, and these two handicaps together compounded a terrible defeat for the Union forces. On September 12, 1862, the Army of Virginia was disbanded and integrated into other armies.

VIRGINIA MILITARY INSTITUTE, the Cadets of—Confederate. The cadets of secluded Virginia Military Institute campus, averaging about eighteen years of age, sewed up a Confederate victory in one of the war's most stirring incidents in the Shenandoah Valley on Sunday, May 15, 1864. The cadets, designated to be used as last ditch reserves, were pressed into action during the Shenandoah invasion by Sigel and Hunter. At the Battle of New Market, the 247 boys were called upon to fill a gap which had opened in the Confederate lines. They found themselves alone when the right side of the Confederate line collapsed under Federal fire from Bushong's Hill. The cadets charged the hill and took the battery after fierce hand-to-hand battle, and delayed the Union invasion. The cadets lost 10 killed and 47 wounded. Their victory and rout of Franz Sigel assured Lee of the Valley's rich wheat harvest for 1864. (See SHENANDOAH VALLEY, the.)

W

WADE-DAVIS BILL, the—Passed by Congress on July 4, 1864. This was a rigid Reconstruction bill which favored harsh measures in the postwar dealings with the returning seceded states. It was sponsored by the radical Republicans, but Lincoln refused to sign the bill.

WALLACE, LEWIS (1827–1905) — Union Major General. Born in Brookville, Ind. Known as "Lew,"

Wallace was a student of law, and devoted most of his time to writing. He served in the Mexican War as a volunteer officer, and returned to practice law in Crawfordsville, Ind., around 1853. When war broke out, he was made adjutant-general of Indiana, and later fought in the West Virginia campaign. He rose to major general (March, 1862) following action at Donelson. Wallace's forces were on hand (but played little part in the fight) at Shiloh. They lost their way to the scene of battle, and Wallace was severely criticized. During the Kentucky campaign, he was in charge of the force assigned to protect Cincinnati, and was given a promotion to corps commander at Baltimore. He was defeated by Early because of a decided lack of Union manpower (outside of Washington in the battle of the Monocacy) in July, 1864. His delaying tactics, however, saved the city from capture.

After the war, he was appointed governor of New Mexico, and later minister to Turkey. His crowning passion remained writing, and his best novel, *Ben Hur,* has brought him more fame than his military exploits.

WARREN, GOUVERNEUR KEMBLE (1830–1882)—Union Major General. Born in Cold Springs, N.Y., and a graduate of West Point, 1850. Warren served with the topographical engineers in the West prior to the war. He also served in the Peninsular campaign, second Bull Run, and Antietam battles in the early part of the war. In September, 1862, he was made brigadier general (at Freder-

icksburg) and rose to major general and chief engineer of the Army of the Potomac by June, 1863.

Warren is credited with discovering the fact that Little Round Top (Gettysburg) was undefended, and ordering troops to take it for the Union. He fought in the campaigns in Virginia, after Gettysburg, as a corps commander. Sherman removed him from his command for "being slow to move" at Five Forks in April, 1865. This action has been much discussed and often disputed by historians. Warren remained in the army after the war as an engineer. In 1879, he was granted a hearing in the Five Forks affair, but was exonerated only after his death.

WATIE, STAND (1806–1871)—Commander of the last Confederate army to surrender.

Brigadier General Watie was a Cherokee chief, and was the highest ranking Indian officer (by virtue of seniority) in the Civil War. His army did not surrender until June 23, 1865. Watie drew his strongest support from the half-breed and former southeastern Indian slaveholders who had been sent west by the Union army in relocation moves. When the Cherokee chief John Ross was "captured" by Union forces, the Cherokee nation split on the allegiance question. following this those favoring the South selected Watie as the head of the Cherokee nation. The Confederate government, anxious to keep their Indian allies, promoted Watie to the rank of brigadier general to honor his rank among the Indians.

195

The Confederates looked upon the Indians as members of their army, but the Indians looked upon themselves as "allies." Watie's Indians covered many of the retreats of the Confederate army in the West, and specialized in harassing raids on supply lines. (See INDIANS.)

WELLES, GIDEON (1802 – 1878)— Union Secretary of the Navy. Born in Glastonbury, Conn. Welles, a well-educated New Englander, was decided upon for a cabinet post by Lincoln himself—one of the few cabinet members to be so selected. Lincoln picked him, however, as a concession to the New England states. The new Secretary of the Navy was totally without knowledge of how to run the Navy Department, but was energetic and sincere in his efforts, and made one of the better cabinet members of the Lincoln administration. From 1861 to 1869, Welles rebuilt the small, inefficient, and outmoded U.S. Navy into one of the strongest fighting forces of that time. Before the end of the war, the navy was blockading over 2,000 miles of coastal waters.

Welles leaned heavily upon the advice of experienced navy men in his department, and was able to gain considerable knowledge of the operations of a navy department in a relatively short time. He reorganized the department accordingly. His department has been described as a "combination of shrewd yankee organization and New England knowledge of the sea." Welles worked well with Gustavus V. Fox (the man who promoted the development of the "Monitor") and President Lincoln. He usually stayed clear of the cabinet squabbles, and made only one enemy during his time in the administration—Secretary of War Stanton. Welles opposed Stanton's every move, but was generally on good terms with the army itself.

He wrote a diary which has become one of the most valued research pieces of the war. After the war, he supported Johnson against the radical Republicans. He was considered a methodical worker who usually got the job done.

WEST VIRGINIA, the Army of—Union. This army was created from troops within the Department of West Virginia, and operated with the Army of the Shenandoah in 1864. Both armies laid waste to the Valley, and ended Confederate resistance in that area.

WHEELER, JOSEPH (1836 – 1906)— Confederate Major General. Born in Augusta, Ga., and a graduate of West Point, 1859. Wheeler fought in the west prior to the Civil War as a lieutenant. He fought at Shiloh as a colonel, and was given command of a brigade in July, 1862, taking over the cavalry of the Army of the Mississippi at that time. While leading the western cavalry through the battles of Murfreesboro, Chickamauga, and Chattanooga, Wheeler rose to major general. He conducted a number of raids, and was particularly effective around Atlanta. He unsuccessfully tried to oppose Sherman's "March to the Sea," but his manpower could not cope with that of the Union force. When the war ended, Wheeler (known as "Fighting Joe") was only twenty-eight years old, and held the rank of major general. He ranks close to Stuart and Forrest among the South's great cavalry commanders.

After the war, Wheeler went into business, but returned to fight in the Spanish-American War and serve as a major general of volunteers in Cuba and the Philippines. He retired as a brigadier general of the regular army of the United States. Although he fought passionately against the North, Wheeler did much to reunite the states after the Civil War ended.

WHITE OAKS ROAD, the Battle of— (See DINWIDDIE COURTHOUSE.)

WHITING, WILLIAM H. C. (1824– 1865)—Confederate major general. Known affectionately as "Little Billy." A graduate of West Point, 1845. Whiting received the rank of brigadier general as a result of work under Johnston at the first Bull Run. He was primarily an engineer in this post. He, like so many others, fell into disfavor with Jefferson Davis as a result of his open disapproval of Davis' plan to organize his army exclusively according to state alignment. Whiting was captured at the fall of Fort Fisher, and died in a prison camp of wounds received. He was captured on January 15, 1865, and died in May of that year.

WILDERNESS, the Battle of the—May 3–7, 1864. In his march toward the heart of the Confederacy, Grant encountered one of his few setbacks at the Wilderness. Here, in a tangled maze of brush and woods, the Union army bogged down and was attacked by Longstreet. Lee's other forces in that area were bunched near the Rapidan River, but Grant (leading Meade's army) slid around Lee's right flank before the heavy fighting began there. The Army of the Potomac was at its greatest strength (119,000 men) at this time, and almost doubled Lee's force.

After minor skirmishing, the forces came face-to-face at a point chosen by Lee near the tangled terrain of the Wilderness so foreign to the Union forces and so familiar to the Confederates. Soon the area was so heavily covered with smoke from guns of the two armies that firing was done by instinct. Brush fires broke out and burned many of the wounded to death. Grant made one of the rare tactical errors of his career at the Wilderness—he allowed Meade's army to be caught between the Confederates at the Wilderness and those at Richmond. However, the Union made a relentless advance through the woods until stopped by a terrific concentration of fire from Gregg's Texans. Although numbering only 800, Gregg's force hit in such concentrated force that the advance stopped long enough to allow the Confederates to regroup. The battle seesawed all day from that point.

However, on the 7th, Longstreet turned the Union flank while Lee moved around the other flank on the right. This was the first show of tactics of the four-day old battle. Confusion spread through the Federal ranks, and the troops began to fall back. On the following day, Grant took his men out of line and assembled to march. To the surprise of most, the order was given to advance southward, bypassing the Wilderness. This was the first time that the Army of the Potomac had suffered a defeat without returning directly to Washington with its "tail between its legs."

Union losses in the encounter almost doubled those of the Confederacy, but the 8,000 men lost by Lee were missed more than the 15,000 troops of the Union who fell. Grant was criticized for his "callous use of manpower." The Wilderness, because of the terrain, was a series of individual and group conflicts rather than one concerted battle. Much of the fighting was done blindly, and many of the dead died from asphyxiation or by fire. The race for Spotsylvania began after the Wilderness battles, and the dead and wounded of the Wilderness were abandoned.

WILKES, CAPTAIN — (See SLIDELL, JOHN.)

WILMINGTON, North Carolina—The last major Confederate port to be successfully closed. When Fort Fisher was finally taken by A. H. Terry, this closed Wilmington (January 15, 1865). The city surrendered on February 22, 1865, to Schofield.

WILSON, JAMES HARRISON (1837–1925)—Union Brevet Major General. Born Shawneetown, Ill., and a graduate of West Point, 1860. Wilson was a topographical engineer, and served with the corps in Virginia and with the Army of the Tennessee at Vicksburg. In October, 1863, he was promoted to brigadier general of volunteers. In 1864, he commanded a division under Sheridan in the Army of the Potomac, fighting at Petersburg. He was given command of the cavalry of the military division of the Mississippi in October of that year, with the rank of brevet major general. His forces made a good showing against Forrest in the Battle of Nashville late in 1864, and and he led his men into Alabama in 1865, in the forefront of the Union advance. They captured Selma, Ala., in April of that year. Wilson was only twenty-nine when the war ended. He was an excellent organizer and a daring leader.

WILSON'S CREEK, the Battle of—August 10, 1861. This was the largest battle fought during the war in the state of Missouri. There were 6,000 troops under Union Captain Nathaniel Lyon pitted against 11,600 under Confederates Benjamin McCullough and Sterling Price. This battle is also called "Oak Hills" and "Springfield." The Confederates defeated the Union force, Lyon was killed, and the Union lost 223 dead, 731 wounded, and 290 missing. The

Confederates lost 257 killed, 900 wounded, and only 27 missing.

According to Carl Sandburg (*Storm Over the Land*, p. 67), describing Lyon in the battle, "Bullets struck him near the ankle, on the thigh; one cut his scalp to the bone, his horse was shot." He fell with a bullet through his heart, after mounting another horse. The Confederates gave his body over to the Union, and he was laid to rest in his native Connecticut. His death raised a controversy which lasted for years. The Battle of Wilson's Creek was used as a "stick" wielded by Congressman Francis P. Blair against General John Charles Fremont, commander of the Department of the West.

WIRZ, HENRY (?–1865)—Confederate Stockade Commander. Wirz was the stockade commander at the infamous Andersonville prison in Georgia. He was of Swiss extraction, and an immigrant to this country. After the war, he was tried and convicted of conspiracy to "impair the health and destroy the lives of prisoners." He was hanged on November 10, 1865. A monument was erected in his memory in 1905, overlooking the 12,884 Union graves at Andersonville cemetery. The monument was erected by Georgians.

"WOMAN ORDER," the—This order was issued by Union General Benjamin Butler while he was in command of New Orleans. It was aimed at Confederate women who played upon their sex to abuse Union soldiers. The order declared that any woman insulting a Union soldier would be regarded as a "woman of the town, plying her avocation." The order stirred up much controversy.

Y

YAZOO CANAL, the— This is the present-day name of the 1863 channel of the Mississippi. The river has changed considerably since the siege.

YAZOO PASS, Mississippi — Almost 300 miles above Vicksburg. There Grant's forces cut the levee in order to send transports down toward the upper reaches of the Yazoo River in an effort to reduce Fort Pemberton. Fort Pemberton lay to the east of Yazoo Pass and north of Vicksburg on the Yazoo River.

YAZOO RIVER, the—The river winds in a meandering fashion south to the Mississippi, just to the west of the city of Vicksburg. Grant attempted to use this river to carry his transports to a point closer to the city during the siege. At the point where the river entered the Mississippi, Pemberton had set up elaborate entrenchments, using the steep bluffs which lined the river, to make his fortifications more formidable.

YELLOW TAVERN, Virginia — The scene of the defeat of a huge Union cavalry force under Sheridan by Confederates under Stuart. This defeat stopped Sheridan in his planned move against Richmond. Stuart was mortally wounded in this engagement. (See STUART, J. E. B.)

YORK, Pennsylvania — Lee's army reached this northern city in June of 1863, in his invasion of Pennsylvania. It was from this point that Lee began his concentration towards Gettysburg.

YORKTOWN, Virginia—It was here, during the Peninsular Campaign, that the Confederates set up a thin line of troops entrenched across the neck of the Peninsula to attempt to stop the Union march on Richmond. McClellan himself scouted the Southern position, yet wasted much valuable time entrenching instead of attacking the thin line of Confederates. At the time, there were only 40,000 additional troops defending the capital of Richmond. McClellan had over 150 huge mortars set up in siege fashion, capable of firing over 400 tons of shells per day. Magruder ("Prince John") duped McClellan into thinking that the lines were manned by thousands more troops than actually were there by marching his men back and forth in view of the scouting party. When McClellan finally decided to attack, he found that Magruder had withdrawn, along with the rest of Johnston's force, to fall back in defense of Richmond.

YOUNG, BENNET H. (1843–1919)— Confederate raider. Young, a graduate of Center College in Danville, Ky., was selected by Confederate Secretary of War James A. Seddon to lead a series of raids on prison camps in Northern territory in late 1864. Young was to recruit from the ranks of those members of the Confederate cavalry who had escaped from Yankee prison camps to Canada. He was also to use Confederate agents in Canada to recruit sympathizers. The size of his force was designated as "no more than twenty."

The youthful lieutenant had recently escaped from Camp Douglass near Chicago in 1863. He had ridden with John Hunt Morgan's raiders until captured in Ohio in 1863. He planned to hit Johnson's Island in Sandusky Bay, Ohio, where a large number of Confederates were being held prisoner. However, word of his plan leaked out, and another target had to be selected. St. Albans, Vt., won the toss, and the plans to throw fear into the hearts of the Northerners, while gaining badly needed funds for the South, came into being.

Young led the St. Albans raid on October 19, 1864, and was captured in Canada by citizens of that town. They were, however, forced to turn him and the rest of the raiders over to Canadian authorities since the arrests had been made by Americans on Canadian soil. Young and his thirteen captured raiders were released by the courts after two trials, because they were labeled officially "belligerents of a nation at war." The move almost caused an international incident of major proportions.

He returned to his native Kentucky after the war, but was refused permission to accept the Johnson Amnesty Proclamation's benefits because of his part in the raid. He went to Europe in 1868, but returned to Louisville to practice law until his death at the age of seventy-six in 1919. (See ST. ALBANS, the raid on.)

YOUNGER, ("COLE") THOMAS COLEMAN (1844–1916)—One of Quantrill's raiders, and one of the West's most infamous outlaws. He and Jesse James are numbered among the 450 members of Quantrill's party which raided Lawrence, Kan., August 21, 1863.

YOUNG'S POINT, Mississippi—This was the site of the camp set up by McClernand and Sherman following the successful attack on Fort Hindman. Here, 50,000 Union troops gathered just twelve miles from the city of Vicksburg, and prepared plans for the attack upon the city.

Chronology of the War

April
23 Democratic Presidential Nominating Convention at Charleston, S.C.

May
3 Democrats adjourn without selecting a Presidential ticket, after the Deep South withdraws over the slavery plank in the platform.
9 The Constitutional Union Party nominates John Bell and Edward Everett at Baltimore.
16 Republicans convene at Chicago to nominate a Presidential ticket amidst rumors that the party might split over the selection.
18 Abraham Lincoln and Hannibal Hamlin win the Republican nominations.

June
18 Democrats convene again at Baltimore.
22 Deep South delegates again pull out of the convention.
23 The remaining delegates choose John C. Breckinridge and Joseph Lane as candidates on the Southern ticket. The northern Democrats select Stephen A. Douglas and Herschel V. Johnson, bringing the total number of tickets to four for the 1860 election.

November
6 Lincoln and Hamlin win the election.

9 South Carolina calls a secession convention.
10 South Carolina's James Chestnut resigns from the Senate, to be followed by his colleague James H. Hammond.
15 Major Robert Anderson assumes command of Charleston, S.C., defenses.
23 Anderson requests supplies and re-enforcements.
28 Anderson, having received no reply, again requests aid.

December
1 Anderson sends for supplies and re-enforcements for the third time.
4 President Buchanan declares secession unconstitutional, but states that the Presidential office cannot deny that the federal government has no power to force any state to remain in the Union if it desires to leave.
8 Secretary of the Treasury, Georgia's Howell Cobb, resigns because he feels that "Secession of my state is imminent."
9 Buchanan assures the South Carolina congressmen that he will not attempt to re-enforce Charleston without first consulting them.
14 Secretary of State Lewis Cass of Michigan resigns because of Buchanan's failure to re-enforce Anderson at Fort Sumter.
18 Senator John J. Crittenden of Kentucky proposes six amendments to the Constitution which will protect slavery.

20 South Carolina secedes from the Union.

22 Lincoln's opposition to the Crittenden proposal protecting slavery in the territories is announced.

24 The Senate Committee of Thirteen rejects the Crittenden Compromise.

26 Anderson withdraws to Fort Sumter, leaving the other harbor forts to the South Carolina forces.

27 Castle Pinckney is seized by South Carolina state troops.

29 Secretary of War John Floyd of Virginia resigns.

30 The U.S. Arsenal at Charleston is seized by state troops.

31 The Committee of Thirteen reports its failure to reach a compromise. Buchanan orders re-enforcements for Anderson.

1861

January

2 Fort Johnson is seized by South Carolina state troops.

5 The " Star of the West " sails from New York with men and supplies for Fort Sumter.

8 Secretary of the Interior Jacob Thompson of Mississippi resigns his post after receiving word that his state is about to secede.

9 Mississippi secedes from the Union.

10 Florida secedes from the Union.

11 The Mississippi River is blockaded at Vicksburg by an artillery battery of Confederates.

12 Alabama secedes from the Union officially after announcing the intention on the 11th.
Secretary of the Treasury Philip F. Thomas of Maryland resigns, and is the last Southener to withdraw from the cabinet.

19 Georgia secedes from the Union.

21 Jefferson Davis and four of his Southern colleagues resign from the Senate.

24 The Augusta (Georgia) Arsenal is seized by 700 state troops.

26 Louisiana secedes from the Union.

29 Kansas is admitted to the Union as the thirty-fourth state.

February

1 Texas secedes from the Union.

4 Virginia's Peace Conference opens in Washington, but is not attended by any representatives from the seceded states. A pro-Union majority takes control of the Virginia Sesession Convention in that state, raising hopes that the state will not leave the Union.

8 The Confederates adopt their first constitution at Montgomery, Ala.

9 Jefferson Davis is elected provisional president of the Confederacy, and Alexander Stephens is elected vice-president.

11 Lincoln leaves Springfield, Ill., for Washington to assume office.

13 Lincoln's election is confirmed by the Electoral College, minus most of the Southern members.

15 The Montgomery Convention resolves to take Fort Sumter and Fort Pickens by "whatever means necessary."

18 Jefferson Davis is inaugurated at Montgomery as provisional head of the newly-formed Confederacy.

23 Lincoln arrives at Washington secretly from Harrisburg, Pa., to avoid assassination attempts.

March

1 Congress refuses to act upon the Peace Conference proposals of the Virginia group.

2 In the absence of opposition, Congress pushes through the Morrill

Tariff Act, which has been opposed by Southern congressmen.

4 Lincoln is inaugurated.

Anderson reports that his supplies at Fort Sumter are running low, and announced that the shortage of food may force his evacuation.

5 Lincoln's cabinet is announced.

6 The Confederate cabinet is announced.

Davis calls for 100,000 volunters.

11 The Confederacy adopts a permanent constitution.

15 After being asked their opinions by Lincoln, all of the cabinet members except Blair advise against the re-enforcement of Fort Sumter. Chase and Seward oppose the move unless Fort Pickens is re-enforced also.

April

4 Lincoln orders a relief expedition to Fort Sumter, but, because of Seward's duplicity, the expedition sails without armed escort.

8 The relief expedition leaves New York.

10 Robert Small, a Negro, who later becomes captain of a Union steamer, terms the day " The dawn of freedom for our race." (Small was a slave.)

12 Confederates fire upon Fort Sumter at approximately 4 :30 A.M.

15 Lincoln calls for 75,000 volunteers to fight against " combinations too powerful to be supressed by the ordinary course of judicial proceedings."

17 The Virginia Convention votes for secession despite a previously heavy balance of power for remaining in the Union.

Nicholas Biddle, a colored man from Pottsville, Pa., joins the Washington artillerists, and becomes the first Negro volunteer.

18 Three free Negroes are taken off the " Star of the West " in Galveston, Tex., taken to Montgomery, and auctioned into slavery.

The Union garrison abandons Harper's Ferry.

Nicholas Biddle is wounded during the Baltimore Passage by a mob, and becomes the first of his race to shed blood in the Civil War, unless Harper's Ferry (John Brown's raid) is looked upon as a Civil War action.

19 The Sixth Massachusetts clashes with a mob in Baltimore during the passage, and Clara Barton comes to the fore as a nurse for the wounded.

20 Frederick Douglass proposes the use of African Zouave Regiments, stating, " Nothing could please me more and bring the race to power, than to see the southern chivalry well whipped by an equal number of blacks. It would indeed to refreshing." His proposal is not considered.

Robert Edward Lee resigns from the U.S. Army.

Confederates seize the abandoned Norfolk Naval Yard.

21 Clara Barton and five Negroes tend the wounded in Baltimore's first make-shift military hospital.

22 Seven Negro seamen among the crew of the " Argo " out of Bath, Me., are seized and jailed in Petersburg.

27 North Carolina and Virginia are included in the blockade.

May

3 Lincoln calls for 42,034 three-year volunteers, and begins to enlarge the regular army and navy.

6 Arkansas secedes from the Union.

7 Tennessee forms an alliance with

the Confederacy, but does not actually secede at this time.

10 Captain Nathaniel Lyon takes over St. Louis after putting down a riot between pro-Union and pro-slavery elements.

12 Troops under General Butler restore order in Baltimore.

George Scott, the first contraband slave at Fort Monroe, becomes a scout in the Union army. His information aids in the battle of Big Bethel, the first major contest of the war.

13 Queen Victoria proclaims British neutrality, thereby unofficially recognizing the Confederacy as a belligerent.

16 The Confederate Congress authorizes the recruiting of 400,000 men.

20 North Carolina secedes from the Union.

21 The Confederate Congress moves to take the capital to Richmond, Va.

23 Virginia votes to join the Confederacy.

24 Major J. B. Cary of the Confederate army, under a flag of truce, is refused permission to reclaim three slaves who have escaped to the Union lines. General Ben Butler proclaims them "contraband" and permits the slaves to remain. On the same day, Butler announces that over $60,000 worth of "contraband" in the form of slaves has escaped to his lines. They are allowed to remain as laborers without pay.

Ten thousand Federal troops enter Virginia, and occupy Alexandria. Major Ephriam Ellsworth is killed while removing a Confederate flag from a hotel roof, and becomes the first officer killed in the war.

26 General George B. McClellan, from the Department of the Army of the Ohio, is ordered to suppress all attempts of insurrection among Negroes.

27 General Butler moves his "contraband" within the confines of Fortress Monroe.

28 Brigadier General McDowell is appointed Union commander of the Department of the Army of Northeastern Virginia.

29 Union forces occupy Newport News, Va.

June

3 Stephen A. Douglas dies at Chicago, Ill.

10 Federal troops are forced to withdraw after the Battle of Big Bethel, the first major battle of the war.

Napoleon declares French neutrality.

11 Western Virginia refuses to secede and sets up a state government which Washington promptly recognizes, calling it the "Loyal Virginia Government."

28 The Tennessee legislature passes an act allowing Negroes to be accepted into the military service, with the governor being given leeway to determine just how many are needed. The Negroes are to be given eight dollars each month, one ration per day, and an annual allowance of clothing.

29 The Tennessee legislature authorizes the governor to accept free male persons of color between the ages of fifteen and fifty for military service.

July

4 A special session of the U.S. Congress convenes.

Confederate spy Belle Boyd kills a Union corporal for "molesting her mother."

11 McClellan wins the battle of Rich Mountain in western Virginia.

16 McDowell's army advances upon Manassas Junction, Va.

20 Major General Joseph E. Johnston's troops from the Shenandoah Valley join Brigadier General P. G. T. Beauregard at Manassas Junction.

21 The first Battle of Bull Run ends in a route of McDowell's Union army.

25 The U.S. Congress passes the Crittenden Resolution declaring the object of the war to be the preservation of the Union rather than the end of slavery.

27 McClellan replaces McDowell as commander of Federal troops in the Washington area.

August

6 The U.S. Congress passes the Confiscation Act for the seizure of the property (including slaves) used against the Union for insurrectionary purposes.

10 Brigadier General Nathaniel Lyon is killed and his army defeated and routed at Wilson's Creek, Mo.

14 Fremont places St. Louis under martial law.

28 Grant is given command of Federal troops in southeastern Missouri and southern Illinois.

30 Fremont proclaims martial law in Missouri and orders the confiscation of property and slaves of Missourians aiding the Confederacy.

September

4 Confederate Major General Leonidas Polk seizes Columbia, Ky., ending the state's attempt at neutrality.

6 Union forces under Grant take Paducah, Ky.

10 A. S. Johnston is given command of the Confederate armies in the West.

11 Lincoln orders Fremont to modify his Missouri slave proclamation to conform to the national Confiscation Act.

17 Judah P. Benjamin succeeds Leroy P. Walker as the Confederate secretary of war.
Thomas Bragg replaces Benjamin as attorney general.

20 Rebels under Sterling Price capture the Union garrison at Lexington, Mo.

October

8 Brigadier General Sherman assumes command of the Federal army in central and eastern Kentucky, replacing Robert Anderson.

21 Federal troops are defeated at Ball's Bluff, Va.

November

1 Winfield Scott resigns as Federal general-in-chief, and is replaced by McClellan.

2 Fremont is relieved of the Western command.

6 Davis and Stephens are elected to full six-year terms as Confederate President and Vice-President.

7 Fort Walker at Port Royal Harbor, S.C., is captured by the U.S. Navy. Grant suffers a tactical defeat at Belmont, Mo.
Fort Beauregard is captured by the U.S. Navy in Port Royal Harbor.

8 Captain Charles Wilkes seizes the Confederate envoys James M. Mason and John Slidell aboard the British mail steamer "Trent."

9 Brigadier General Don Carlos Buell replaces Sherman in the Tennessee-Kentucky area.

19 Major General Henry W. Halleck replaces Fremont in command of Union forces in Missouri.

30 The British government demands the release of Mason and Slidell and an apology for their seizure.

December
17 A skirmish on Chisholm's Island, Goosaw River, S.C.
20 The Joint Committee on the Conduct of the War is organized, consisting of U.S. Senators Wade, Chandler, and Andrew Johnson, and Representatives Gooch, Julian, Covode, and Moses F. Odell.
20 The first "Stone Fleet" is sunk at the entrance to Charleston Harbor.
27 Seward announces the release of Mason and Slidell, and acknowledges Wilkes' error in seizing them.

1862

January
1 Land and naval forces engage at Page's Point, Port Royal Ferry, S.C.
11 Simon Cameron resigns as U.S. secretary of war, and is replaced by Stanton.
19 George Thomas defeats the Confederates at Mill Springs, securing the state of Kentucky for the Union.
20 The second Stone Fleet is sunk at the entrance to Charleston Harbor.

February
6 Grant and Foote lead a successful army-navy attack upon Fort Henry.
7 Albert S. Johnston retreats from Kentucky.
8 Ambrose E. Burnside leads a Federal expedition successfully against Roanoke Island, N.C.
10 Skirmishes on Barnwell's Island, S.C.
13 Grant invests Fort Donelson on the Cumberland River.

16 Brigadier General Simon B. Buckner unconditionally surrenders 15,000 Confederates to Grant at Fort Donelson.
22 Jefferson Davis is inaugurated.
25 The Confederates abandon Nashville.

March
2 Polk abandons Columbus, Ky.
3 Andrew Johnson is appointed military governor of Kentucky by Lincoln.
6 Lincoln proposes to Congress the gradual compensated emancipation of border state slaves.
The "Monitor" leaves New York.
7 The "Merrimac" enters Hampton Roads, and destroys or damages three wooden U.S. warships.
The confederates lose the battle of Pea Ridge, giving the Union control of Missouri.
9 The "Merrimac" and the "Monitor" meet in the first battle of ironclads, with no decisive victor, at Hampton Roads.
11 Halleck takes over all Federal forces in the West.
11 McClellan is removed as general-in-chief of Federal forces, but remains in command of the Army of the Potomac.
12 A Union naval force takes Jacksonville, Fla.
14 Burnside takes New Bern, N.C.
Southern forces evacuate New Madrid, Mo., giving the Federal forces a clear path to attack Island No. 10 in the middle of the Mississippi River.
17 Grant takes over the army at Pittsburg Landing (Shiloh).
Davis completes his organization of the Confederate cabinet. J. P. Benjamin moves up from secretary of war to secretary of state.
23 Thomas J. Jackson ("Stonewall")

is defeated at Kernstown, Va., in the battle of the Shenandoah Valley campaign for the Union. Shield was the victor.

28 The Confederate invasion of New Mexico is halted at the Battle of Glorieta, called the "Gettysburg of the West."

29 Albert S. Johnston reassembles his forces at Corinth, Miss.
The affair of Edisto Island, S.C.

April

4 McClellan's army starts its Peninsular campaign towards Richmond, Va.

5 McClellan besieges the Confederate defenses at Yorktown, Va.

6 The Confederates surprise Grant at Shiloh. A. S. Johnston is killed; Beauregard takes command of the Confederate army.

7 Buell re-enforces Grant at Shiloh, turning the tide of battle in favor of the Union. Beauregard retreats to Corinth, Miss.

8 Over 5,000 Confederates on Island No. 10 surrender to Pope, opening the Missisippi more to Union traffic.

11 Fort Pulaski falls to Federal troops. thereby completing the blockade of Savannah, Ga.

12 The Andrews Raid ends in northern Georgia, with Federal raider James J. Andrews and seven of his men hanged as spies. The others (who escaped from prison after being captured) returned North and received the first Congressional Medals of Honor ever issued.

16 The Confederate government votes conscription of able-bodied men between the ages of eighteen and thirty-five; owners of twenty or more slaves are exempted, and the hiring of a substitute or payment of $500 exempts those who can afford it.

Lincoln signs the bill abolishing slavery in the District of Columbia.

25 Farragut captures New Orleans after running the guns of Fort Jackson and St. Philip. These forts surrender when New Orleans falls.

29 Halleck takes over Grant's army and advances on Beauregard's force at Corinth.
There are engagements at White Point, S.C., Pineberry Battery near there, and Willtown, S.C.

May

1 Butler moves into New Orleans and sets up what has been described as "one of the most corrupt administrations in the city's history."

4 The siege of Yorktown ends when J. E. Johnston and his force retreat.

5 Longstreet successfully defends against McClellan at Williamsburg while the Confederates retreat.

8 Jackson defeats Milroy at McDowell, Va., as part of the Confederate Shenandoah Campaign to keep re-enforcements from reaching McClellan.

9 McClellan advances on Richmond and forces the Rebels to abandon Norfolk, Va.

10 Union forces occupy Pensacola, Fla.

11 The Confederates burn the "Merrimac" to prevent its capture.

12 Union troops occupy Baton Rouge, La.

15 Butler issues the famous "Woman Order" in New Orleans to halt unladylike insults to his troops from Confederate women.

20 The Homestead Act passes the U.S. Congress.

23 Jackson recaptures Front Royal, Va.

25 Jackson routs Banks at Winchester, Va.

Halleck arrives at Corinth after taking twenty-six days to march twenty miles.

Engagement between James Island and Dixon's Island, S.C.

30 Beauregard evacuates Corinth in the face of Halleck's force.

31 Joe Johnston is severely wounded at the inconclusive battle of Fair Oaks on the Peninsula.

June

1 Lee succeeds to the command of the Confederate force in Virginia in front of Richmond.

4 Fort Pillow, Tenn., is evacuated by the Confederates.

6 Federal forces occupy Memphis after a naval battle.

8 Fremont loses to Jackson at Cross Keys, Va.

10 Skirmishes take place at Grimball's plantation, James Island, S.C.

15 J. E. B. Stuart completes his famous ride around McClellan's entire army.

16 A battle take place at Secessionville, S.C.

17 Jackson's army leaves the Shenandoah to re-enforce Lee at Richmond.

19 Slavery is abolished in the U.S. territories.

21 There is an engagement at Simmon's Bluff in S.C.

25 McClellan attacks Oak Grove, Va., beginning the Seven Days battles.

Union gunboats enter the South Santee in South Carolina.

26 Lee attacks McClellan's right wing at Mechanicsville, Va., but fails to destroy the Union corps under Fitz-John Porter.

Pope is given command of the Federal army of Virginia, newly formed from various commands around Washington.

Farragut's fleet bombards Vicksburg, Miss.

27 Lee breaks through the Gaine's Mill line and forces McClellan to retreat towards the James River.

29 Lee attacks the Army of the Potomac again at Savage's Station, Va.

30 McClellan successfully retreats to Frayser's Farm, Va., and gets past Lee to the James River.

July

1 Lee is repulsed at Malvern Hill, Va., ending the Seven Days battles and allowing McClellan to retreat across the James River.

The U.S. Congress authorizes construction of a transcontinental railroad.

2 Lincoln calls for 300,000 three-year enlistments.

The U.S. Congress passes the Morrill Act, providing land grants to states with which to set up agricultural colleges.

3 McClellan entrenches at Harrison's Landing on the James River.

4 There is a skirmish at Port Royal.

11 Halleck becomes general-in-chief of the Union armies.

14 Pope leads an advance upon Gordonsville, Va.

17 The U.S. Congress passes a second Confiscation Act — almost exactly the same as that which Fremont issued and for which he was relieved of his command in Missouri.

22 Lincoln presents his draft of the Emancipation Proclamation to his cabinet, and is convinced to release it at another time.

The North and South sign a prisoner exchange cartel.

29 The "Alabama" leaves Liverpool, England, to begin its attacks upon

northern shipping lanes, under the captaincy of Raphael Semmes.

August

4   Lincoln issues another call for 300,000 nine-month militiamen.

9   Jackson defeats Banks at Cedar Mountain, Va.

Lee attempts to destroy Pope's force before McClellan can reinforce the Union arm.

14   General E. K. Smith begins the Confederate invasion of Kentucky at Knoxville.

McClellan begins a withdrawal from the Peninsula under orders from Halleck.

26   Pope's supply depot at Manassas is destroyed by Jackson. Pope attempts to pursue but is unable to pinpoint the Rebel force.

28   Jackson engages King at Groveton, Va., revealing his position to Pope.

30   Longstreet sweeps Pope's flank, and the second Battle of Bull Run ends in another humiliating defeat for the Federal forces.

Buell orders the pursuit of Bragg and Kirby Smith in Kentucky after the former Confederate commander had left Chattanooga to join Smith in Kentucky.

September

1   Union Major Generals Kearny and Stevens are killed as Jackson hits Pope's army at Chantilly, Va.

2   Pope is replaced by McClellan outside of Washington.

Kirby Smith occupies Lexington, Ky.

5   Lee crosses the Potomac into Maryland, opening his Northern invasion.

7   The Confederates reach Frederick, Md.

9   Lee divides his force, sending Jackson to Harper's Ferry to prepare

for an invation of Pennsylvania after the Maryland invasion is successful.

13   McClellan is handed a copy of Lee's battle order, found in a nearby meadow, and is given detailed information of the deployment of the Confederate troops. He fails to act upon these orders immediately.

14   McClellan hits South Mountain passes, winning battles at Crampton's Gap and South Mountain, forcing Lee to move towards Sharpesburg, Md.

15   Jackson takes Harper's Ferry, capturing 12,000 Federals.

16   McClellan moves into position at Antietam to block further Confederate advances. Lee calls Jackson to reinforce his army.

17   Lee's army withstands a number of Federal assaults, but is stopped. This is called the bloodiest single battle of the war.

18   Lee retreats to Virginia, ending his first invasion threat.

19   Rosecrans is ordered to engage Price at Iuka, Miss.

22   Lincoln issues the preliminary Emancipation Proclamation to become effective January 1, 1863.

Bragg reaches Bardstown, Ky., abandoning his move on Louisville, and seeks to reunite with Kirby Smith.

29   Buell reaches Louisville, Ky.

October

4   Rosecrans defeats Van Dorn at Corinth, Miss., completing the isolation of Bragg in Kentucky.

8   Bragg and Smith retreat towards Tennessee after a battle between Buell's force and the Southerners fails to give either side a clearcut victory at Perrysville. The Rebel invasion of Kentucky is ended.

12 Stuart completes his second ride around McClellan's army, after destroying property at Chambersburg, Pa.

30 Rosecrans replaces Buell as commander of the Army of the Cumberland.

November

2 Grant begins a campaign to capture Vicksburg, Miss., from the Tennessee state line.

4 The Republicans suffer a setback in both Congressional and state elections in the North, raising doubts as to whether Lincoln will be re-elected in 1864.

7 Burnside replaces McClellan as commander of the Army of the Potomac.

17 Burnside moves towards Fredericksburg, Va., reaching the banks of the Rappahannock River opposite the city.

21 Lee's force entrenches in a strong defensive position in front of Fredericksburg.
James A. Seddon succeeds George W. Randolph as Confederate secretary of war.

30 Jackson arrives at Fredericksburg from the Shenandoah Valley with re-enforcements for Lee.

December

11 Burnside's force starts to cross the Rappahannock at Fredericksburg.
Nathan Bedford Forrest launches a cavalry attack upon Grant's communications lines in Tennessee.

13 Lee stops Burnside with heavy losses in the Battle of Fredericksburg.

15 The Army of the Potomac is forced to retreat across the Rappahannock River.

20 Van Dorn hits Grant's Holly Springs, Miss., supply depot, doing great damage, and halting the Federal advance towards Vicksburg temporarily.

21 John Hunt Morgan and his Confederate raiders began a cavalry raid on Union supplies in Tennessee.

29 Sherman's force suffers heavy losses in a futile attack upon Chickasaw Bluffs up the river from Vicksburg.

31 The "Monitor" sinks in a storm off Cape Hatteras, N.C.
Rosecrans gets the worst of the first day of battle at Murfreesboro, Tenn.

1863

January

1 Lincoln announces that the Emancipation Proclamation is now in effect.

2 Bragg attacks Rosecrans again at Murfreesboro, but fails to carry the position.

3 Bragg withdraws from Murfreesboro after a tactical victory.

8 John P. Usher becomes U.S. secretary of the interior, succeeding Caleb S. Smith.

11 Federals take Fort Hindman on the Arkansas River.

23 Burnside's offensive against Lee fails in the " Mud March."

26 Major General Joseph Hooker takes over as commander of the Army of the Potomac, succeeding Burnside.

February

2 Grant attempts to hit Vicksburg from the rear by cutting a passage through at Yazoo Pass, Miss., but is halted.

25 The U.S. Congress authorizes a national banking system as set up by Salmon P. Chase, the secretary of the treasury.

212

March

3 The U.S. Congress passes the first conscription act which lists all men between the ages of twenty and forty-five as eligible for draft. The act provides for the exemption of a man if he hires a substitute or pays the government $300 which will be used to pay bounty to an enlistee.

8 Grant fails to bypass Vicksburg's defenses via the Yazoo River Canal and by the Lake Province route.

17 The Yazoo Pass is blocked by rebel forces at Fort Pemberton.

21 Dixon's ironclads have to be rescued by Sherman's troops after being trapped in Steel's Bayou. This ends still another attempt to get to the rear of Vicksburg's defenses.

25 Burnside is appointed commander of the Department of the Ohio, and is ordered to concentrate on eastern Tennessee.

April

2 Bread riots in Richmond, Va.

7 Rear Admiral Samuel F. Du Pont fails to take Fort Sumter, S.C.

11 Longstreet begins the siege of Suffolk, Va.

16 The Union fleet under Porter runs the guns of Vicksburg, setting up Grant's new campaign against Vicksburg below the city.

17 Colonel Grierson begins his famous raid through Mississippi in the hopes of drawing Pemberton out of Vicksburg to meet him. Confederate communications to Vicksburg are cut off.

29 Stoneman leads a cavalry raid behind Lee's lines in Virginia.

30 Hooker crosses the Rappahannock and the Rapidan in a move towards Chancellorsville, Va.

Grant moves his force across the Mississippi to the Vicksburg side near Bruinsburg, Miss.

May

1 Grant takes Port Gibson, Miss.

2 Jackson is killed accidentally by his own men after his forces have routed the Federal right flank at Chancellorsville, Va.

3 Grierson reaches the Union lines at Baton Rouge, after having devastated the Mississippi - Louisiana countryside.

Lee launches a second invasion of the North from Fredericksburg.

9 As a result of a cavalry battle at Brandy Station, Va., the Union commander realizes that the Confederates are making another attempt to invade the North.

15 Ewell leads Lee's invasion into Winchester, Va., destroying the garrison there.

20 The "loyal Government of Virginia" is admitted to the Union as the thirty-fifth state, with the name of West Virginia.

23 Rosecrans moves towards Tullahoma to dislodge Bragg.

25 Stuart leaves on his third ride around the Army of the Potomac, leaving Lee without a scouting force of any major size. His plan is to screen Lee's advance into Pennsylvania.

The mine at Vicksburg is exploded, but fails to breach the defenses sufficiently to make the attack a success.

The Army of the Potomac crosses the Potomac River to check Lee's move northward.

28 Early's division seizes York, Pa.

Meade replaces Hooker as commander of the Army of the Potomac.

29 Lee moves toward Gettysburg; Stuart is still moving around the Federal force; Union troops are concentrated north of the Potomac.

July

1 Hill and Ewell engage Meade's advance force, routing them. The Southerners set up on Seminary Ridge; the Northerners occupy Cemetery Ridge.

2 Lee's attacks on the Federal flanks fail.

3 Pickett's charge on the Federal middle fails, and the Confederates retire, ending the three-day battle. Pemberton asks Grant for terms at Vicksburg.
Bragg retreats to Chattanooga after being outmaneuvered by Rosecrans.

4 Vicksburg surrenders, turning over 30,000 troops.

5 Lee retreats from Gettysburg without opposition.

8 Lee entrenches at Williamsport, Md., unable to cross the flooded Potomac River. Still Meade does not attack him.

9 Port Hudson, La., surrenders following the fall of Vicksburg, giving the Union complete control of the Mississippi, and adding 6,000 prisoners to the tally.
Morgan leads his raiders across the Ohio River against orders.

13 The draft riots begin in New York, lasting four days, and involving a mob of over 50,000 persons.

14 Lee succeeds in withdrawing across the Potomac with Heth fighting a rearguard action at Falling Waters, Md.

16 Front-line troops are called in to restore order in New York, and fire upon the mob.

19 Over half of Morgan's raiders are captured at Buffington, Ohio, leaving the raider stranded in northern Ohio.

24 Lee masses his force at Culpeper, Va.

26 Morgan surrenders to one of his own prisoners at New Lisbon, Ohio.

August

15 Burnside opens his campaign against Knoxville, Tenn.

16 Rosecrans moves on Chattanooga.

21 Quantrill's raiders attack and burn Lawrence, Kan.

September

2 Burnside enters Knoxville.

4 Rosecrans chases Bragg across the Tennessee River and moves on Chattanooga.

7 Union forces take Fort Wagner.

8 Dahlgren fails in an attempt to take Fort Sumter.

9 Rosecrans enters Chattanooga, deserted by Bragg, who was forced to retreat into north Georgia.

10 Steele seizes Little Rock, Ark., for the Union.

17 Rosecrans chases Bragg to Chickamauga Creek, Ga.

18 Longstreet re-enforces Bragg at Chickamauga.

19 The Battle of Chickamauga begins.

20 Longstreet breaks through the Federal lines, but is delayed by Thomas long enough to allow the Union forces to evacuate safely to Chattanooga.

23 Bragg entrenches on Missionary Ridge and Lookout Mountain, and lays siege to Chattanooga.

24 Hooker leaves Virginia with 15,000 men to re-enforce the besieged forces at Chattanooga.

October

9 Lee attacks the Army of the Potomac near Bristoe Station, Va.

17 Grant takes over as supreme commander of the Western forces.

19 Rosecrans is replaced by Thomas in command of the Army of the Cumberland.

23 Grant arrives at Chattanooga.

27 W. F. Smith forces open a supply line into Chattanooga.

November

4 Longstreet's troops leave Bragg in order to hit Burnside at Knoxville.

10 Lee retreats to the Rapidan River after fighting an indecisive battle at Bristoe Station, Va.

19 Lincoln delivers his Gettysburg Address.

20 Sherman arrives at Chattanooga with re-enforcements.

23 Thomas opens the Battle of Chattanooga by overrunning the Orchard Knob in front of Missionary Ridge.

24 Bragg evacuates Lookout Mountain under pressure from Hooker.
Sherman hits Missionary Ridge from across the Tennessee River.

25 Bragg stops Sherman, but is unable to stop the reckless charge of Thomas' men at Missionary Ridge. Bragg retreats into Georgia.

26 Meade crosses the Rapidan River and engages a small Confederate force at Mine Run, west of Chancellorsville.

27 Morgan escapes from the Ohio State Penitentiary where he and his officers have been held on criminal charges.

29 Longstreet attacks Fort Sanders guarding Knoxville, but is beaten back.

December

1 Meade ends his campaign in Virginia for the winter, after finding the Confederates too firmly entrenched at Mine Run, Va. His army digs in at Culpeper, Va.
Bragg becomes military adviser to Jefferson Davis, and is removed from command of the Army of Tennessee.

4. Longstreet retreats into Virginia after failing to take Knoxville and lift the siege.

8 Lincoln proposes his "One-Tenth" reconstruction plan for restoring seceded states to the Union.

27 Joseph E. Johnston takes over as commander of the Army of Tennessee.

1864

January

4 George Davis replaces Thomas Watts as attorney general of the Confederacy.

February

17 The Confederate submarine "Hunley" sinks the U.S.S. "Housatonic" off Charleston, becoming the first submarine in history to sink an enemy vessel in combat.

20 Union forces under Seymour lose the Battle of Olustee, Fla.
The Pomeroy circular distributed by Senator Pomeroy of Kansas is issued, calling for the nomination of Chase instead of Lincoln for the Presidency. The secret letter is uncovered.

22 Forrest defeats W. S. Smith's cavalry at Okolona, Miss.

March

2 Kilpatrick and Dahlgren lead a raid on Richmond in an abortive attempt to release the prisoners at Libby Prison. Dahlgren is killed and

implicated in an assassination plot to kill Jefferson Davis.

4 Sherman's troops return to Vicksburg after staging a month-long raid on the countryside around Meridan, Miss.

Civil government is restored in Louisiana.

12 Grant goes east to receive promotion to lieutenant general, and command of the Union armies.

15 Porter's fleet reaches Alexandria, La., and spearheads the Red River campaign.

18 Grant appoints Sherman to head the western armies.

23 Steele moves out of Little Rock, Ark., to take part in the Red River campaign.

25 Banks is given command of the Red River campaign.

April

8 Confederate General Taylor stops the Red River campaign at Shreveport, La.

10 Napoleon III succeeds in getting Archduke Maximilian of Austria crowned as emperor of Mexico, violating the Monroe Doctrine. The U.S. is too involved in the Civil War to do anything about it.

11 Civil government is restored in Arkansas.

12 The Fort Pillow massacre takes place when Forrest captures Fort Pillow and massacres almost all of the captured Negro troops there. Few escape the butchery.

17 Grant ends the prisoner exchange policy, increasing the strain on the Confederate manpower.

25 Porter's gunboats are trapped by low water in the Red River.

30 Steele is defeated by the Confederates at Jenkins Ferry, Ark., and retreats to Little Rock.

May

4 Grant moves across the Rapidan to attack Lee.

5 Lee hits Grant at the Wilderness, with the battle ending in a stalemate.

6 Longstreet arrives with re-enforcements for Lee and halts Grant's offensive at the Wilderness completely. He is wounded by his own men in the fighting.

Sherman begins the Atlanta campaign.

7 Grant moves southward despite the setback at the Wilderness, bypassing Lee's army in a race for Spotsylvania Courthouse.

8 Lee wins the race to Spotsylvania, with Stuart clearing the way. Grant's advance units are defeated.

9 Lee entrenches at Spotsylvania.

Sedgewick is killed by a Confederate sharpshooter.

Sheridan launches an attack on Richmond. One of the heaviest cavalry raids of the war.

Sherman fails to outflank Johnston at Dalton, Ga.

10 Grant fails to breach Lee's lines at Spotsylvania.

Butler withdraws from the Bermuda Hundred after an unsuccessful strike at Petersburg.

11 Sheridan's raid on Richmond is stopped at Yellow Tavern. Jeb Stuart is mortally wounded in the fighting.

12 After a day-long fight, at the "Bloody Angle," Lee is able to plug the gap in his lines at Spotsylvania.

Butler attacks the Richmond defenses at Drewery's Bluff on the James River.

13 Johnston is forced to withdraw from Dalton to Resaca, Ga.

Porter's flotilla is able to move

216

back down the Red River past Alexandria. Banks continues his withdrawal.

15 Sherman again attempts to outflank Johnston, forcing the Confederates to abandon Resaca.

Breckinridge defeats Sigel at New Market, Va., ending the Union Shenandoah Valley campaign.

16 Butler is driven from Drewry's Bluff by Beauregard, and is forced to again move back to Bermuda Hundred.

·17 Grant continues his move to outflank Lee at Spotsylvania.

19 A Confederate counterattack under Ewell fails at Spotsylvania.

Sherman succeeds in flanking Johnston out of his Cassville, Ga., defensive position.

24 Lee is able to repulse the Union thrust at North Anna River, after Grant has left his Spotsylvania lines to again try to outflank the Confederates.

25 Johnston and Sherman engage in a four-day fight at New Hope Church, Ga.

28 Grant and Lee begin a four-day skirmish at Totopotomoy Creek, Va.

31 Fremont and John Cochrane are nominated by dissatisfied Republicans in a convention at Cleveland. The dissident group met before the regular Chicago convention.

June

1 Lee entrenches at Cold Harbor, Va., with Grant taking up a position facing him.

3 The Union force is repulsed with great loss, and entrenches.

Congress passes the National Banking Act, providing for a national currency.

4 Johnston moves to check Sherman's advance at Lost Mountain,

Pine Mountain, and Brush Mountain.

8 The regular convention nominates Lincoln and War Democrat Andrew Johnson for their ticket at the Republican convention.

10 Forrest defeats Union General Sturgis at Brice's Crossroads, Miss.

12 Sheridan's cavalry raids in the Shenandoah Valley are stopped by Wade Hampton at Trevilian Station, Va.

14 Grant begins a crossing of the James River in a move to attack Petersburg, Va.

Confederate General Polk is killed in the action at Pine Mountain.

15 Grant's force is unable to take weakly-held Petersburg.

C. G. Memminger resigns as Confederate secretary of the treasury and is replaced by George A. Trenholm.

16 Beauregard moves out of the Bermuda Hundred lines to protect Petersburg.

17 Lee's army reoccupies the Bermuda Hundred lines before Butler can move forward.

18 Grant begins the siege of Petersburg after assaults fail.

David Hunter replaces Sigel in the Shenandoah Valley and is defeated by Early at Lynchburg, Va.

19 Johnston moves from Pine Mountain to Kennesaw Mountain in Georgia.

The "Alabama" is sunk by the U.S.S. "Kearsarge" off Cherbourg, France.

23 A. P. Hill stops the Federal advance on Petersburg via the Weldon Railroad.

Early begins a Confederate offensive in the Shenandoah Valley.

27 Johnston repulses Sherman's frontal attack at Kennesaw Mountain.

30 Chase resigns as U.S. secretary of the treasury after a spat with Lincoln over a postal appointment. He is replaced by William Fessenden.

July

3 Johnston moves his Confederate troops from Kennesaw Mountain to the Chattahoochee River defenses in order to avoid being flanked.

4 Congress passes the Wade-Davis Bill, but Lincoln refuses to sign it.

6 Early crosses the Potomac into Maryland.

9 Johnston withdraws from the Chattahoochee to defend the city of Atlanta.

Early wins a victory at Frederick, Md. (Monocacy), and stirs fear in the capital.

11 The Army of the Potomac sends re-enforcements to the units defending Washington.

12 Early withdraws to the Shenandoah Valley after being repulsed in the outskirts of Washington.

15 Union General A. J. Smith defeats Forrest at Tupelo, Miss., but is forced to withdraw because of his precarious position.

17 Hood replaces Johnston in front of Atlanta to the surprise of all concerned.

20 Hood is repulsed in an attack upon the Union forces at Peachtree Creek. Sherman moves to cut Atlanta's rail connections.

22 Major General James B. McPherson is killed as the Union forces halt a Confederate counterattack.

24 Early defeats pursuing Union forces at Kernstown, Va., in the Shenandoah Valley.

28 Federal troops, feinting at Richmond, Va., are repulsed at Deep Bottom, Va.

Confederates under Hood fail to stop Sherman's move to Ezra Church, Ga.

30 The Battle of the Crater turns out to be a Union defeat, as the Confederates stop an attempted Union breakthrough at Petersburg.

Union cavalry under General George Stoneman attempts to liberate the prisoners at Andersonville, Ga., but Stoneman is captured by forces under Joseph Wheeler at Macon, Ga.

August

5 Farragut is victorious at Mobile Bay.

7 Sheridan is assigned to command Union forces in the Shenandoah.

10 Wheeler begins an extended cavalry raid on Union communications lines between Atlanta and Nashville.

21 Grant seizes the Weldon Railroad leading south from Petersburg, following the Battle of Glove Tavern.

22 Kilpatrick's five-day cavalry raid fails to hurt Hood's supply lines below Atlanta.

29 The Democrats nominate McClellan and Pendleton as their Presidential ticket.

31 Union forces sever the Macon and Western Railroad connection into Atlanta.

September

1 Hood evacuates Atlanta after Sherman takes Jonesboro south of the city.

2 Hood sets up a line of defense at Lovejoy's Station south of Jonesboro, Ga.

Sherman moves into Atlanta.

4 Civilians are ordered out of Atlanta by Sherman.

Confederate raider Morgan is killed at Greeneville, Tenn.

8 McClellan accepts the Democratic nomination for President, but refuses to endorse the peace platform of the party.

19 Sheridan defeats Early at Winchester, Va., in the Shenandoah Valley.

Sterling Price begins a Confederate raid in Missouri.

22 Early is routed by Sheridan at Fisher's Hill, Va.

Fremont refuses to run for President, withdrawing his name from the list of candidates.

24 Lincoln asks for the resignation of Montgomery Blair and replaces him as postmaster general with William Dennison.

28 Hood strikes at Sherman's supply lines across the Chattahoochee.

29 Grant captures Fort Harrison, but fails to take Fort Gilmer in the Battle of New Market Heights, Va., outside of Richmond.

October

4 Hood hits Sherman's rail communications at Big Shanty, Ga.

5 Hood repulsed at Allatoona, Ga.

6 Sheridan puts the torch to the Shenandoah Valley, and withdraws to Winchester, Va.

7 Union forces at Darbytown and New Market Roads repulse Confederate thrusts.

13 Hood destroys Sherman's communications rails, and Sherman is forced to move his troops to Resaca from Atlanta.

19 Early is again defeated by Sheridan at Cedar Creek, Va., completely driving the Confederate forces out of the Shenandoah Valley.

Confederate raiders hit St. Albans, Vt., from Canada, stirring fear in the northern reaches of the Union.

23 Price's rebel raiders are defeated at Westport, Mo., and driven out of the state.

27 A. P. Hill repulses Grant's forces at Hatcher's Run, Va.

Lieutenant William Cushing sinks the Confederate ram "Albermarle" at Plymouth, N.C.

30 Schofield is sent by Sherman to reenforce Thomas at Nashville and halt Hood's attempted invasion of Tennessee.

31 Nevada is admitted to the Union as the thirty-sixth state.

November

8 Lincoln and Johnson win the election for President and Vice-President of the U.S.

15 Sherman begins his "March to the Sea" at Atlanta.

19 Hood, re-enforced by Forrest's cavalry, begins a drive on Nashville, Tenn.

23 Sherman reaches Milledgeville, Georgia's capital, and burns the countryside.

25 The Confederate plot to burn New York City fails.

29 Schofield escapes Hood's trap and moves to Franklin.

30 Hood hits Schofield at Franklin but fails to stop the Union retreat to Nashville. The Confederates lose five generals in this campaign.

December

1 James Speed replaces Edward Bates as U.S. attorney general.

2 Hood sets up a defensive line south of Nashville.

6 Lincoln appoints Salmon P. Chase to the post of Chief Justice of the Supreme Court following the death of Roger B. Taney.

13 Sherman takes Fort McAllister, clearing the Savannah and establishes contact with forces under

Dahlgren which are blockading the port.

15 Thomas hits Hood at Nashville.

16 Hood is defeated soundly and forced to retreat into Mississippi.

21 Hardee evacuates Savannah allowing Sherman to occupy the city, completing his "March to the Sea."

25 Butler's joint army-navy expedition is repulsed at Fort Fisher, N.C.

1865

January

15 Major General A. H. Terry takes Fort Fisher, closing Wilmington, N.C., the last major Confederate port.
Hood is relieved of command at his own request.

31 The U.S. Congress submits the Thirteenth Amendment, abolishing slavery, to the states.

February

1 Sherman moves toward the Carolinas.

3 The Hampton Roads Conference.

6 Lee takes over as commander-in-chief of the Confederate armies.
Breckinridge replaces Seddon as Confederate secretary of war.

17 Sherman occupies Columbia, S.C., capital of the state. The city is "mysteriously" destroyed by fire that night.

18 Fort Sumter is abandoned, and the Union forces take over Charleston, S.C.

22 Wilmington, N.C., surrenders to Schofield.
Johnston reassumes command of the Army of Tennessee, now operating in North Carolina.

March

2 Sheridan destroys Early's remaining

troops in the Shenandoah Valley at Waynesboro, Va.

4 Lincoln is inaugurated for his second term.

7 McCulloch replaces William Fessenden as U.S. secretary of the treasury.

11 Sherman reaches Fayeteville, N.C.

17 Canby opens an attack on Mobile, Ala.

18 The Confederate Congress adjourns for the last time at Richmond, Va.

19 Sherman stops Johnston's attack at Bentonville, and the Rebels retreat toward Raleigh, N.C.

22 Wilson begins a raid in northern Alabama.

23 Sherman takes Goldsboro, N.C.

25 Gordon captures Fort Stedman but is forced to evacuate under heavy Federal fire.

27 Sheridan rejoins the Army of the Potomac.

28 Grant, Sherman and the President discuss plans for peace aboard the "River Queen" at City Point, Va.

April

1 Sheridan turns Lee's flank at Petersburg by defeating Pickett at Five Forks, Va.

2 Grant breaks through Lee's Petersburg line. Confederate A. P. Hill is killed.
Lee begins a retreat westward towards Amelia Court House, abandoning Petersburg.
Wilson's Federal cavalry captures Selma, Ala.

3 Union forces enter Richmond.

4 Lincoln visits Richmond in person.

5 Sheridan blocks Lee's escape route south from Amelia Court House, forcing the Confederates to veer towards Lynchburg, Va.
Civil government is restored in Tennessee.

6 Grant cuts off and captures Lee's

rear guard commanded by Ewell at Sailor's Creek, Va.

7 Federal troops fail in an attack upon Lee at Farmsville, Va.
Grant and Lee correspond concerning surrender.

8 Sheridan reaches Appomattox Station to cut off Lee's retreat.

9 Lee surrenders to Grant at Appomattox Court House, Va.

12 Wilson's Union cavalry captures Montgomery, Va.
Federal troops enter Mobile, Ala.
Johnston informs Jefferson Davis that further resistance is futile.

13 Sherman enters Raleigh, N.C.

14 Anderson raises the same flag above Fort Sumter that he was forced to lower at the beginning of the war.
John Wilkes Booth shoots Lincoln at the Ford Theatre in Washington.
Lewis Paine wounds Secretary of State Seward in a separate attempt.

15 Abraham Lincoln dies, and Johnson becomes President.

18 Sherman offers Johnston broad armistice terms at Raleigh, N.C.

21 Johnson and the cabinet refuse to honor Sherman's terms and send Grant to North Carolina.

26 Johnston accepts Grant's terms which are the same as offered Lee.
Booth is captured and either kills himself or is killed by Federal cavalry near Bowling Green, Va.
The Confederate cabinet meets for the last time in Charlotte, N.C.

May

4 Taylor surrenders to Canby, ending Confederate resistance east of the Mississippi.

10 Jefferson Davis is taken prisoner at Irwinsville, Ga., by Union cavalry.

13 The last major fighting takes place at Palmito Ranch near Brownsville, Tex.

23 The Federal armies parade in grand review in Washington.

26 Kirby Smith surrenders the Confederate troops west of the Mississippi ending the Civil War. The last force did not surrender, however, until June 23, when Stand Watie surrendered his Indian forces.